Big Data for Small Business

FOR
DUMMIES®
A Wiley Brand

by Bernard Marr

FOR
DUMMIES®
A Wiley Brand

Big Data for Small Business **For Dummies**®

Published by: **John Wiley & Sons, Ltd., The Atrium, Southern Gate, Chichester,** www.wiley.com

This edition first published 2016

© 2016 by John Wiley & Sons, Ltd., Chichester, West Sussex

Registered Office

John Wiley & Sons, Ltd., The Atrium, Southern Gate, Chichester, West Sussex, PO19 8SQ, United Kingdom

For details of our global editorial offices, for customer services and for information about how to apply for permission to reuse the copyright material in this book, please see our website at www.wiley.com.

For general information on our other products and services, please contact our Customer Care Department within the U.S. at 877-762-2974, outside the U.S. at 317-572-3993, or fax 317-572-4002. For technical support, please visit www.wiley.com/techsupport.

Wiley publishes in a variety of print and electronic formats and by print-on-demand. Some material included with standard print versions of this book may not be included in e-books or in print-on-demand. If this book refers to media such as a CD or DVD that is not included in the version you purchased, you may download this material at http://booksupport.wiley.com. For more information about Wiley products, visit www.wiley.com.

A catalogue record for this book is available from the British Library.

Library of Congress Control Number: 2015955036

ISBN 978-1-119-02703-4 (pbk); ISBN 978-1-119-02704-1 (ebk); ISBN 978-1-119-02758-4 (ebk)

Printed and Bound in Great Britain by TJ International, Padstow, Cornwall.

10 9 8 7 6 5 4 3 2 1

A Wiley Brand

Contents at a Glance

Table of Contents

Part IV: Show Time! Making Big Data Work for Small Business 149

Introduction

Almost everything we do now leaves a digital trace. If you bought this book online, you left a trail of digital crumbs in your wake, from browsing the online retailer's website, to the transaction itself. Even if you walked into a physical bookstore and paid with cash, there's still likely to be a digital trail of your activities, including CCTV (closed-circuit television) footage and location data from your own phone.

These digital traces can be summed up in one phrase: big data. *Big data* refers to the ability to collect and analyse the vast amounts of data now being generated in the world. This ability to harness the ever-expanding amounts of data is completely transforming our ability to understand the world and everything within it – from healthcare and science to how entire cities and countries are run. And, of course, it's transforming the way we do business.

Some business owners and managers dismiss big data as being only for big-budget corporations. I think this is a huge mistake. Of course it's true that some companies have eye-watering budgets for big data analytics, but most simply don't. In fact, I work with plenty of small- and medium-sized businesses that successfully harness the power of data without spending a fortune.

The key is to start with a clear strategy. This allows you to focus solely on the data that's right for you – the data that will help you achieve your long-term business goals. Having a clear strategy helps you cut through the hype and noise surrounding big data and get straight to how it can realistically help you improve the way you do business. That's why I wrote *Big Data for Small Business For Dummies*: to help SMEs (small and medium enterprises) use big data in a practical and strategic way.

Whether you're planning a one-off data project or want to incorporate data into your ongoing business operations, this book can help you understand what big data is, how you can apply it to your business, how to create your own big data strategy and get underway and how to build a culture that emphasises data-based decision making and continuous improvement.

About This Book

Think of this book as a no-nonsense tour guide to help you on your big data journey. There are lots of inspirational examples of how other businesses are already using data, but the focus remains on practical tips to get you using data in *your* business. As well as examples and tips, the book is packed with step-by-step guidelines and lists designed to help you get the most out of big data. All the information is designed to be accessible and easy to understand. And where I have to resort to technical jargon, I give clear definitions. Sidebars (the grey boxes) contain nice-to-know but not essential information, so you can easily skip over them if you like.

The book is designed as a resource that you can dip in and out of and return to time and time again. As such, you don't need to read it from cover to cover (although, if you want to, go ahead!). It's designed to be read in whatever order works best for you.

Finally, if you decide to visit a website listed in the book then you just need to copy the URL (uniform resource locator) exactly as it appears in the book. This is true even if the address falls between two lines or two pages – no extra characters (such as hyphens) were inserted.

Foolish Assumptions

Every author has a target audience in mind when he writes. For this book, I assume that you're the owner of a small/medium business or a manager in such a business. I assume that you've heard a little about big data already – perhaps what a powerful tool it can be for businesses – and you want to know more. I don't assume you have any prior technical knowledge whatsoever. Crucially, whether you're a business owner or manager, I assume that you want to improve the way you do business and you're in a position to make strategic decisions . . . and then act upon them.

If you would like to supplement this book with more technical information, you might like to check out *Big Data For Dummies* by Judith Hurwitz, Alan Nugent, Fern Halper and Marcia Kaufman, published by Wiley.

Icons Used in This Book

When I see a huge wall of text, I start to switch off. So in this book I use a number of icons to break the text up, and to make it easier and more enjoyable to read. The icons also help you spot key information quickly.

These indicate expert advice or suggestions to help your big data journey go more smoothly. They help you save time, energy or money and are based on my experiences working with other businesses.

 This icon flags critical material that you should store away in your memory for later use. But don't worry – they're usually very short.

 As the name suggests, this icon flags potential pitfalls that you need to avoid as you start using big data.

 Where I've had to use data-related jargon (for example, if it's a key industry term that you need to know), I highlight it using this icon.

 I believe real-life examples bring information to life and I included tons of examples throughout the book that show how other businesses are already using big data. Some of these are small-scale data projects, others are much larger, and some are just plain weird and wonderful! But all are designed to demonstrate the exciting potential of big data and give you a few practical ideas for your own business.

Beyond the Book

In addition to the material in the print or e-book you're reading right now, this product also comes with some access-anywhere goodies on the Web.

Check out the free Cheat Sheet at www.dummies.com/cheatsheet/ bigdataforsmallbusiness for some helpful key information and check-lists. It's designed as a quick-check reference for some crucial big data information, including a handy list of key terminology.

There are also some useful bonus articles and an additional Part of Tens chapter available on the website. Head to www.dummies.com/extras/ bigdataforsmallbusiness to access these.

You may also like to check out the website of the Advanced Performance Institute, which I founded and head up. There you'll find many relevant case studies, white papers and reading material on big data: www.ap-institute. com. I also write regularly for *Forbes* magazine on all things big data and

you can find my articles at www.forbes.com/sites/bernardmarr.
My LinkedIn page also contains a wealth of articles and posts on big data:
www.linkedin.com/in/bernardmarr.

Where to Go from Here

The short answer is: It's up to you. You don't have to start at Chapter 1 and
work your way through the book in a linear way – but you can if you want to.

If you're completely new to big data, I recommend you start with the
Chapters in Part I for an explanation of what big data is and the main ways
it can be used in business. Otherwise, simply use the table of contents to
find what you're most interested in and jump straight to that section. If you
want to start by finding out exactly how to create a big data strategy, turn
to Chapter 10. If you're interested more in big data skills and competencies,
start with Chapter 8. Wherever you go from here, you'll find a wealth of
information and tips to help you start using big data in your business.

Part I
Getting Started with Big Data Basics

getting started with

big data basics

In this part . . .

- ✔ Understand what big data is and why you need to know about it.

- ✔ Find out the key characteristics that define big data.

- ✔ See why there's so much hype around big data right now – and why all the fuss is justified.

- ✔ Check out key big data uses for small businesses.

Chapter 1

Introducing Big Data for Small Businesses

*B*ig data has been making big headlines over the last couple of years, but it's much more than just a buzz phrase or the latest business fad. The phenomenon is very real and is producing concrete benefits in so many different areas – from business to medical research to national security.

The basic idea behind big data is that everything you do is increasingly leaving a digital trace (or data), which you (and others) can use and analyse. *Big data* therefore refers to that data being collected and the ability to make use of it.

In this chapter, I look at how this phenomenon is transforming the way you do business. I also look at what sorts of data are available these days and introduce my step-by-step processes for using big data in business.

Personally, I don't love the term *big data* because I think it places far too much emphasis on the sheer volume of data, when, as I talk about in this chapter, what you do with the data is much more important than how much of it you have. I have a feeling the term will gradually disappear and what's now called *big data* will, in the future, just be known as *data*.

Why Big Data Matters to Every Business, Big and Small

Given all the hype around big data, it's no surprise that market researchers Gartner found in 2014 that 73 per cent of businesses have already invested in a big data plan or are planning to do so in the next few years.

The online behemoths that have come to dominate business in the Internet age – Google, Facebook, Amazon, you know the ones – all base their business models on big data. It's by collecting and analysing huge amounts of information from us that they're able to determine precisely what we want. The data also enables them to sell advertising services capable of precisely targeting their clients' preferred demographics.

But big data isn't just for giant corporations, it matters to every company – no matter how small or traditional. To cater for this huge demand, many companies have sprung up to offer services to other businesses, enabling them to launch big data initiatives of their own.

I've found that the term *big data* can scare some business owners off, especially the *big* part. Some think it doesn't apply to their small business – or that it'll be prohibitively expensive to use. The truth is, in the current business age, if you want to grow, you need to start using data strategically. And yes, some companies have massive big data budgets. Most companies, however, are working with much smaller budgets but are still able to use data to gather insights that help their business grow.

Entering a world filled with data

Of course, data collection itself isn't new. But technological advances like chip and sensor technology, the Internet, cloud computing and the ability to store and analyse data have changed the quantity of data you can collect.

Activities that have been a part of everyday life for decades – shopping, listening to music, taking pictures, talking on the phone – increasingly happen wholly or in part in the digital realm and therefore leave a trail of data.

And the amount of data being generated every day is staggering. For example, users of Facebook upload around one billion pieces of content to the social network site every day. In industry, machinery and vehicles are fitted with sensors and trackers that record their every move, and whenever you call a call centre, an audio recording of your conversation is made and stored in a huge digital database.

Big data statistics to blow your mind

The following statistics give you a flavour of the sheer volume of data being generated in today's world:

- Every two days we create as much information as we did from the beginning of time until 2003.

- Over 90 per cent of all the data in the world was created in the past two years.

- It's expected that by 2020 the amount of digital information in existence will grow from 3.2 zettabytes today to 40 zettabytes. (A zettabyte is a unit of data measurement roughly equal to one million terabytes; a terabyte is one trillion bytes.)

- Every minute we send 204 million emails, generate 1.8 million Facebook likes, send 278 thousand Tweets and upload 200 thousand photos to Facebook.

- Google alone processes on average over 40 thousand search queries per second, making it over 3.5 billion in a single day.

- Around 100 hours of video are uploaded to YouTube every minute and it would take you around 15 years to watch every video uploaded by users in one day.

- 570 new websites spring into existence every minute of every day.

- This year, there will be over 1.2 billion smartphones in the world (which are stuffed full of sensors and data collection features), and the growth is predicted to continue.

- The boom of the Internet of Things will mean that the amount of devices that connect to the Internet will rise from about 13 billion today to 50 billion by 2020.

- 1.9 million IT jobs will be created in the US alone by 2015 to carry out big data projects. Each of those will be supported by three new jobs created outside of IT – meaning a total of 6 million new jobs thanks to big data.

Understanding the infinite ways to use big data

Eventually, every aspect of your lives will be affected by big data. However, there are some areas where big data is already making a real difference today – in business and in other areas. Let's look at the main areas where big data is most widely used right now.

- **Understanding and targeting customers:** This is one of the most common uses of big data today. Here, big data is used to better understand customers and their behaviours and preferences.

- **Understanding and optimising business processes:** Big data is also increasingly used to optimise a wider range of business processes, including stock control, supply chain and delivery routes and HR processes.

- **Optimising personal quantification and performance:** Individuals can now benefit from the data generated from wearable devices such as smart watches and smart bracelets – data like calorie consumption, activity levels and sleep patterns.

- **Improving healthcare and public health:** The computing power of big data analytics enables scientists to decode entire DNA strings in minutes and allows them to find new cures and better understand and predict disease patterns. What's more, big data analytics allow researchers to monitor and predict the developments of epidemics and disease outbreaks by integrating data from medical records with social media analytics.

- **Improving sports performance:** Most elite sports have now embraced big data analytics. Video analytics track the performance of every player in a football game, and sensor technology in sports equipment such as golf clubs allows you to get feedback (via your smartphone) on your game and how to improve it.

- **Improving science and research:** Science and research is currently being transformed by big data. Experiments with the Large Hadron Collider, for example, generate huge amounts of data. The CERN (European Organization for Nuclear Research) data centre has 65,000 processors to analyse its 30 petabytes (a petabyte is one quadrillion bytes) of data.

- **Optimising machine and device performance:** Big data analytics help machines and devices become smarter and more autonomous. For example, big data tools are used to operate Google's self-driving car.

- **Improving security and law enforcement:** I'm sure you're aware of the revelations that the National Security Agency (NSA) in the US uses big data analytics to foil terrorist plots (and maybe spy on us!). Others use big data techniques to detect and prevent cyber attacks and police forces use big data tools to catch criminals.

- **Improving and optimising cities and countries:** Big data is used to improve many aspects of where we live. For example, it allows cities to optimise traffic flows based on real-time traffic information as well as social media and weather data.

- **Optimising financial trading:** High-Frequency Trading (HFT) is an area where big data finds a lot of use today by using big data algorithms to make trading decisions.

Using big data in small businesses

Big data might seem like it's something that only big business can make use of. When people first hear that massive volumes of information are being used to fight terrorism, cure cancer or predict the spread of Ebola, it sounds expensive, difficult and time-consuming. But that doesn't have to be the case.

Huge datasets on everything from demographics to weather and consumer spending habits are freely available online for small businesses to use. Plus, the basic tools to make sense of the data are also free and becoming increasingly simple for anyone to use. For example, if you're using Google's AdWords to track what your customers are searching for online, you're engaging in big data analysis, even if you don't know it.

In many ways, big data is much better suited to small businesses than to big corporations – smaller companies tend to be more agile and able to act on the insights that data provides in a more timely fashion. In the end, even the most impressive data set and the most potent insights are worthless if you don't act on them.

Plenty of small businesses are already using big data to better understand and target customers. Retailers can predict what products will sell, car insurance companies can understand how well their customers actually drive and detect potential fraud and takeaway companies can tailor their services to meet local customer preferences and demand. Social media has become a particularly valuable source of data for understanding customers, trends and markets.

Big data can also help improve business processes. Retailers are able to optimise their stock levels based on what's trending on social media, what people are searching for on the web or even weather forecasts. Supply chains can be optimised so that delivery drivers use less gas and reach customers faster. And you can use data to understand and improve staff engagement or improve your hiring process.

There's more detail on the many big data uses in Chapter 3 – and there are examples dotted throughout the book. Just look out for the Example icon.

Too often I see big data analysis being done in an infrequent, unstructured or ad hoc way (and that's in businesses of all sizes). You really need an underlying strategy in order to get the most out of big data, and there's more on that in Chapter 10. Without an underlying strategy, you may stumble across the odd valuable insight, but with proper planning and preparation, those insights are more frequent and more useful.

Understanding Big Data in More Detail

The first thing to understand is that data in itself isn't a new business phenomenon. Business data is as old as, well, business itself. Just think of sales and financial ledgers or, in more recent history, customer databases. It's specifically *big* data that's the new phenomenon. But, as I mention at the start of the chapter, big data isn't just about how *big* it is. In fact, volume is just one of the key defining factors of big data.

In practice, some of the data you use in your business may not exactly qualify as big data (as defined by the four Vs I explain in the next section), and that's fine. If the best data for you isn't strictly big data, don't lose any sleep over it. So long as you're using data in a strategic way to meet your goals and grow your business, that's all that really matters – not what it's called.

Breaking big data down into four Vs

To understand big data, and what separates it from normal data, you need to understand four main factors, which all handily start with a V. It's these Vs that define what's really special about big data, why it's different to regular data and why it's so transformative for businesses. You can find more information on the Vs in Chapter 2.

The four Vs are:

- ✔ **Volume** refers to the vast amounts of data generated every second.
- ✔ **Velocity** refers to the speed at which new data is generated and the speed at which data moves around.
- ✔ **Variety** refers to the different types of data you can now use.
- ✔ **Veracity** refers to the trustworthiness of the data.

I'd include a fifth V that's perhaps more important than all the others: value. It's all well and good collecting vast volumes of data or accessing a wide variety of data, but if you can't turn that data into value (which in the case of business means *growth*) then it's useless.

Why big data is so big right now

I think there are three main reasons why big data is in the news so much these days:

- ✔ Big data has incredibly powerful predictive capabilities.
- ✔ Big data helps you make much smarter decisions.
- ✔ Big data challenges traditional notions of causality.

I look at each of these reasons in Chapter 2.

Another exciting aspect of big data is that it's only going to get bigger and more widely used. As the tools to collect and analyse data become less and less expensive and more and more accessible, we'll develop more and more uses for it – everything from smart yoga mats (no, really) to better healthcare tools and a more effective police force.

Whether you're all for the benefits big data can bring or worried about Big Brother watching everything you do, it's important to be aware of the power of big data. If you live in the modern world, it's not something you can escape. And if you're in business, it's something you should be positively embracing. Having said that, there are some ethical and moral points of debate around big data, such as who owns your data and the need for companies to be more transparent with their customers about what data they collect and why. I explore these issues in Chapter 2.

Turning data into big data

It may seem like big data has exploded onto the business scene out of nowhere. But in fact it's been a more like a gradual evolution: from dusty archive rooms to the microfiche to databases and on to data centres. I think it's part of human nature to want to continually gather information and make sense of what's going on around us – we've just developed sleeker technology for it over the years.

It's fair to say, however, that the pace of this development has ramped up enormously since the invention of digital storage and the Internet. In particular, three technological advances came together to create the perfect conditions for big data: huge advances in storage capacity, faster networks and more powerful analytic technology.

There's more detail on the technology changes that underpin big data in Chapter 6. But here's a short overview of these three advances.

Data storage used to be limited to mainframe computers, hard disks or company servers. Now you have connected computers and servers that give you more storage capacity than ever before. Large amounts of data can be broken up into smaller chunks and stored across a range of machines in different locations. This is called *distributed computing*.

Distributed computing gives you greater storage capacity, but it also allows you to connect data faster than ever before. With data being spread across many different locations, you need to be able to bring that data back together quickly. This is where faster networks come into play.

These massive increases in storage and computing power make number crunching possible on a very large scale. Without faster networks that connect data sets together for analysis, big data just wouldn't be possible for the average business. Now you can break up the analysis of data into manageable chunks, meaning that no one machine has to bear the whole load. This makes analysis faster and far more efficient – and cheaper.

For the first time you're able to analyse large, complex and messy data sets (which previously would have been far too big to store). And thanks to new analytic programs, the data can be in just about any form – structured or unstructured, messy or neat, text, audio, video, sensor, images. We now have the ability to extract insights from almost any type of data.

Data, Data Everywhere

It used to be that data would fit neatly into tables, spreadsheets and data-bases: think of data like sales figures, customer records, wholesale prices and so on. But now you can look at all sorts of data – including emails, Facebook posts, photos, blog comments and voice recordings – and extract meaning.

With big data technology you can now harness different types of data and bring them together with more traditional, structured data. It's this ability to analyse and use a wide variety of data that's especially exciting to me, as it means you can now extract more business-critical insights than ever before.

In this section I give an overview of the different types of data, but you can find more detail (and some great examples) in Chapters 4 and 5.

Discovering structured, unstructured, internal and external data

There are two main types of data: structured and unstructured.

Structured data refers to any data or information located in a fixed field within a defined record or file, usually in a database or spreadsheet. Examples include sales and transaction records, financial data, website hits and customer details.

Structured data has three main things going for it: it's usually cheap to use, it's easy to store, and it's easy to mine for information. But, on the downside, it represents only a small proportion of all the data available these days – as the digital traces you leave behind get bigger and bigger, only a small amount of this data is structured in format.

Another downside is that structured data is simply less rich in insights than unstructured data, meaning it can be more difficult (maybe even impossible) to really understand what's going on if you're using only structured data. For best results, structured data often needs to be paired with other data to get a fuller picture. For example, structured data can tell you that hits on your website increased 20 per cent last month, but you need other forms of data to explore why that happened.

Unstructured data is basically all the data that doesn't fit neatly into traditional formats or databases. Examples includes email conversations, social media posts, video content, photos and voice recordings. *Semi-structured data* is a cross between unstructured and structured data. It may have some structure that can be used for analysis (perhaps tags such as date or author, for example) but it lacks the strict structure of databases or spreadsheets.

Unstructured and semi-structured data tends to be much more difficult to store (not least because so darn much of it is created every day). Now, thanks to massive increases in storage capacities and the ability to tag and categorise this data, as well as huge leaps in analytical technologies, you can finally make use of this data.

The advantages of unstructured and semi-structured data are that there's absolutely loads of it (it accounts for around 80 per cent of all business-relevant data being generated today), and it providers a richer picture than structured data. However, it's harder to store and more difficult to analyse, which makes it more expensive to work with.

Unstructured/semi-structured data is undoubtedly seen as the sexier, more exciting kind of data – as a result, people often make a beeline for it and neglect poor old structured data. But there's value in both. Both can offer up interesting and useful insights that can help your business. In fact, the real value often comes in combining structured and unstructured data to get a really rich picture of what's going on.

Internal data accounts for everything your business currently has or could access. This may be structured in format (for example, a customer database or transactional records), or it could be unstructured (conversational data from customer service calls or feedback from employee surveys, for instance). Many people think internal data isn't very exciting, but it can provide a wealth of information.

The beauty of internal data is that it's cheap (or maybe even free) and, as you own the data, there are no access issues to deal with. But, the downsides include having to maintain and secure the data (especially if it includes personal data). You may also find that internal data on its own doesn't provide enough information to meet your strategic goals and you may need to supplement it with external data.

External data is all the information that exists outside your business, whether it's publically available or privately held by a third party. It can also be structured or unstructured in format. Examples include social media data, census data and weather data.

External data is powerful because it gives you access to information that's often more up to date and richer than any information you could gather yourself. And, as it's someone else's data, you have the added bonus of not worrying about the security and data protection issues. But, the obvious downside is that you don't own the data, and you usually have to pay for access (although not always – check out Chapter 15 for some great free data sources).

When it comes down to it, no type of data is really better than any other type. What's best for one business may not be best for yours. The key is to start with a strong data strategy and let that strategy guide you to the best data for you, whether it's structured, unstructured, internal or external or a combination.

Getting acquainted with new types of data

You leave more and more digital traces of your activities than ever before. If you think about what you've done today so far, most of those activities have left some digital trace (data) that can and is being collected and analysed. Some of the data you can now collect is new; some has been around a while but we've only just found ways to really analyse it.

Some of the exciting new types of data include:

- ✔ **Activity data:** This is the computer record of human actions or activities that occur online or in the offline physical world.

- ✔ **Conversation data:** Conversations are increasingly leaving a digital trail behind – whether it's an SMS message, email, blog or social media post (which are all forms of text data) or as an audio recording of a telephone, teleconference or Skype call.

- ✔ **Photo and video image data:** Digital cameras and, more recently, smartphones have resulted in an explosion of this type of data, largely driven by ever-increasing connectivity and a desire to share every aspect of our lives on social media platforms!

- ✔ **Sensor data:** Sensors are increasingly being built into products, from phones and cars to golf clubs, all of which results in a vast amount of new data.

- ✔ **The Internet of Things (IoT):** Related to sensors and increasing connectivity, the IoT is all about objects being manufactured with embedded sensors and the ability of those objects to communicate with each other.

Making Key Big Data Decisions

There are three keys areas of decision making that relate to big data: one is pulling out insights from the data and using that information to guide your decision making, another is deciding how to build your big data skills and competencies, and the final aspect relates to infrastructure decisions. I look at each in turn in the next sections.

Understanding the value of insights

In today's competitive business world, success often comes down to a company's ability to learn faster than the competition and act on what they learn faster than the competition. The process of turning data into insights and actionable knowledge is the key to that success.

No matter how much data you gather, it's worth very little unless you can turn it into insights and actionable knowledge. Data-based insights help you to make better business decisions. Crucially, you then need to *act* on those decisions. It's this action that creates the fifth V of big data: value.

A key part of this process is making sure the *right information* is delivered to the *right people* at the *right time*. In order to aid decision making and ensure the necessary action is taken, insights need to be presented in a clear, concise and interesting way. People are less likely to act if they have to work hard to understand what the data is telling them.

Data and insights can also feed into the machines in your company, as well as your people. This applies to any machine or technology that's a key part of how the business operates on a day-to-day basis, such as stock control systems or machinery on a production line. Connecting data and machines allows businesses to increase efficiency, improve product quality, cut costs and much more. Processes and systems can also be connected with data, so that you can improve how you do things based on what the data shows.

There's more on focusing on insights and feeding data to your people, machines and systems in Chapter 7.

Building big data skills and competencies

There's currently a skill shortage in big data, meaning there's more demand for big data experts than there are available experts. This can make it hard for smaller businesses to recruit good data staff. But there are alternatives to hiring in-house staff. You can try training up your existing people, working with external data providers (of which there are now many, big and small) and partnering with other organisations, such as universities.

Whether you want to hire new people or boost your existing skills, I think there are six key skills required to successfully use big data in business:

- ✔ Analysing data
- ✔ Being creative
- ✔ Applying mathematics and statistics
- ✔ Understanding computer science
- ✔ Grasping the business side of things
- ✔ Communicating insights

There's more on these skills in Chapter 8.

I think developing your existing staff is a brilliant place to start. So, as a first step, think about whether your existing people have the potential to meet some or all of these needs (with a little extra training in all likelihood). There are some brilliant big data-related courses out there, many of them online and many of them free. I list my favourites in Chapter 8.

If data is going to be a key part of your business, then it's a good idea to consider hiring a data scientist to work in-house. The six skills I list are a good starting point when you're searching for the right person, and I also list some helpful recruitment questions in Chapter 8. If you don't have any tech experience at all then recruiting in the tech field can seem daunting – with these questions and by focusing on the core skills, you'll be able to assess candidates with confidence.

In a competitive recruitment environment where demand outstrips supply, you may need to get a little creative when it comes to tapping into big data skills. It's all about finding creative ways to pull the necessary skills together in whatever way works for you. For example, you may find someone with statistical and analytical skills who falls short on business insights, but your own people could help supplement those skills.

Getting the infrastructure in place

Your ultimate goal is to gather insights which will lead to better decision making and improved business performance. In order to do this, you'll need to invest in some tools or services.

By *infrastructure* I mean the software and hardware that will enable you to turn big data into insights. There are four key elements to a big data infrastructure:

✔ **Data collection:** If you need to source new data, this may require new infrastructure investments, such as sensors, cameras, or systems to collect text or audio data. For example, if you want to collect machine data from your factory operations or vehicles, you'll need to invest in sensors to collect the data.

✔ **Data storage:** You need to think about where to store all this data. The main storage options include: data warehouses, data lakes, distributed or cloud-based storage systems, company servers and hard disks.

✔ **Data analysis/processing:** Now you have your data, the next step is to sort and tidy up the data and analyse it to extract information.

✔ **Data visualisation/communication:** If the key insights aren't clearly presented, they won't result in action. For most small businesses looking to improve their decision making, simple graphics or visualisation platforms are more than enough to present insights from data.

I explore the main options for each element in Chapter 9, along with some of the most commonly used software packages.

The first step is to assess your existing infrastructure so, for each of these four elements, you need to consider what related technology or resources you already have in-house and how they might need to be improved or supplemented. For example, you may already be collecting useful customer data through your website or customer service department but don't yet have the analytics in place to work with that data.

If you're accessing someone else's data (using Facebook or Twitter, for instance), then the data capture, storage and processing elements may not apply to you – or they may apply to a lesser degree (you may want to partner someone else's data with some of your own internal data). In the last few years many businesses have sprung up offering cloud-based big data services to help other companies and organisations solve their data dilemmas. This type of big data as a service can cut costs because you pay only for the data you use.

Making Big Data Work for You

In the furore about big data it's easy to forget that it's all just data at the end of the day. There may be more of it than ever before, and there may be new forms of data but that data is still only really useful if you can use it to answer your strategic business questions and improve the way you do business.

Starting with a plan

Implementing a data strategy in an intelligent, structured way is what differentiates a big data-driven enterprise from one that is simply using data on an ad hoc basis. And the basics are no different for a small, agile and growing company than they are for the tech industry giants who have been using big data for years.

Whether you're planning on building a team of analysts or simply making the most of what your iPhone tells you about your Google AdWords and social reach, it's important to know what you're trying to achieve and why. Do you want to increase sales? Make your customers more satisfied? Or retain staff for longer? The strategic questions you're hoping your data will answer are just as important as the answers themselves – so make sure you're very clear about what questions you need answers to before you start.

After all, most small companies don't want to stay small, right? Data analysis can lead to big things for small business – but it's much more likely to happen if you go about it in a smart way. Therefore, every company, big or small, in any industry needs a solid big data strategy. Chapter 10 takes you through the process of developing a big data strategy and making a business case for using big data.

You need to know what questions you need answers to before you dive into data. Focusing on strategic questions allows you to forget about big data and focus on smart data instead. By working out exactly what you need to know, you can hone in on the data that you really need.

I believe that's a key aspect of using data successfully: finding the best data for *you* – the data that gives you the insights needed to grow your business . . . and then, of course, making sure you *act* on those insights!

Using big data to change your decision making

I believe data should be at the heart of strategic decision making in all businesses, from Fortune 500 companies to the local taxi firm. Data can provide insights that help you answer your key business questions such as 'How can I improve customer satisfaction?' or 'How can I improve staff retention?'.

Data leads to insights. Business owners and managers can turn those insights into decisions and actions that improve the business. This is the power of data.

By using data to make better decisions, you can improve the customer experience, increase employee satisfaction, enhance your business performance and gain competitive advantage. You can solve problems and react to opportunities. The power of data is in how you use it.

I developed a ten-step process for applying data to your decision making:

1. **Develop a big data strategy.**

2. **Hone in on the specific goals and challenges for each area of your business.**

3. **Identify your unanswered strategic questions.**

    For example, what do you need to know in order to meet your goals?

4. **Identify the data that will help answer those questions.**

5. **Look at what data you already have access to.**

6. **Assess whether the costs and effort are justified.**

7. **Collect the data.**

8. **Analyse the data.**

9. **Present and distribute the insights.**

10. **Incorporate what you've learnt into the business.**

Chapter 11 walks you through this process in more detail.

After you do all that you can with the data and communicate your insights to the key people in the company, it's time to review the evidence so that everyone in the business can move toward more fact-based decision making and leverage data to meet your objectives.

Moving to fact-based decision making should be a company-wide effort, meaning, as much as possible, everyone in the business should be using data as the basis for what he does. This requires a change in organisational culture away from gut-based decision making to basing strategic decisions on data. There's more on building a culture of data-based decision making in Chapter 13.

Transforming your business operations

Many businesses start by using data to inform their decision making, and this remains the most widespread way that businesses use data. But data can also integrate very successfully into your daily business operations.

This aspect is not really about extracting insights from data to improve decisions; it's about how data can help you run your business more smoothly. Therefore, it's less about your people making better decisions and more about using systems and algorithms that automate and improve processes.

Thanks to new technologies, you're seeing more businesses successfully integrate data and algorithms into their everyday operational processes. Increased connectivity, especially the Internet of Things (which I talk about in Chapter 5), has played a big role in this change. Just imagine how having your systems – production, stock control, distribution and security systems – all connected and talking to each other could make your business more efficient.

In Chapter 12 I set out an eight-step process for using data to transform your business operations. In brief, the steps are:

1. **Re-evaluate your business model.**

2. **Source the data you need.**

3. **Weigh up the costs and benefits and make a solid business case.**

4. **Secure ownership.**

5. **Manage the data (which includes making sure it's secure).**

6. **Establish the infrastructure and technology.**

7. **Test and pilot the algorithms and infrastructure.**

8. **Transform your operations and review progress.**

How you use data in your business is up to you – it depends on your business goals. Using it to improve decision making is perhaps the most obvious way, followed by making processes more automatic and efficient. But these options aren't an either/or thing. You might want to focus on decision making for now and see if the data throws up any operational opportunities further down the line.

Data can also lead to bigger changes in your business – it could even lead to you reshaping your business model. Many companies are now using their data to create new income streams (for example, by selling data back to clients). For some, it's even resulted in a complete change in business model. There's more on this in Chapter 13.

Thanks to big data, the world is getting smarter every day. Businesses that don't embrace the data revolution run the risk of being left behind. Those that do embrace it can become smarter, more efficient and much more competitive.

Chapter 2

Digging into the Essence of Big Data

*H*aving picked up this book, you've likely already come across articles or blogs championing big data. You've heard some of the buzz and want to know why big data is such a big deal right now.

Data in itself isn't a new business phenomenon. But big data is. And not all data is big data, even if there's plenty of it. Don't be alarmed, it gets easier!

The truth is, companies have had a lot of data for a long time – consider big mainframe computers and early data centres. Data in itself isn't a new invention. Until recently, this data was limited to what's called *structured data* (see Chapter 4), meaning it was typically in spreadsheets or databases. However, even though there was lots of it, this data wouldn't count as *big data* because big data is defined by more than just how, well, *big* it is. As I show in this chapter, there are other factors that define big data.

For the purposes of this chapter, I talk strictly about big data as defined by the four Vs – volume, velocity, variety and veracity – I cover in the following section. In practice, some of the data you use in your business may not exactly qualify as big data, and that's fine. The key to successfully using data is finding the best data for *you* – the data that gives you the insights needed to grow your business – and then making sure you *act* on those insights. (The chapters in Part IV set out this process in detail.) If the best data for you isn't strictly big data, so what? Nobody is going to call the big data police!

Breaking Big Data into Four Vs

Big data is not a passing fad; it's here to stay. And it's going to change the world completely. But to really understand big data, and what separates it from normal data, you need to understand four main factors: volume, velocity, variety and veracity, commonly known as the four Vs of big data. By exploring each of the Vs, you can get a feel for how big data can revolutionise the way you do business.

The four Vs define what is really special about big data, why it's different to regular data, and why it's so transformative. For data to be classed as 'big data' it must satisfy at least one of the Vs: volume, velocity, variety and veracity.

I look at each of the Vs in turn in the next sections.

Growing volumes of data

Volume refers to the vast amounts of data generated every second. Just think of all the emails, Twitter messages, photos, video clips and sensor data you produce and share every second (and those are just for starters). On Facebook alone, ten billion messages are sent, the Like button is clicked 4.5 billion times and 350 million new pictures are uploaded each and every day. You're no longer talking about humble gigabytes of data, but petabytes and even zettabytes or brontobytes of data. To put this in perspective, if you take all the data generated in the world between the beginning of time and the year 2000, the same amount of data is now being generated every minute!

Data on this scale is simply too large to store in traditional ways, such as on a disc or a mainframe computer. Neither can it be analysed using traditional database technology. This is where distributed computing and cloud computing (see Chapter 6) come into their own. Here the storage burden can be shared across lots of computers and servers. Effectively, the data is broken up into parcels which are stored in different locations. The data is managed and brought together by an overarching software program such as Hadoop. I talk a little more about Hadoop in Chapter 9 but, in a nutshell, the system uses a little of the power from each computer to analyse large volumes of data. This is much faster and more efficient than relying on one (very powerful and expensive!) machine to do it.

Theoretically, using distributed systems you can cope with any amount of data, which is a good job when you consider that rates of data are growing at a mind-boggling speed.

This means you talk about big data when the volumes are so big that the data no longer fits into traditional storage systems, such as a single database or data warehouse. For example, if you have an enormous customer database with two million rows of information, it may be a large amount of data, but it's not strictly big data.

Increasing velocity of data

Velocity refers to the speed at which new data is generated and the speed at which data moves around. Just think of social media messages going viral in seconds, the speed at which credit card transactions are checked for fraudulent activities or the milliseconds it takes trading systems to analyse social media networks to pick up signals that trigger decisions to buy or sell shares. Some data is being generated at such a speed that makes it not worth storing – it's out of date seconds later.

For instance, in the example of checking credit card transactions for fraudulent activities (such as a transaction in Rome one minute and a transaction in India ten minutes later), the analysis is done in real time, as the transaction is taking place. There's absolutely no point storing this data and accessing it later. The credit card company needs to analyse it right then and there, on the fly, and has no use for it later.

This is typical of the way many companies use data today. Big data technology, specifically in-memory technology, allows you to analyse the data as it's being generated, without ever putting it into databases.

Exploding variety of data

Variety refers to the different types of data you can now use. In the past, the focus was on structured data that neatly fits into tables or databases, such as financial data. In fact, the vast majority of the world's data is now unstructured, and therefore can't easily be put into tables (think of photos, voice recordings and social media updates). I talk more about the different types of data in Chapters 4 and 5.

With big data technology, you can now harness different types of data, including messages, social media conversations, photos, sensor data, video data and voice recordings, and bring them together with more traditional, structured data. This ability to analyse and use a wide variety of data is really powerful, and you can now extract more business-critical insights than ever before.

For me, variety is the most interesting and exciting aspect of big data. While businesses have been capturing and analysing data for years, the ability to harness a wide range of data is completely transforming your ability to understand the world and everything within it – including, most importantly for business, your customers.

Variety, velocity and volume are very closely linked. Because we're now able to extract information from messy (unstructured) data like Facebook posts and video images, the volume and velocity of data have increased accordingly. The amount of data out there and the rate at which we're generating new data is frightening – and I'm a data expert! The digital universe is doubling in size every two years. At that rate, by 2020 there will be nearly as many bits of information in the digital universe as there are stars in the physical universe.

Coping with the veracity of data

The first three Vs – volume, velocity and variety – formed the original definition of big data by IT (information technology) analytics firm Gartner. Experts have attempted to add on a number of other Vs over time (some useful, some less so), but those three remained the core. However, veracity is a useful and valid fourth V, and it's now widely accepted as a key feature of big data.

Veracity refers to the messiness or trustworthiness of the data. You used to only be able to analyse neat and orderly structured data, data that you trusted as accurate. But now you can cope with unruly and unreliable data.

With many forms of big data, quality and accuracy aren't controllable – just think of Twitter posts with incorrect hash tags, abbreviations, typos and colloquial speech, as well as the reliability and accuracy of the content. But big data and analytics technology now allow you to work with messy data like this. Because there's so much of it, you can make sense of it. In this way, the volumes often make up for the lack of quality or accuracy.

Introducing a fifth V – Value

I'd argue there's another important V to take into account when looking at big data – *value*. Having access to vast amounts of data and many different varieties of data is wonderful, but unless you can turn it into value, it's useless. Data has to earn its keep and provide positive outcomes for your business, such as understanding your customers better or making your production line more efficient. So, while people get giddy with excitement over the volume, velocity and variety of big data, when it comes to business, it's actually value that's the most important V.

It's also important that businesses make a strong business case for any attempt to collect and leverage big data. It's all too easy to fall into the buzz trap and embark on big data initiatives without a clear understanding of the costs and benefits to your business. Therefore, I always advise clients to start by building a business case and developing a data strategy – there's more on this in Chapter 10.

Understanding Why Big Data is Such Big News

Big data seems to have really captured people's imaginations, and I see more and more articles or blogs on the topic each week. Far from a flash-in-the-pan thing, it's becoming a mainstream part of the how businesses operate and make decisions.

Why is big data such a big deal? Well, partly it comes down to the wide applications of big data, which go far beyond business. Big data has a huge role to play in activities as diverse as healthcare, disaster relief efforts and making cities safer, better places to live. Sure, it helps companies sell a lot more stuff, but it's also capable of much, much more.

I think there are three main aspects of big data that make it so newsworthy: its powerful predictive capabilities, how it helps you make much smarter decisions and the way it challenges traditional notions of causality. I look at each of those in turn in the next sections.

Promising predictability

It's no exaggeration to say that with big data you can predict the future. It's kind of like a crystal ball – but made of wires and networks and software.

Thanks to the ever-increasing amount of data and exciting new analytic technologies, experts have the ability to build predictive models for just about anything. This is called *predictive analytics*. Predictive analytics can be used to predict who will buy what when and how many units of a product you'll sell next year; it can be used to predict crop yields for a specific type of seed planted in a certain site; it can even predict civil unrest or outbreaks of viruses.

Making more fact-based decisions

For businesses, the real power of data is that it helps you make smarter decisions that change your business for the better. Want to understand more about your customers so you can run more targeted promotions? Data can help. Want to understand how customers navigate your website so you can make improvements to the site? Data can tell you that. Want to understand what makes your employees tick so you can increase employee satisfaction and reduce staff turnover? You guessed it, data can help.

Big Brother gains a sibling

Researchers have realised that Twitter updates can more quickly and more accurately predict flu outbreaks than traditional CDC (that's the US Center for Disease Control and Prevention) tracking methods. In fact, Twitter data can predict an outbreak up to eight days in advance with more than 90 per cent accuracy. In another example, the African company CellTel realised a similar predictive capability when it noticed an uptick in prepaid phone cards before major incidents of violence and unrest in Congo. CellTel realised that the cards were denominated in US dollars, and people bought them to have something portable and valuable to take with them to protect against local inflation.

These predictive models can also be more than a little disconcerting as one Minneapolis father found out. After his local Target store sent his 15-year-old daughter coupons for discounted maternity products, he visited the store to complain. Absolutely furious, he said to the manager 'My daughter got this in the mail! She's still in high school, and you're sending her coupons for baby clothes and cribs. Are you trying to encourage her to get pregnant?'

The manager could clearly see that the coupons had been sent to the daughter so he apologised on behalf of the company and put it down to an error. In fact, the manager was so disturbed by the mailer that he called a few days later to apologise again to the father. Only by this time, things had changed. 'I had a talk with my daughter,' the father explained. 'It turns out there's been some activity in my house I haven't been completely aware of. She's due in August. I owe you an apology.'

Astonishingly, big data and analytics meant that Target knew a high school girl was pregnant before her own father did. How did they know? Well, the company had been able to identify 25 products that, when analysed together, allowed their statistician, Andrew Pole, to assign each shopper a 'pregnancy prediction' score. Sending coupons congratulating people on their pregnancy was obviously going to freak them out and make them feel uncomfortable (hello, Big Brother!) so what they ended up doing was mixing baby-related merchandise coupons in with other coupons that they knew the client would not be interested in so that it looked random. The predictive model worked, increasing Target's revenue from $44 billion in 2002 (when Pole was hired) to $67 billion in 2010.

So much of business is based on experience or good old gut reactions. And there's still a place for that to some degree. But in this day and age you have the ability to base your decisions on so much more than instinct and what's worked in the past. Today, almost everything in business can be measured, quantified and analysed, and, in doing so, you can dramatically improve your decisions. That's not to say there's no room for gut instinct or that all decision making must be a sterile, concrete process. On the contrary – I'd argue the smartest decisions are those based on the hard facts of data viewed with the wisdom of experience.

In Chapter 11, I set out a step-by-step process for using data to improve decision making in your business. It's an approach I use all the time with clients. But there's also a bigger, cultural shift required to transform decision making across your company, and I explore that in Chapter 13.

Challenging causality

One of the big discussions in big data is that it allows you to challenge traditional models of *causality*, or cause and effect.

With big data, it's all about correlations, rather than causality. So, when I buy Product A from Amazon, the site tells me 'People who bought Product A also bought Product B'. Amazon uses the correlation between the products to sell more, but they don't necessarily need to understand *why* people who bought Product A also bought Product B. Nor does the customer, for that matter. In this way, causality becomes less important. You no longer need to understand why one thing leads to another, you just listen to what the data tells you.

Turning science on its head

This focus on correlations potentially challenges the whole scientific method. In the past if you wanted to know something, you developed a hypothesis and ran experiments to establish whether the hypothesis was correct or not. The experiments that took place would vary depending on what you were trying to find out but, regardless of whether you were seeking to understand consumer behaviour or the efficacy of a new drug, the experiment would always take a sample of data, people, ingredients or components in order to test the hypothesis. The sample was always therefore limited in size and the results were then extrapolated out to make assumptions or best- and worst-case scenario predictions for everything from the spread of disease to the accumulation of credit card debt.

This approach has worked well and is credited with many breakthroughs in just about every area of human endeavour. But big data could change all that. If you test a hypothesis on consumer behaviour, for example, the sample of people you test the hypothesis on is based on the assumption that the sample is representative of all consumers (N = all). It's not. But it was the best option considering the lack of data. The advent of big data – and specifically the technology to store, collate and analyse that data – means lack of data is no longer the problem. Theoretically, at least you can use a sample where N really does equal all.

The danger, of course, is that N does not equal all any more than the sample equals all. For example, if an insurance company is able to use all claim information and finds a correlation between fraud and the amount of time taken to complete an online claim form, it doesn't need to know *why* time is an indication of fraud, it just needs to know that it is so it can initiate an investigation of all claims over a certain time period. But what about the person who is not very computer literate, or the person who was interrupted by her sleeping toddler waking up crying? The correlation isn't representative of all people all of the time. Similarly, with the Target pregnancy indicator example from the sidebar 'Big Brother gains a sibling', what if the customer was buying products for a friend or for a non-pregnancy-related use? (A lot of people, for instance, use nappies, or diapers, in plant pots to help provide the plants with extra nutrition.)

There's a real danger that you could be pigeonholed by all sorts of organisations and businesses based on probability, not reality. What happens when someone is refused a mortgage because some algorithm identifies that person as a high risk even though she's never actually defaulted on a mortgage before? What happens if your insurance premium is increased based on your probability to claim in the future even though that future hasn't arrived yet?

When correlations go crazy

If you ever took a science class in school, you might have heard the phrase, 'Correlation does not equal causation'. For example, if data tells you that men over six feet tall spend more money online, that doesn't mean their height *caused* them to spend more money.

And that can be the problem when data analysts are looking at these strange and interesting new truths that emerge from the mass quantities of data to which they now have access. If you take it as true that orange used cars are more reliable, the question then becomes why. Are owners of orange cars more careful? Does the colour prevent people from getting in accidents? Or does the colour orange have some other magical property that keeps a car running well? The data has no answers, it just tells you what is.

Tyler Vigen posts funny charts to his website, Spurious Correlations (www.tylervigen.com), that show the danger of simply matching two data sets without any deeper understanding of how the things are related. For example, if correlation is all you need to go by, then you can assume that the more films Nicolas Cage appears in in any given year, the more people drown in swimming pools. Or you can assume that an increase in US spending on science will result in an increase of suicides by hanging. Spurious indeed, you hope, or US researchers and Nic Cage's film career are in trouble.

Don't take absolutely everything that data tells you at face value and never ever change your business strategy based on potentially bogus correlations. If your data throws up some strange and interesting correlations, try validating those findings using other data sets to see if there really is a genuine link.

Three companies that really get the big data buzz

If you're still unsure what all the fuss is about, or don't understand how companies can really put big data to work, check out these amazing new companies making data work for them. I also look at big data uses for businesses in more detail Chapter 3.

✔ **Metamind:** Metamind creates natural language processing, image recognition and artificial intelligence software. Founder Richard Socher merged mathematics with language to create deep learning systems with potentially groundbreaking applications in industry and for consumers. Launched in 2014 after raising $8 million in funding, the technology is designed to make machines think and act more like people. For example, teach the machine what a flower looks like by showing it an image, and it should be able to recognise flowers when it sees another picture of them – allowing it to categorise the data accordingly. Internet giants like Google and Facebook are known to be putting a huge amount of effort into making interacting with computers more like interacting with humans, and technology like Metamind's could be a big step forward.

✔ **Flatiron Health:** Flatiron Health is putting big data to work in one of the most important battles facing doctors and scientists today – the fight against cancer. By automatically analysing terabytes of data collected during the diagnosis and treatment of cancer patients, the company hopes its OncologyCloud will harvest insights from the 96% of available patient data which is not yet collected or processed. In 2014, it received $130 million in funding, with the majority coming from Google, and it recently acquired cloud-based medical records provider Altos Solutions. The plan is to use Altos Solutions technology to make OncologyCloud's data and insights available to as many healthcare professionals as possible.

✔ **Affectiva:** Affectiva is another name you might not have heard of, but you might find yourself using (or creepily, and more likely, being used by its software) in the near future! Affectiva creates 'emotional measurement technology' – generally based on facial-recognition – that allow photos and videos to be analysed to determine the mood and feeling of the people featured. The technology can be used for judging the reaction of audiences to adverts, measuring the mood of people pictured interacting with a company's brand or service, or judging the mood of the audience of a political debate. Coca Cola and Unilever have both used the firm's software to carry out analysis, and the technology is likely to become more widely used in marketing and many other applications.

Why Now? A Cloud Full of Data

You understand what defines big data and what makes it so exciting. But why is it such a big deal at this particular point in time? Like planets aligning, several factors have come together at the right time to make harnessing big data a reality.

I talk more about the key technological advances that make big data possible in Chapter 6, and I go into building a big data infrastructure in Chapter 9. Here, I give a quick overview of the main technological advances: better storage, faster networks and more powerful analytics. All of these advances come together to create big data.

Harnessing more storage than ever before

In the past, if you wanted to house a lot of data, you needed to invest in some pretty heavy-duty kit, like mainframe computers. Now, companies big and small can buy inexpensive, off-the-shelf storage systems that are connected to the Internet.

Now you have connected computers and servers which give you more storage capacity than ever before. Data can be parcelled up and stored across a range of machines in different locations. Massive increases in storage and computing power, some of it available via cloud computing, make number crunching possible on a very large scale and at declining cost.

In addition, these advances in computer storage and processing power have meant that for the first time you are able to analyse large, complex and messy data sets (which previously would have been far too big to store).

For example, we've been able to record video data for a long time but a lack of storage capacity or a way to really analyse those recordings limited their utility. But all that is changing. In days gone by the only video data that was collected was security closed-circuit data (CCTV). The purpose of that data was to monitor retail or business premises for shoplifting, malicious damage or employee wrongdoing. Most of the security systems would loop recordings which meant that they would record continuously onto video tapes or digital hard drives and then after a set number of days the recording would loop back and re-record over the old data. If there was no incident in the area being recorded then the data was useless so it was erased over and over again. However, with the advances in video and image analytics all that is changing. The data is now being viewed as useful in ways that were not even considered before, such as understanding how customers move around a store and how the placement of products and staff affects their buying decisions. Like all big data and analytic changes, this has come about primarily because of the quantum leap in storage capability. Ten years ago it would have been unheard of to record and store all that CCTV footage – you'd have needed a warehouse just to keep the old tapes, which would degrade if not kept in a temperature-controlled environment! No business in its right mind would swallow the massive costs involved in storing all that video, especially as there was no way to really analyse it at the time.

When you consider that the amount of stored information grows four times faster than the world economy, and the processing power of computers grows nine times faster, it's easy to see how all that stored data could now become useful.

Fuelling big data with faster networks

Distributed computing gives you greater storage capability than ever before, but it also allows you to connect data faster than ever before. With data being spread across many different locations, the ability to bring that data together in a split second is key.

Without faster networks that connect data sets together for analysis, big data just wouldn't be a practical option. With these faster networks and overarching data software like MapReduce, Big Table and Hadoop, you can break up the analysis of data into manageable chunks, meaning that no one machine has to bear all the load. This makes analysis faster and far more efficient.

There's more on using systems like this and building your own big data infrastructure in Chapter 9.

Taking advantage of new and better analytical capability

Our improved analytical capability is closely related to better networks and increased storage. Without the ability to store and access all this data, you wouldn't be able to analyse it and extract useful insights.

Analytical advances can be summarised by three key factors:

- ✔ Thanks to distributed computing you can analyse data much faster than ever before, often in real time as something is happening (think of the credit card transactions).

- ✔ You can also analyse a much wider variety of data: faces, videos, speech and so on. It's no longer all about rows and columns in a spreadsheet.

- ✔ You have innovative new ways of analysing the data itself. For example, you can analyse tone of voice in conversations between call centre staff and customers.

In the past if you wanted access to data or wanted to be able to gain insights from that data, it needed to be contained in a structured relational database and you needed to use SQL query tools (see Chapter 4) to extract any value. That's now no longer the case – the data can be in just about any form, structured, unstructured, text, audio, video, sensor, imagines, messy or neat – and you can still extract value from it.

In the past, the only way to analyse CCTV video was to physically sit and watch it frame by frame. The latest video analytics tools are changing all that because they now use algorithms that go through video, scene-by-scene, shot-by-shot, and actually capture what is in the video. And then they index that information and use it to identify patterns or cross reference it with other analytic tools.

What Next for Big Data?

Big data is an exciting field with the power to completely change the way you do business. And it's easy to get so caught up in the positives that you overlook the potential negative aspects of big data. Although I'm a strong advocate for using big data, I do believe it's important to be aware of the ethical issues. This is especially important in business, as reputation is so critical to success. Thanks to social media, scandals can travel around the world in the blink of an eye and reputations that took years to build up can be damaged in just a few seconds.

When you hear about these predictive models and what companies are doing with big data and analytics, there's a real danger that privacy will give way to probability. And there's also clearly an issue of transparency – an issue that I believe businesses need to manage very carefully.

There are still significant moral and ethical dilemmas to be ironed out in this area. Big data is a little like the gold rush – a lawless frontier of extraordinary opportunity for those willing to take the early risk. But the law will catch up as more and more people become increasingly uncomfortable about what's being collected, how it's used and what's now possible.

Bracing for the big data backlash

I've predicted for a while that there'll be a backlash to big data. At every seminar or keynote speech I give, people are always shocked by the level of data collection going on that they weren't aware of. You sign your life and privacy away so easily these days with very little thought. Few people are fully aware of just how much analysis Facebook is doing and how much it can understand about you based on what you like and what you upload.

Like most brilliant innovations, big data can be used for good and bad. The possibilities of face recognition software alone are more than a little frightening, and whilst that software can help to prevent crime and thwart terrorist activities, it can also be used to spy on ordinary people for commercial purposes. And therein lies one of the biggest challenges – most people have absolutely no idea what's going on in darkened rooms in places that don't officially exist or in the basements of giant corporations that have access to masses of data and futuristic technology.

You don't know what data is being compiled about you. Even if companies or applications tell you in their terms and conditions, you, like most people, don't read them. Or even if you do read them, you may not understand them or understand the implications of what you agree to.

One of my favourite examples of the lack of understanding in this area comes from a short experiment in 2014 designed to highlight the dangers of public Internet. Customers in a London café were asked to agree to terms and conditions as they logged on to use the free Wi-Fi. In the terms was a clause which stipulated the user would 'assign their first-born child' to the company in return for free Wi-Fi access. Several people willingly agreed!

Lots of small businesses use Google's email service, Gmail – it's free, it's reliable and you get tons of storage. But did you know that, as it's offering you that free service, Google feels that you can't legitimately expect privacy when using the service. Basically Google believes it is okay to read and analyse the content of any and all emails sent or received from a Gmail user. This revelation was put forward in a brief that was filed in a US federal court as part of a lawsuit against Google. Google is accused of breaking US federal and state laws by scanning the emails of Gmail users and in its defence put forward this statement (which was recently exposed by Consumer Watchdog):

> *Just as a sender of a letter to a business colleague cannot be surprised that the recipient's assistant opens the letter, people who use web-based email today cannot be surprised if their communications are processed by the recipient's ECS provider in the course of delivery.*

So, essentially, if you sign up to use Gmail, you waive all rights to privacy, and Google can use what it discovers using text analytics to better target its advertising. My guess is that probably 95% of the 400+ million users of the Gmail service don't currently realise this. But it's not just Google. Facebook is famous – or rather infamous – for constantly tinkering with privacy policy and privacy settings.

Everyone understands that companies need to make money and providing a free email service such as Gmail may be reward enough for some people. Many people may not care about privacy. But if we're to navigate these murky waters safely, then I believe there needs to be much, much more transparency about what's being collected and how the data is being used or could potentially be used.

What your Facebook Likes say about you

Today everything is potentially data, and even the most innocuous piece of information can be turned into insight if you apply analytics to a large enough data set.

Did you know, for example, that your Likes on Facebook are used to expose intimate details about you as well as personality traits and preferences that you might not otherwise share? Most of us don't want to share personal details such as our religious beliefs, political views, sexual orientation or how much alcohol we drink. It's none of anyone's business!

And yet, a study conducted by researchers at Cambridge University and Microsoft Research Labs showed how the patterns of Facebook Likes can be used automatically to very accurately predict a range of highly sensitive personal attributes. Using the Like data of 58,000 volunteers the study also illustrated that the ,Likes can have little or nothing to do with the actual attributes they help to predict. Often a single Like is enough to generate an accurate prediction.

The study found that a Like for:

- Curly Fries, Science, Mozart, Thunderstorms or *The Daily Show* predicted high intelligence.

- Harley Davidson, Lady Antebellum and I Love Being a Mom predicted low intelligence.

- Swimming, Jesus, *Pride and Prejudice* and Indiana Jones predicted satisfaction with life.

- iPod, Kickass, Lamb of God, Quote Portal and Gorillaz predicted dissatisfaction with life.

- So So Happy, Dot Dot Curve, *Girl Interrupted, The Adams Family* and Kurt Donald Cobain predicted being emotionally unstable or neurotic.

- Business Administration, Skydiving, Soccer, Mountain Biking and Parkour predicted being emotionally stable or calm and relaxed.

- Cup Of Joe For A Joe, Coffee Party Movement, *The Closer,* Freedomworks, Small Business Saturday and Fly The American Flag predicted that you were old.

- Body By Milk, I Hate My Id Photo, Dude. Wait, What?, J Bigga and Because I Am A Girl predicted that you were young.

- Kathy Griffin, Adam Lambert, Wicked The Musical, Sue Sylvester Glee and Juicy Couture predicted you were a homosexual man.

- X Games, Foot Locker, Being Confused After Waking Up From Naps, Sportsnation, WWE and Wu-Tang Clan predicted you were a heterosexual man.

When you click Like, you want to show your friends on Facebook that you feel positive or supportive of specific online content such as status updates, photos or products, books, music or other individuals such as celebrities. What you may not realise is that by doing so you openly share information about yourself that can then be used to predict other, more personal, attributes that you would never dream of sharing so openly.

When it comes to data and the law, many legal systems are playing catch-up. In Scandinavian countries, for example, data protection laws are much more stringent than the UK and US. I predict that new legislation will be implemented in the UK and US to tighten up data protection and individual privacy. I believe (and I hope) companies will need to be much more upfront about what they collect and why, and consumers will have a more obvious opt-in/opt-out choice regarding their data.

Encouraging transparency and ethics

I feel that a lot of data collection practices aren't very ethical. Facebook, for example, buries a lot of what it does with data in a 50-page user agreement that nobody reads. I think it's vital that businesses explain to their customers what data they're collecting and how they intend to use it.

If you weren't a terribly ethical company and your goal was simply to collect as much data as possible without caring much about what anyone thought, then that approach would probably work fine for you in the short term. You probably could collect a load of data. But that's not a very sustainable long-term approach to business.

The more ethical you are, the more valuable your data is in the longer term. If you aren't upfront about what information you're collecting and storing about your customers, then there's a danger that data could be taken away from you or your reputation could be damaged. If people understand what data they're giving over to your company and how you'll be using it, they're generally happy for it to be used. Nobody likes finding out they've been duped!

Say I buy myself a shiny new Apple watch. I'm happy for Apple to collect certain data on me (such as sleep patterns or how many steps I take a day) because the company is clear about what it's tracking and the data it collects helps me lead a healthier lifestyle, so I'm getting something in return. But, hypothetically speaking, imagine if Apple then started selling my data to my health insurance company, who used that information to alter my premiums. I don't know about you, but I'd be livid. I'd feel that was a huge invasion of my privacy and not at all what I signed up for – and I'm not getting anything in return except for potentially higher premiums.

Follow these tips for data transparency and your customers will thank you for it:

- ✔ If you collect personal information on your customers or employees, be upfront about it.
- ✔ Explain why you're collecting that information (for example, so that you can provide a better service).

✔ Don't hide this information in lengthy user agreements or terms and conditions that no one will read. Keep it short, easy-to-understand and put the information in an obvious place. A few sentences when customers register their details to shop online is a good example.

✔ Offer customers something in return for parting with their precious data (such as a discount for customers who take part in a survey, or making the online ordering process much easier in future once you have their data on record).

✔ Always give customers the option to opt out. Even if this means they can no longer use your service, or parts of your service, it's far better to give them the choice.

✔ Use *aggregated data,* data that is not tied to any specific individual, wherever possible. Facebook, for example, provides information to interested third parties on trends and hot topics that isn't tied to individual users. Depending on what you're using data for, you may not need data on individuals, just a bigger picture on what a collective of people are up to.

Making sure you add value

When you're collecting data on people, it's not just important to be honest about it, it's a good idea to add value for them – something that makes it worth their while.

For example, I have one of the latest smart televisions from Samsung that allows me to program the television and, using the inbuilt camera, it detects the faces of my children and limits what they can watch. I don't mind Samsung knowing what I watch, when I watch and how long I watch my smart television because Samsung is helping me and my wife to protect our children from stuff they shouldn't see. Samsung did, however, get into trouble when it came out that it's actually counting the number of people watching television. I think this sort of problem could be avoided with greater transparency and by delivering increased value to the user.

Make it beneficial for people to share their information with your business, either through better or cheaper products or services. Always seek to add value so that the people providing the data, be they customers, employees or other stakeholders, feel it's a fair and worthwhile exchange. Aim for a win-win for all parties.

If you provide value, most people will be happy for you to use their data – especially if you're able to remove personal markers that link them as an individual to the information. If you can demonstrate that you're using the data ethically, people will respond positively. Ultimately, this makes the data more valuable to you in the long term – it's no good using data to understand more about your customers if they leave in droves because they feel you've invaded their privacy.

Chapter 3

Identifying Big Data Uses in Small Businesses

*I*n 2014, market research revealed that 70 per cent of businesses had either launched a big data strategy, or were planning one for the near future. You may think this applies to big-budget corporations only, using data to get even bigger. Does big data provide the same opportunities for small business and independent traders? Absolutely!

While the big players can rely on their own customer databases and monitoring processes to improve their analytics, the average small business has less self-generated data. But this doesn't mean big data is off limits. Small businesses can benefit from existing big data that's already out there, buy big data services and become more focused on collecting their own data.

In many ways, big data is suited to small business in ways that it never was for big business – even the most potent insights are valueless if your business is not agile enough to act on them in a timely fashion. Small businesses generally have the advantage of agility, making them perfectly suited to act on data-derived insights with speed and efficiency.

To help you get a feel for how data could help your business, in this chapter I look at the main uses of big data, with plenty of real-life examples. I also look at some compelling big data facts and figures in the sidebar 'Astonishing big data statistics every business owner should know' later in the chapter.

Understanding Your Customers and Markets

Three key strands allow you to understand your customers and markets: one is getting a full and rich picture of your customers (who they are, where they are, what they want and so on); the second is identifying bigger picture trends in your industry that could lead to new product or service offerings; and the third is seeing what your competition is up to. Big data can help with each of these areas. Social media has become a particularly valuable source of data – activities such as identifying niche markets and analysing customer feedback are much easier when you're tuned into the possibilities of social media.

Getting a 360-degree view of your customers

This is one of the biggest and most publicised areas of big data use today. Here, businesses use big data to better understand customers and their behaviours and preferences. Businesses can gain a full understanding of customers – what makes them tick, why they buy, how they prefer to shop, why they switch, what they'll buy next and what factors lead them to recommend a company to others. Companies can also better interact and engage with customers by analysing customer feedback in order to improve a product or service.

Getting a more complete picture of your customers may involve a combination of traditional in-house data, social media data and browser logs, as well as text analytics and sensor data (there's more on different types of data in Chapters 4 and 5). Small businesses can also take advantage of large, public data sets to glean in-depth insights on their customers.

Aggregators or hub companies are springing up in most industries that provide data services to small companies. One example of this is Factual. com, which provides location data to help companies serve their own customers with more personalised experiences and recommendations. Other services and tools exist to make it easier for businesses to dip their toes into the water and see if the results will be worth the investment. For example, Silverpop, which was acquired by IBM, Adestra and Marketo all offer marketing automation driven by data – either from the business's own data, or from bought-in or public records.

Food delivery outlets have been quick to jump on board the Just Eat and Hungry House bandwagons, which allow customers to order food straight from their smartphones to their homes. The thousands of restaurants they have signed up all have access to data telling them what their customers usually order, what days of the week they like to get food delivered and what other restaurants they patronise in the local area. Restaurant owners can use this to find the optimum locations for their delivery outlets as well as to schedule offers and promotions and tailor their own menu to suit their customers' tastes. They also get access to valuable metrics, such as how far away their average customer lives, how much they spend and what time of day they like to eat. TripAdvisor.com offers similar data services to owners of hotels, restaurants and leisure companies (big or small).

Harnessing the power of social media

Social media is an obvious and powerful source of data for any small business. All of the big platforms, including Facebook and Twitter, offer targeted advertising, allowing you to precisely target the age groups and geographical areas where your products and services will sell. An effective social campaign provides you with a wealth of Likes, Shares and Comments which gives insight into who you are reaching and how they are responding.

Even without spending a penny, social media platforms can be used to see who is talking about what – and determine how that is likely to affect demand for products or services (if this appeals to you, check out the section on conversation data in Chapter 5). Twitter – where almost all conversations are effectively held in public – is easier to mine than most platforms, and its ongoing status as the second most popular social media network cements its value.

In 2014, IBM announced a partnership with Twitter, offering new services to help businesses pull insights directly from tweets. The companies involved in the early testing of the service have not been named, but IBM gave several examples of the kinds of insights which have been unearthed. These included a communications company which was able to reduce customer churn by 5 per cent by predicting where customers were most likely to be affected by loss of service due to bad weather. Also mentioned was a food and drink retailer which discovered that high staff turnover was one of the factors that negatively affected the value of their most loyal customers.

Making retail more customer focused

I've worked with a number of bricks-and-mortar retailers who are starting to use data to compete with online retailers.

In a trial recently announced by House of Fraser, customers approaching mannequins in one outlet will receive information on their phone about the clothes the dummy is wearing, directions on where to find them on the racks and the option of buying them immediately from the online store. The communication is two-way – as well as giving customers information, the system is designed to receive information about customers, including their location in the store, their pattern of movement and, of course, what they eventually spend money on. This allows managers to spot patterns in how altering the store layout or pricing affects sales.

If this seems beyond the scope of smaller retailers, think again. These days, many customers carry smartphones which can be used to track movement through a store. And inexpensive sensors in store windows can measure footfall and how many people stop to look in your window – great for testing window displays or special offer signs.

Understanding (and predicting) trends in your industry

Wouldn't it be great to be able to predict the future? If you had a crystal ball or a time machine, you could remove all of the guesswork from making business decisions. You'd directly see the products of your labour and instantly know whether or not your present efforts were on the right track. This is where trend spotting comes into play. Whether you intend to buck them or follow them, as a business person, you seek to identify trends in industrial practices, customer behaviour and anything that could make a difference to your bottom line.

Spotting and monitoring behaviours and patterns allows you to take a stab at predicting where things are heading, how demand for your products or services will change over time and what will prompt that change. What can you do to respond to it? To increase demand when it's low and ensure supply when it's high? Until recently, trend analysis and prediction often came down to *gut instinct* – that feeling that people who are confident in their abilities get, and which they often feel puts them at the top of their game or gives them an edge over their competitors. Now, big data is taking a lot of the guesswork out of that process – it's the closest thing you have to a crystal ball!

Marketing is a great example of understanding and predicting trends. With the advent of social media and the Internet, people are used to (knowingly or unknowingly) sharing vast amounts of data about themselves, their interests, habits, likes and dislikes – and savvy marketers have been quick to tap into this. Trending topics flash across Facebook and Twitter every day, making it easier than it has ever been before to work out what people are looking for and what they want. Products and services can then be marketed to fill those needs. Services such as Trendera and Trend Hunter collate this data and use it to answer specific questions for their business customers.

The ability to know what the public wants before they know it themselves is every business's Holy Grail. In retail, online and offline customer behaviour can be measured to microscopic detail. That data can be compared with external data, such as the time of the year, economic conditions and even the weather, to build up a detailed picture of what people are likely to buy and when. If you run an organic farm shop, for example, weather data can help you identify in advance when you're likely to sell a truck load of sausages and ice cream. This information can also inform your production and stock levels and marketing activity.

Much of this technology is based on free, open-source software, or inexpensive, software-as-service cloud-based solutions. And a lot of businesses have gained very valuable insights from the free, huge public datasets made available by companies like Google (Google Trends is a fantastic tool) and government services such as data.gov.uk. In fact, I devote a whole chapter (Chapter 15) to the top ten free data sources for small businesses. Technology like this makes it perfectly viable for many small and medium-sized enterprises to have a crack at predicting the future themselves. You might not yet have the technology to actually see into the future, but now you have the ability to remove the guesswork and replace it with cold, hard data-driven insights.

Reviewing the competition

In the past, understanding your competition was limited to industry gossip or looking around rivals' websites or shops. Some competitors might go as far as pretending to be customers in order to find out more about a service or product. These days, however, you hardly need to leave your desk to find out what the competition is up to.

Today you can access a wealth of data on your competitors: financial data is readily available, Google Trends can offer insights on the popularity of a brand or product, and social media analysis can illustrate popularity (how often a company is mentioned, for example) and show what customers are saying. Twitter is particularly transparent and a brilliant place to start. All the information you gather can be compared with your own brand; for example, does your competitor get more mentions on Twitter? How do their Twitter conversations with customers compare with yours? Does their Facebook page have more Likes and Shares than yours? Now you can get a much richer picture of your competitors than ever before.

The flip side of course is that your competitors will be able to glean just as much information on your company. There's not much to be done about this, unless you want to withdraw from online life and social media platforms altogether (not at all recommended for modern businesses!). The best way to stay one step ahead is to keep up-to-date on advances in big data – by reading books like this – and treat it as an ongoing part of your business life, not just a one-off project or investment.

Improving Your Operations

Big data is also increasingly used to optimise business processes and everyday operations. With any business process that generates data (for example, machinery on a production line, sensors on delivery vehicles, customer ordering systems), you can use that data to make improvements and generate efficiencies. There's more information on using data to transform operations in Chapter 12; here I look at some of the key options.

Gaining internal efficiencies

For companies with a manufacturing or industrial focus, machines, vehicles and tools can be made 'smart', which means they can be connected, data-enabled and constantly reporting their status to each other. Machine data can include anything from IT machines to sensors and meters and GPS devices.

By using this data for operations analysis, organisations can gain real-time visibility into their operations. This increases efficiency by allowing every aspect of an industrial operation to be monitored and tweaked for optimal performance. It also reduces costly down-time – because machinery will break down less often if you know exactly the best time to replace a worn part.

This use of data isn't limited to manufacturing businesses. In retail, for example, companies are able to optimise their stock based on predictions generated from social media data, web search trends and weather forecasts. This allows stores to stock up on the most popular items, ensuring they don't miss out on sales and reducing the amount of unwanted stock lying around. Depending on the systems you choose, this process can even be automatic, with stock automatically replenished when certain conditions are identified, such as on-hand stock of an item drops below a set number.

Challenging your business model

Data can even become a part of your business model, leading to exciting new ways to generate revenue. Facebook, for example, is free to users but has historically generated income from advertising. Now the company is capitalising on the huge amount of data it has on its users, by making certain data available to businesses. Some of this data is available for free but some of it you have to pay for, creating a new income stream for Facebook.

You may not be a big data giant like Facebook, you may not even be generating data on a 'big' scale, but data could still influence your business model. If you have the ability to generate data, you may find that data could prove valuable above and beyond what it was originally intended for (see the sidebar, 'Planting the seeds of a great app' for an example of this).

Obviously, this way of using data is an 'icing on the cake' sort of thing. Most businesses set out with a very particular goal (or goals) they want to achieve with the help of data, and many are happy sticking to that. But, when it comes to data, it's always a good idea to stay open to new possibilities. If this appeals to you, check out Chapter 13 for more information on building a big data culture and incorporating data into your business model.

Planting the seeds of a great app

A popular local garden centre created a free app for customers to help them record their gardening activities – a bit like a gardening journal but on your phone or tablet. Customers could purchase seeds and plants through the app, record what they planted and when, note pests and diseases and record when the plants flowered (or, in the case of vegetables, were harvested). The firm's original goals were to increase sales and encourage customer loyalty. But, the data itself turned out to have an additional value above and beyond the original goals.

The data was providing a detailed picture of local gardening conditions, including which varieties of plants and vegetables worked best in the local climate and what the common problems and pests were. While not on a big data scale, the data was still incredibly valuable because of its regional focus. The centre introduced a premium version of the app which provided this information to customers for a small fee. Paying customers could get reliable information on which varieties flowered earliest and for the longest, which were vulnerable to disease, how prevalent the dreaded tomato blight was and many other green-fingered tips – all targeted to their geographic region.

Optimising your supply chain

Supply chain, or delivery route, optimisation is one business process that benefits heavily from big data analytics, largely because it's an area that's so rich in data. Here, GPS and sensors are used to track goods or delivery vehicles and optimise routes by integrating live traffic data and so on. Inexpensive sensors can be placed on vehicles or individual pallets, or businesses can use their drivers' smartphones to track progress.

One great example comes from a pizza delivery company that tracks drivers very simply using the GPS sensors in their smartphones. This gives the company new insights into how to optimise delivery routes – by tracking where their drivers are and monitoring traffic conditions using publicly available data, they're able to deliver to customers faster and more efficiently. This means fewer free pizzas given away for late delivery (and your tasty pizza arriving in your belly earlier)!

Astonishing big data statistics every business owner should know

Big data is changing the world as we know it. If you don't believe me, check out some of these staggering statistics:

✔ Ninety per cent of the data in existence was created in the last two years.

✔ Every two days we create as much information as we did from the beginning of time until 2003.

✔ Big data was a $28.5 billion market in 2014, predicted to grow to $50.1 billion overall in 2017.

✔ Companies that use big data analytics are five times more likely to make decisions faster than their competition.

✔ Retailers could increase their profit margins by more than 60 per cent through the full exploitation of big data analytics.

✔ Customer experience enhancement is expected to be the largest big data business category, and the one with the most growth, with forecasts saying this sector will grow from $0.75 billion in 2015 to $3.57 billion in 2020.

✔ AT&T is thought to hold the world's largest volume of data in one unique database – its phone records database is 312 terabytes in size and contains almost two trillion rows.

✔ If you burned all of the data created in just one day onto DVDs, you could stack them on top of each other and reach the moon – twice.

Tackling Your Key Business Enablers

Business enablers are all the things that make your business successful, whether it's your people, your systems, or your ability to create a brilliant product. Big data has a role to play in improving almost every aspect of your business, but here I focus on some of the key enablers, namely your people, your IT and security and research and development.

Recruiting and managing talent

Companies are nothing without the right people. More often than not it's the people that give a small business its competitive edge. It's therefore absolutely vital that businesses find, recruit and retain the right people. Data can help you find the most successful candidates, understand whether your current recruitment channels are effective and help keep your existing employees happy.

A client of mine wanted to recruit self-driven people able to take initiative. By analysing different data sets from the type of people they wanted to recruit and those they wanted to avoid, the company found that candidates who filled out applications with browsers that weren't pre-installed on their computers and that had to be installed separately (such as Firefox or Chrome) tended to be better for that particular job. This was a simple thing to measure but it streamlined the process (eliminating those that didn't meet the criteria before interview stage) and meant the company could find the right sort of people more easily. Another one of my retail clients is now able to analyse social media profiles in order to very accurately predict the level of intelligence as well as the emotional stability of potential candidates.

The applications go way beyond recruitment. For a seemingly people-focused area, HR (human resources) processes generate a surprising amount of data. Much of this is related to staff performance and engagement, such as absenteeism figures, productivity data, personal development reviews and staff satisfaction data. In addition to these traditional types of data, companies can now collect so much more data that wasn't available before: capturing employees on closed-circuit television (CCTV), taking screenshots when staff are using company computers, scanning social media data, analysing the content of emails and even monitoring where employees are using the data from geo-positioning sensors in corporate smartphones. The challenge is to establish what data is really going to make an impact on your company performance. What's really useful? It might, for example, be increasing employee satisfaction in order to reduce staff turnover and sick leave.

With more than half of human resources departments reporting an increase in data analytics since 2010, it's obvious that data-driven HR practices are here to stay. While capturing data on this scale may all seem a bit Big Brother, the benefits to businesses can be huge. The benefits to a company able to accurately identify why one particular customer sales representative outperforms his colleagues are obvious. The same is true in sports, where big data analytics is playing an increasing role in boosting performance – as shown in the sidebar 'How sports team use data to get the most out of people'.

Crunching employee data could prove disastrous if a company gets it wrong. In workplaces where morale is low or relationships between workers and managers are not good, it could very easily be seen as a case of taking snooping too far. It's vitally important that staff are made aware of precisely what data is being gathered from them and what it is being used for. Everyone (and certainly those running the operation) needs to be aware that the purpose is to increase overall company efficiency rather than assess or monitor individual members of staff.

Dealing with IT and security

Big data can help optimise IT (information technology) resources, which, in a small company, can be especially precious. Data and algorithms can be used to identify vulnerabilities in IT systems, reduce risk, detect fraud and monitor cyber security in real time.

One way big data allows businesses to detect fraud is by analysing credit card transactions in real time. This includes the ability to shut down transactions that are suspicious or not feasible, for example, purchasing something in New York City at 2 p.m. and in New Deli at 3 p.m. On a much grander scale, big data analytics are also used to detect terrorist activity and cyber security attracts by constantly monitoring and processing data including phone conversations, social media messages and emails as well as sensor and machine data.

A great example comes from the insurance industry, which has made great strides in using data to detect fraud. By analysing the length of time taken to complete a claim online, or by analysing whether a client goes back and changes information on a previous page, they can flag a potentially fraudulent claim.

How sports teams use data to get the most out of people

The 2011 film *Moneyball* (and the Michael Lewis book it's based on) stoked public interest in the way data are used in sports. After showing the way Oakland Athletics general manager Billy Beane used analytics to reverse the fortunes of his ailing MLB team, development of data approaches to sports has continued to grow and evolve. Teams and the analytics providers have come up with increasingly sophisticated ways of monitoring and capturing ever-growing volumes of data. Cameras, sensors and wearables record every aspect of player performance. Managers, coaches and athletes are using data to track calorie intake, training levels and even fan interaction in the chase for better performance on the field.

In the UK, Premier League football team Arsenal recently invested millions in developing its own analytics team to make better use of the data it collects. One important data stream comes from eight cameras installed around its stadium to track every player and player interactions. The system by sports analytics provider Prozone tracks ten data points per second for every player – 1.4 million data points per game. The system is also used to monitor 12,000 soccer matches around the world, which are all analysed using automated algorithms as well as manual coding of every interaction with the ball to increase the accuracy and value of the analysis.

In addition to video analytics, wearable devices are increasingly used to track performance even more closely. Football's international governing body, FIFA, long opposed the use of wearables during games. However, FIFA has recently announced changes including allowing players to wear monitoring equipment during matches for the first time.

Data collected during professional games is also immensely valuable to the armies of sports scientists, nutritionists and medical personnel involved in the industry. Having detailed access to records of player performance and activity helps to assess the impact of training schemes and diets and predict recovery times after injuries.

I recently worked with an Olympic sports team that also analyses how well their athletes sleep. Data is collected from wearable devices athletes wear at night and is then correlated with track performance. At important competitions, the coaches can now assemble their team not only on past performance but also on the level of sleep team members had the nights before the event.

Some critics of the union between big data analysis and sports have said that it takes away from the fundamental principle that sport is about humans competing on the track or field. Isn't there a danger that it will become more about techies competing in the analytics lab? But the truth is the days when any major international sport was purely played on the field are long gone. Due to the money up for grabs by the winners, teams and athletes have long been supported by an entourage of coaches, physiotherapists, psychologists and experts of any flavour to give them a competitive edge. Why shouldn't they have statisticians and analysts at their disposal too?

Transforming research and development

One area that's really embracing big data and analytics is healthcare. In 2003, when scientists decoded the human genome, it took a decade of intensive work to sequence three billion base pairs of DNA. Today, the computing ability of big data analytics enables scientists to decode that much DNA in a day! This data now allows scientists to predict the likelihoods of getting certain diseases, which in turn can lead to preventative actions and early interventions.

The battle against cancer is using gaming to advance research, providing another fascinating insight into what's possible in a smarter world. By some estimates, 81 million people worldwide spend up to nine and a half hours a week playing mobile phone and online games like Candy Crush Saga, Flight Control and Angry Birds. Today scientists are tapping into that obsession in an effort to solve a whole host of important medical problems. New games are being created with the potential to pinpoint key information about killer diseases like cancer and diabetes. In one example game developers in Dundee created a mobile phone game similar to Space Invaders called Genes in Space that could help to cure cancer. Although to the gamer it looks like he's navigating through stars and galaxies, what he's actually navigating through are graphics made up of the DNA information of thousands of tumour samples. Every time a player completes a level it means that one DNA sample has been mapped and the data automatically sent back to the lab at Cambridge University for analysis. In the month following the game's release, the lab received 1.5 million analyses from gamers. Considering that one analysis normally takes five minutes to map, it would have taken the research team 125,000 non-stop hours or 14 years to cover the same amount of data that the gamers had covered in just one month!

Obviously there are some massive players in the healthcare and pharmaceutical industry, but a lot of innovation is driven by small start-ups. These small companies can leverage big data to conduct research based on a huge range of factors – for example, which drug is most effective for which genetic makeup.

Predicting Performance

Closely related to spotting trends, predictive analysis is a key use of big data. In a nutshell, it comes down to predicting what people want (and when), or what will work in your business and testing those assumptions. There are millions of ways data can help businesses with this, but I look at some key examples here.

Unlocking connections in data sets

A common mistake companies make with data is to only ever look at data in little silos. But by looking at combinations of data you can spot really interesting and illuminating connections.

The value of data is in the combination of data sets and the connections spotted between them. By looking at more than one data set, you can build a more complete picture of your customers, your sales, the success of your product and so on. To do this, you'll probably need a combination of internal and external data and traditional structured and messy unstructured data (see Chapter 4 for an explanation of the different data types).

Say you want to understand your customers better and to predict which customers you should be focusing your marketing efforts on. To really explore this, you'll need a combination of data: internal data, such as transactional and finance data (are certain customers more profitable than others?), and external data, such as geographic and demographic data. Using this combination of data you can gain insights on which customers are the ones you should be targeting in future – you may be surprised by the results.

Unleashing weather data

Weather data is really valuable for small businesses, especially because it's free to access, meaning absolutely anyone can get it – from a big-box style retailer to a local window cleaner. I rate it so highly, it features in my top ten free data sources (see Chapter 15).

One of my clothing retail clients has an ordering system that works with weather data, allowing the client to easily stock up on popular items based on the weather forecast. So, the ordering system makes sure the store has sufficient stock of rain macs, wellies and umbrellas for the rainy spells (which, let's be honest, in the UK is not limited to the obvious winter months), hats and gloves for those unexpected first frosty days that always catch people unawares and flip-flops for the first really warm days of the year. It's partly common sense, yes, but the weather data takes the guess work out of the ordering process for this company.

Using big data as your test bed

This sounds very scientific doesn't it? Please don't be put off! What I mean by this is simply running business experiments, for example, using data to try things out and see whether new ideas are working.

Everything useful that human beings have done has been based on some degree of experimentation. From the wheel to penicillin, from the airplane to the iPhone, ideas have been conceived, tested and failures improved and retested. Using big data as a test bed allows you to test different assumptions, measure the impact on various factors (like customer satisfaction) and analyse the results so that you can come to an evidence-based conclusion. If the conclusion is positive, then you move forward with the product or service. If not, then you abandon it, or restructure and retest it.

Testing assumptions is good business sense. And it's something businesses have been doing for years and years – think focus groups and market-research surveys. Data just adds an extra dimension and rigour to the process.

All business experiments start with a testable hypothesis or assumption. Say, for example, you want to test the assumption that rolling out a new customer service training program will increase customer satisfaction and profit margins. It seems like a reasonable assumption, but whether it's true or not has to be tested – not just assumed. The next step is to design a suitable test, such as training only some of your staff and not others (thereby seeing what results you get if you do nothing). The data is then analysed to determine the results and appropriate actions, for example, should all staff be trained in this way? In this example, you analyse the difference between the performance of those who were trained and those who weren't and see whether what you expected to happen (increased customer satisfaction and profit margins) actually did happen.

Small companies can learn a lot from business experiments that big corporations run, albeit with scaled down budgets and expectations. eBay is the master of testing website changes. Its managers have conducted thousands of experiments with different aspects of its website and, because the site garners over a billion page views per day, they're able to conduct multiple experiments concurrently. For smaller businesses, simple A/B experiments (in this case, comparing two versions of a website) can be easily implemented to see how changes to your website impact on overall *stickiness* (how long customers spend on the site) and sales.

Given the wealth of data and analytics tools now at your disposal and the increasing connectivity with customers and other stakeholders, running business experiments is a relatively straightforward approach for testing proposed new products, or product or service enhancements. But note the idea is to test, not to prove an assumption (an easy trap to fall into). Organisations that punish failure in such experiments should remember that getting things wrong is usually a vital stepping stone to getting things right!

Part II
Unpacking Big Data

Five Types of Data to Get to Grips With

- **Structured data:** Any data or information located in a fixed field within a defined record or file, such as a database or spreadsheet.

- **Unstructured data:** All the data you can't easily store and index in traditional formats or databases, such as email conversations, social media posts, video content and photos.

- **Semi-structured data:** A cross between unstructured and structured data, it may have some structure that can be used for analysis but lacks the strict structure found in databases or spreadsheets.

- **Internal data:** All the data your business currently has or could potentially access or generate in future.

- **External data:** The infinite array of information that exists outside your business.

Go to www.dummies.com/extras/bigdataforsmallbusiness for free online bonus content to help you make the most of big data in your business, including a handy cheat sheet.

In this part . . .

- ✔ Break down the different types of big data.
- ✔ Check out the new and exciting types of data that businesses are tapping into.
- ✔ Get to grips with the technology that makes big data possible.
- ✔ Understand the different ways data can be analysed.

Chapter 4

Unpacking the Many Types of Data

In This Chapter

▶ Understanding the difference between structured and unstructured data

▶ Delving into internal and external data

▶ Deciding what's right for your business

*H*istorically, data used to be a very ordered and neat thing. Even before computers, humans used data to impose order on business actions and processes – think of accounting ledgers or stacks of paper transaction records. Computers, and particularly spreadsheets and databases, gave you a way to store and organise data like this on a large scale in an easily accessible way; instead of ploughing through paper archives, business information was available at the click of a mouse. This absolutely revolutionised business processes (imagine doing your tax return or sending out a customer mailing with only paper records to help you). For a long time this form of *structured data* reigned supreme; anything that wasn't easily organised into rows was simply too difficult to work with and was ignored.

Now, though, advances in storage and analytics means that the masses of messy, unstructured data out there can finally be harnessed to the advantage of businesses big and small. It's no longer all about the humble spreadsheet and database.

But what exactly do I mean by structured and unstructured data? And what sort of data is typically available in-house in the average business? What can you source externally? In this chapter, I explain the key features of structured and unstructured data (semi-structured too, for that matter), plus internal and external data. I also give examples of the different types of data and weigh up the pros and cons of each.

Deploying Order: Structured Data

Structured data refers to any data or information located in a fixed field within a defined record or file. This includes data contained in relational databases and spreadsheets. As the name suggests, structured data refers to data that's organised in a predetermined way, usually in rows and columns.

Structured data gives names to each field in a database or spreadsheet and defines the relationships between the fields. For example, if you look at a standard customer database, the defined fields include name, address, contact telephone numbers, email address and so on. Within those fields, conventions may also be set (for example, the telephone number field will only accept numeric information). These conventions can also include drop-down menus that limit the choices of the data that can be entered into a field, thus ensuring consistency of input (for example, a Title field may only give you certain options to choose from: Mr, Ms, Miss, Mrs, Dr and so on.).

Despite its fixed nature, this data can be queried and used in lots of different ways, such as understanding how many units of a product you sold in a given month and how that compares to the same month last year. Or, in the case of customer records, if you pull all the names and email addresses of customers who bought a certain product (if you wanted to offer a discount on a related product, for example), then you're already mining structured data very successfully.

Structured data is often managed using *Structured Query Language* (SQL) – a programming language originally created by IBM in the 1970s for managing and querying data in relational database management systems.

SQL represented a huge leap forward over paper-based data storage and analysis, but, not everything in business fits neatly into a predefined field.

At present, structured data provides most current business insights. Despite this, it's often considered old hat and a bit dull, especially in comparison to its rock star cousin, unstructured data. Like the Eagles sang, there's a new kid in town – unstructured data is the Johnny come lately, and everybody loves him. Good old structured data can be overlooked as a result (I can't help but picture an unloved spreadsheet in the corner of a party, miserably mainlining Twiglets and hoping someone will talk to it). But I think it's a big mistake to ignore structured data as it still has plenty to offer businesses – particularly when it's combined with unstructured data.

Digging into the pros and cons of structured data

Think about a library for a moment. A library has a database of all the books it holds with everything neatly categorised into fields such as book title, author name, ISBN (International Standard Book Number, the identification number given to a book by the publisher) and the library's own identification number (pinpointing where the book can be found). The database will also record when the book is checked out and by whom. This system is very easy to use and maintain: When a new book arrives, its details can be easily added to the system; when a customer asks about a particular book, the librarian can look up the information without specialist analytical help. Nor does the system require specialist storage or a huge data warehouse, instead sitting happily on the library's computers.

This is the beauty of structured data – anything that can be put into rows and columns is incredibly easy to categorise, store and access. Most of the time it can be used by anyone in the organisation without any in-depth technical knowledge.

The main advantages of structured data are:

- ✔ It's easy to input.
- ✔ It's easy to store.
- ✔ It's simple to analyse and mine for information.
- ✔ It's often the least expensive data option.

It's not all rosy, though. The downsides of structured data are as follows:

- ✔ It provides a rather limited view that rarely tells the whole story.
- ✔ It's only a small proportion of the total data available in the world.

The fact is, structured data is less rich than unstructured data (which I talk about in the upcoming section, 'Coping With Messy Data: Unstructured or Semi-Structured Data'), and, used alone, it's difficult (if not impossible) to get a really full picture of what's going on. Often you need to use other data sources to get a better understanding. For example, structured transactional data will tell you that there was a 40 per cent increase in online sales in June, but it won't tell you *why* that happened or how happy customers were with their purchases. To get a fuller picture, you'd need to combine that data with other information, such as a customer survey, demographic data, social media conversations and maybe even weather data.

And, while structured data is (for now) still the most commonly used, it represents just a fifth of all the data available in the world: 20 per cent of the world's data is structured; everything else in unstructured. Therefore, if you use only structured data as the basis of your business decisions, you're missing out on a *lot* of information!

Examples of structured data

If you know that structured data is all the data that can be easily categorised into rows and columns, you can build a picture of the many examples of structured data that the average business has access to. Examples include:

- ✔ Customer data
- ✔ Sales data and transactional records
- ✔ Financial data, such as cash flow
- ✔ Number of website visits
- ✔ Any kind of machinery data points, such as temperature logs in a refrigerated storage unit or number of products manufactured on a production line

Here's an example of the power of structured data: Walmart handles more than a million customer transactions each hour and imports those into databases estimated to contain more than 2.5 petabytes of data – that's equivalent to 2,500 terabytes or 2.5 million gigabytes of data. (To put that in perspective, it's estimated that all the content from US academic research libraries equals just two petabytes, which makes Walmart's databases look pretty astonishing.) The company is able to combine this structured customer data (particularly who bought what, when) with a variety of sources including customers' mobile phone location data, Walmart's internal stock control records and external weather data to create tailored sales promotions. So, if you bought any BBQ-related goods from Walmart, happen to be within a three-mile radius of a Walmart store that has the BBQ cleaner in stock, and the weather is sunny, you might receive a voucher for money off the cleaner delivered to your smartphone!

Your own structured data may not be nearly as impressive as Walmart's massive databases, but it can still provide an excellent starting point for gathering insights, especially if you combine that data with other sources to get a more detailed picture of what's going on.

Coping With Messy Data: Unstructured or Semi-Structured Data

Unstructured data is all the data you can't easily store and index in traditional formats or databases. It represents all the data that can't be so easily slotted into columns, rows and fields. It includes email conversations, social media posts, video content, photos, voice recordings, sounds and so on. It's usually text heavy, but may also contain data such as dates, numbers and facts or different types of data such as images. These inconsistencies make it difficult to analyse using traditional computer programs.

Up until relatively recently, technology just didn't have the grunt to store, never mind analyse, anything other than structured data. Everything that didn't fit into databases or spreadsheets was usually either discarded or stored on paper or microfiche in filing cabinets or storage facilities. Now, thanks to massive increases in storage capabilities and the ability to tag and categorise such data, not to mention advances in analytical tools, you can finally make use of this data.

Semi-structured data is a cross between unstructured and structured data; it's data that may have some structure that can be used for analysis but lacks the strict structure found in databases or spreadsheets. In semi-structured data, tags or other types of markers are used to identify certain elements within the data, but the data itself doesn't have a rigid structure. For example, a Facebook post can be categorised by author, date, length and even sentiment, but the content is generally unstructured. Another example is a Microsoft Word document; as I draft this chapter, the document metadata details my name as the author and when it was created and amended, but the content of the document is still unstructured. It might be possible to automatically analyse the content of the document, but not using traditional analytical methods – I would need a specialist text analysis tool.

The process of turning unstructured data into semi-structured data used to be quite laborious. For example, in the case of a video of a cat playing with a ball of string, the video would have to be watched and heavily tagged according to certain terms: cat, cute, ball, funny and so on so that people searching for funny cat videos could find it easily. Now videos can be automatically categorised (no pun intended!) using algorithms; computer programs can watch the video, automatically detect what's in it (sometimes even who is in it, thanks to face recognition software) and produce tags automatically.

Unstructured and semi-structured data are like the popular kids at school: Everyone is talking about them, and they represent the sexy new frontier in big data. There's no denying that this type of data and the advances accompanying it are truly exciting for businesses. The trick is to not get swept up in the excitement and lose sight of the value that traditional structured data still holds.

Many companies are starting to use unstructured data analytics to complement their traditional data analysis in order to get richer and improved insights and make smarter decisions. I always advise clients that combining this messy and complex data with other more traditional structured data is where a lot of the value lies.

Understanding the pros and cons of unstructured or semi-structured data

It's estimated that 80 per cent of business-relevant information originates in unstructured or semi-structured data. Think about that for a second: The overwhelming majority of data out there relevant to the average business is unstructured or semi-structured in nature. It massively outweighs structured data when it comes to sheer volume.

Not only is there more of it, but it tends to be richer in insights, too. So, while structured data – all those neat rows and columns of information – usually tells you the who, what and when; unstructured or semi-structured data can help you get to the heart of trickier insights, like why, what do they have in common or when will it happen again.

The advantages of unstructured and semi-structured data include:

- ✔ There's absolutely loads of it – significantly more than structured data.
- ✔ It provides a richer picture than structured data.

Exciting though unstructured and semi-structured data is, there are some downsides (pretty big ones too):

- ✔ It's harder to store.
- ✔ It's much more complicated to analyse and, therefore, to extract insights from.
- ✔ Because of both these factors, it's usually more expensive to use than structured data.

Messy data like this is complex stuff to work with, usually requiring specially designed software and systems. For one thing, it tends to be bigger than structured data, meaning you need bigger and better storage. It's also trickier to organise and mine for insights – not impossible at all, just harder to do. As a result, the costs can add up. It can also be easy to fall prey to *mission creep*, getting so excited by the possibilities of data that you lose sight of the value for your business. It's therefore really important to come up with a clear and robust data strategy before you start delving into the data possibilities. Head to Chapter 10 for more information on creating a data strategy.

Examples of unstructured or semi-structured data

Thousands of examples of unstructured and semi-structured data are out there, but, broadly speaking, they fall into the following categories:

- Photos and images
- Videos, including CCTV
- Audio conversations
- Website text
- Text – including emails, documents, blog posts, social media posts and so on.

I take a closer look at many of these in Chapter 5.

Brands are starting to mine these new types of data as part of their everyday marketing activities. An example of this comes from a friend of mine who runs conferences for a living. One of the conferences he ran was for a well-known electronics manufacturer. Just before the conference started, he shared a picture on Twitter of the main stage, ready for the first speaker. The picture included the brand's sign and logo behind the stage, but he didn't mention the company explicitly using a hashtag or their Twitter handle. The next week he kept seeing targeted ads online for that particular brand. The company knew he was talking about them because their analytical software searches for text and photo that is related to the company and their products. In this case it didn't result in him buying a hoover, but you can see the very powerful potential for businesses looking to get closer to their customers.

These aren't just whizzy marketing tools, the wider applications are enormous. US border control is experimenting with a new avatar system at border control points in the US. After getting off a plane, visitors are greeted by a virtual border agent who asks questions such as 'Where have you arrived from?' 'What is your destination' and 'How long are you staying for?' Your answers are then cross-checked against information already in the system (for example, from the flight operator) to spot any inconsistencies. The system also monitors factors such as eye movement, pupil dilation, gestures, changes in your voice pattern and so on. to see if you're telling the truth.

Don't fall into the trap of thinking tools like this are for big corporations only. Plenty of analytical tools are relatively inexpensive and easy to use. Twitrratr, for example, helps you monitor how people talk about your company on Twitter, separating out the positive and negative tweets that reference your brand or product.

Discovering the Data You Already Have (Internal Data)

Internal data accounts for everything your business currently has or could access. This could be structured in format (for example, a customer database) or it could be unstructured (for example, conversational data from customer service calls). Internal data is your private or proprietary data that is collected and owned by your business – crucially, you control access to the data, no one else does.

Internal data includes data that you already have, plus any data that you don't yet have but have the *potential* to collect. For example, you could run a customer survey in order to gather information about customer habits and what they think of your product. This would be internal data, owned and controlled by your company.

Again, like structured data, internal data isn't considered very sexy or innovative and a lot of businesses run giddily towards external data that they currently don't have. But I think that's a big mistake.

There's real value in your internal data because it's naturally tailored to your business or industry. Sure, you may need to look at some external data alongside it (in fact, I'd encourage you to) but never overlook internal data altogether.

Weighing up the pros and cons of internal data

The main advantages of internal data are:

- ✔ There are no access or ownership issues to contend with
- ✔ It's cheap to use (maybe even free)

Because you own your internal data, you're never at the whim of a third party that can stop supplying it any time or charge the earth for access. You can use the data without problems whenever you need to. For really business-critical information, access and ownership are key issues and not something to take lightly.

Another feather in the cap of internal data is the price – it's usually cheaper to work with than buying access to external data. That's not always the case (say, if you had lots of information held on microfiche, the costs of digitising that data could be pretty hefty) but it's generally true. For this reason, internal data is a good place to start when you're weighing up your data possibilities.

The downsides of internal data are:

- ✔ It may not provide a full enough picture to achieve your strategic goals (although it might!)
- ✔ You have to maintain and look after this data
- ✔ You are legally obliged to make sure personal data is secure

It costs money to properly maintain and secure data, keeping it up-to-date and protected from criminals. This is particularly true of personal data, which is a big legal issue these days. And of course laws do change, so you'll need to keep abreast of your changing legal obligations. Therefore, while using internal data is generally cheaper than buying in external data, you do need to factor in costs for maintenance and protecting that data in a responsible way. There's more on data governance in Chapter 9.

Examples of internal data

Examples of internal data include:

- ✔ Customer survey data
- ✔ Conversational data from calls to your customer service team

- ✔ Employee satisfaction survey data
- ✔ HR data
- ✔ Sales data
- ✔ Financial data, such as cash flow and profit/loss statements
- ✔ CCTV (closed-circuit television) video data
- ✔ Customer record data
- ✔ Internal documents
- ✔ Website data, such as number of visitors, or how customers move around the site
- ✔ Stock control data
- ✔ Sensor data from company machinery or vehicles

This is by no means an exhaustive list, and there are many, many more examples of internal data. Some of these will not be relevant to your business, and some factors not listed here may be absolutely critical to your industry (imagine, for example, the data gathered by a company that calibrates engineering equipment).

You may think big data bras is a figment of the imagination, but you'd be wrong. Online retailer True&Co is using data to help women find better fitting bras. Statistics show that most women wear the wrong bra size, and so the website has stepped up to try to solve that problem. Customers fill out a fit questionnaire on the site and, based on the responses, an algorithm suggests a selection of bras to choose from. The company also uses customer feedback and the data it collects to influence the design and development of its own in-house brand of bras. This is a brilliant example of a company generating and mining its own data to gather insights that improve its product, increase sales and create happy customers.

With all this internal data within touching distance, how do you know where to start? Are some forms of internal data better than others? In short, no (sorry!). There's no pecking order as each business has different needs. Instead, to work out which internal data is most useful to you, you'll need to work out what it is you're trying to achieve in your business. Once you know your goals, you can work out which data can help you get there. There's more on this in Part 4.

Accessing the Data That Is Out There (External Data)

External data is the infinite array of information that exists outside your business. This can be publically available or privately held. It can also be structured or unstructured in format.

Public data is data that anyone can obtain — some of this might be available for free (for example, from government websites), and some you might need to pay for. *Private data* is data owned by a third party and that isn't available for public consumption — you usually have to source and pay for this data from another business or third-party data supplier.

There are plenty of ready-made datasets, both public and private, that are available to suit a range of needs (census data being a good example). Sometimes, though, what you need isn't available as an off-the-shelf solution. In this case, you can pay a third-party provider to gather the data for you.

Delving into the pros and cons of external data

The pros of external data are

- It offers access to information much wider and richer than anything you could create yourself.

- It's often fresher and more up-to-date than anything you could replicate in-house.

- Someone else is responsible for storing and maintaining that data and keeping it up-to-date.

- You don't have to worry about security and data protection issues.

Companies like Walmart, Amazon and Facebook have the ability to generate (and manage) huge amounts of data. And that's great for them but, generally speaking, it's way beyond the capability of the average business. External data sources, however, give any business the capability to access and mine big data — without many of the hassles that come with storing and managing that data on a day-to-day basis.

For a small business, it's often nice not to have the burden of maintaining data and worrying about keeping it secure. By buying (or accessing free) data from an external provider, the provider bears that responsibility so you don't have to.

And the cons of using external data are

- You don't own the data.
- You may have to pay for access.

The major disadvantage of not owning the data you use is that you're reliant on an external source. There's a risk that the provider could stop supplying the data or put their costs up significantly. This is an especially big risk if you've become reliant on that data for key business functions, such as marketing activity.

Ultimately, the risks and the costs of accessing external data need to be weighed up against the risks and costs of *not* using that data. Would you have to go to the trouble of creating it yourself? Would your business suffer if you didn't use that data? Would it stop you meeting your strategic goals? You may find that, overall, the benefits far outweigh the risks.

Examples of external data

Examples of external data include

- Weather data
- Government data, such as census data
- Economic data
- Social media profile data
- Social media text and activities, such as tweets, likes and shares
- Google Trends or Google Maps data

A beautiful example of using external data comes from a website called FallingFruit.org. The site aims to remind urbanites that agriculture and natural foods do exist in the city. The site combined public information from the US Department of Agriculture, municipal tree inventories, foraging maps and street tree databases to create an interactive map of trees. City folk can use the site to see which fruit trees might be dropping fruit right now in their own neighbourhoods.

When it comes to external data, it's hard to know what is actually available and where to look. As a starting point, I recommend checking out Chapter 15 which lists my top ten free data sources. I also strongly recommend working with a good data consultant. A consultant can help you hone in on the best external datasets and providers to suit your business needs. This doesn't need to cost the earth and it's absolutely money well spent, saving a lot of time and potentially wasted resources.

What Type of Data is Best for Me?

A lot of the big data hype focuses on unstructured data and the allure and promise of external data, often at the expense or dismissal of internal or structured data.

The truth is, no type of data is really 'better' than any other type. Unstructured data isn't necessarily better or more valuable than structured. What's best for one business may not be best for yours. The key is to start with a strong data strategy (see Chapter 10), establish your key strategic questions (see Chapter 11), and let those guide you to the best data for you, whether it's structured, unstructured or a combination.

The same goes for internal versus external data – there's no rule as to what's right or wrong. There will always be internal data that's easier to collect and analyse but that may not provide you with everything you need to grow your business.

A taxi company can collect data on where its drivers are around the city. This is easy to do and it's really useful information, so it makes perfect sense to collect it and use it. But, if you're the owner of the company, knowing where drivers are isn't the whole picture. You may also want to know where most people want to be picked up from when it's raining so you can position your drivers accordingly. For this, you'll need to combine your own information on pickups with weather data. You could create your own weather data that you control but that would probably be a waste of resources because weather data is so easy to access externally for free (see Chapter 15 for the best free sources). This external weather data is also pretty low risk to use, since it's government data – the UK and US governments have made strong commitments to data transparency so it's highly unlikely that they will withdraw access or start charging for it. In this example, there's a really strong case for making use of this external data.

The waters get a little murkier when you start looking at purchasing external data from a commercial provider. There are big advantages to buying in external data versus creating your own, since the provider bears all the burden of securing and maintaining that data, saving you valuable time and resources. But you need to consider the risk of price hikes or the withdrawal of that data, particularly if the data is absolutely critical to your business. Some companies prefer to create their own data, for example by collecting more detailed personal information on customers. But the risks then become about maintaining and securing that data, rather than ensuring access.

Ultimately, whatever type or combination of data you choose, there will always be some risks and pros and cons. You need to weigh up what's right for your business.

Finally, a word on not putting all your eggs in one data basket. I always advise my clients that a combination of datasets is better than relying on one for business decisions; otherwise you can end up with a very limited picture. As a rule, two datasets is better than one . . . but three is ideal. With three different datasets, you can create a much richer picture by looking at the data from different perspectives. This means you can verify insights rather than plunging ahead with decisions based on false assumptions.

With this in mind, the ideal data for you may actually be a combination of different types of data. To meet your strategic goals (which I talk about in Chapter 10), you may well need some structured internal data (like sales data), plus some structured external data (for example, demographic data), alongside some unstructured internal data (such as customer feedback) and unstructured external data (for example, social media analysis). Really smart businesses, the ones that will thrive in the future, are those that combine data to get the most useful insights for them.

Chapter 5

Discovering New Forms of Data

*T*he world is becoming increasingly datafied. Being *datafied* means that an activity or action (such as purchasing something) has been turned into data. This is also known as *datafication*.

Datafication is leading to new forms of data. Some of the data we can now collect is new, some has been around a while but we've only just found ways to make it genuinely useful. In this chapter I look at the main forms of data that are being collected, stored and analysed.

In this chapter, I give some examples on how you might use these types of data in your business. There's more on big data uses for small businesses in Chapter 3. To understand the technology advances that underpin these new forms of data, see Chapter 6.

One of the simplest ways to understand the datafication process is to think about the difference between a traditional paperback book and the same book on an e-reader. Using digital files, you can store hundreds of books on an electronic gizmo that's often smaller than a printed book. But just because the book is digital does not mean it's datafied. Some e-books are just digital copies of the physical book. A datafied book is so much more. A datafied book allows the reader to change the font size, add notes, highlight text and search the book for a particular phrase or paragraph. Plus, when you read a datafied book on an e-reader, data is being gathered and sent back to companies like Amazon or Barnes & Noble about your reading habits. Data is being collected about what you read, how long you read for, how fast you read, whether you skip pages and what pages you highlight or add a note to.

Of course, this information is extremely useful to booksellers, publishers and authors. As an author, I'd love to know if I was losing my audience at a particular part of my book! This information could prompt a second edition and hopefully a more committed readership. Publishers could figure out what is being consistently highlighted and establish whether those things indicate trends around which they could commission a new book. And booksellers could alert the reader when he's getting close to the end of the book with recommendations about what to buy next based on his previous purchases. Amazon, of course, already does this.

Tracking Activity Data

Essentially, *activity data* is the computer record of human actions or activities that occur online or in the offline physical world.

Unless you're a *Luddite,* completely disconnected from and opposed to technology, living in a shack on some remote island, paying for everything you need in cash (unlikely, considering you're reading a book on big data!), you're creating data in your wake. This data is valuable. Analysing it provides insights on everything from your personal health to crime prevention to increased sales, improved customer service and elevated business performance.

Think about your typical daily activities: Most of them leave some digital trace (data) that can be and is collected and analysed. If you make a phone call, a trace of that call exists as *call data;* depending on whom you call, the content might also be recorded. If you go shopping and use your credit or debit card, the trace is *transaction data* – what you buy, when, where and for how much. If you browse the Internet, a digital record is created showing where you accessed the Internet from (using the computer ISP, or Internet service provider), what sites you visited, how you navigated through them, what held your attention and how long you stayed. Even if you choose not to work and go for a run instead (pat on the back for you!), if you wear a Fitbit or UP band your movements create data showing how fast you moved, how many steps you took and how many calories you burned. CCTV (closed-circuit television) cameras also probably recorded you at various locations as you enjoyed your run!

More and more of the activities you engage in both online and offline leave a digital signature or data trail.

IACP Center for Social Media: Fun facts on activity data

The IACP Center for Social Media conducts annual surveys on social media activity. Here are just some of their astonishing findings:

- Consumers spend around $373,070 (£243,288) shopping on the Internet every minute.

- Approximately 47,000 apps are downloaded from Apple every minute.

- Brands and organisations on Facebook receive approximately 34,722 likes every minute.

- Approximately 571 new websites are created every minute.

- Tablets took just two years to reach 40 million users in the United States. It took smartphones seven to reach the same figure.

- Facebook drives around a quarter of all Internet traffic.

- Facebook has 2.317 billion monthly active users.

- Ninety-two per cent of companies use social media as a recruitment tool. Of those, 93 per cent use LinkedIn.

- YouTube is the second largest search engine in the world.

Pros and cons of activity data

Activity data allows you to monitor how your customers interact with your business, brand, products and services over time.

The main advantages of activity data are:

- It allows you to see what your customers actually do as opposed to what they say they do. This can provide useful insights on product development or service improvement.

- It is never ending because human beings are in constant activity so it provides a rich vein of insight.

- It is often self-generating. As long as you have the infrastructure set up to collect the data it will be collected in the normal course of everyday business.

Saving premature babies

The monitoring of heart rate variation (HRV), plus other data points, is being used to save premature babies. HRV measures the tiny variations in the interval between each heartbeat and has been proven to be a significant metric for predicting health problems. For example, big data analytics alert doctors about life threatening problems in premature babies at the Hospital for Sick Children in Toronto.

Doctors have discovered that premature babies are particularly susceptible to *late-onset neonatal sepsis,* a blood infection that usually occurs several days after delivery. Born early, these babies are not as strong and their natural defences are often lower than

a full-term baby. By monitoring data such as respiratory rate, heart rate, blood pressure and blood oxygen saturation, and then analysing the vast data streams, doctors can monitor an infant's vital signs in real time and detect changes in his condition.

Complex algorithms examine about 1,200 data points every second looking for patterns and features that are known to occur before the infection becomes clinically apparent. When found, the doctor is alerted and the baby receives life-saving antibiotics *before* he becomes ill. This early intervention is already saving tiny lives and many similar interventions are becoming more and more commonplace.

The main disadvantages of activity data are:

✔ The sheer amount of potential activity data that you can collect is staggering – even in a small business. It can therefore be confusing as to what to collect and why. Focusing on your strategic questions (Chapter 11) can help you concentrate on the data that's most helpful for your business.

✔ The majority of activity data is unstructured, and this can potentially be harder to analyse and draw insights from.

Activity data around your website (such as Google Analytics) lets you know how many visitors your site gets, where they go and where they lose interest and jump out. This information can therefore help you to revise or update your website to make it more *sticky* (meaning that visitors stick around on your website for longer) and provide more of what your customers' actions indicate they want.

Using activity data

The applications for activity data are as endless as the activities about which data can be collected and analysed.

Lady Gaga playlist

Activity data is also collected when you listen to music using a smartphone or digital music player. This data tells iTunes and other providers what you're listening to, how long you're listening and what tracks you're skipping past. And artists like Lady Gaga are using this data to create playlists for live gigs and influence future song creation.

In fact, Lady Gaga took data collection and fan interaction to a whole new level in 2012 with the launch of her own social network hub, www.littlemonsters.com. Lady Gaga's manager Troy Carter, along with financial backers and Lady Gaga herself, created the hub so they could communicate directly with fans and work out what they wanted and listened to. Carter told *Wired* magazine that while Lady Gaga still has a deal with Universal Records, 'there will come a time when she'll release music through her own site. It's not just going to be about sells. It's going to be about the streams coming through the site. For us, it's important to be able to identify who's listening to what. We want to own that data. We have to own that data.'

Of course, this makes total sense when you consider that Lady Gaga has some 42 million Twitter followers and more than 67 million Facebook likes! And she's not afraid to use those fans and followers to exert influence. For example, Lady Gaga brought attention to the effort to repeal the anti-gay 'Don't Ask, Don't Tell' policy in the US armed services. She also generated worldwide support for her anti-bullying initiative, the Born This Way Foundation. Littlemonsters.com features a Monster Code that encourages kindness, tolerance and acceptance.

Activity data tells you what people are doing and these insights can help you improve everything from sales to website traffic to your understanding of aspects of human experience, such as sleep and exercise.

For example, Jawbone, the company that makes the activity band, now collects health, movement and sleep data from millions of people around the world (including me). This means that Jawbone has access to 60 years' worth of sleep data – every night! No company has ever had so much sleep data, which means that Jawbone is able to analyse the data to understand more about sleep, sleeping patterns and what disrupts those patterns. Jawbone could, for instance, look at the data and work out how many hours of sleep are lost, on average, when the Super Bowl is broadcast in the US or how long it normally takes for business travellers to return to normal sleeping patterns after international travel.

Getting your hands on activity data

How best to get your hands on activity data depends on what activity you seek to understand and whether that data currently exists or could exist in your business.

You could ask your target audience questions regarding the activity you want to understand more about. This can be done through a market research survey or focus group. Or you could put a mechanism in place to capture their answers as part of the activity in question. For example, if you want to know more about why someone bought a particular product online, you could add the question to the checkout page so he needs to answer it to complete the purchase process.

Activity data that most businesses already have is transaction data – although it may not always be digital or datafied. Depending on what strategic questions you're seeking answers to (see Chapter 11), it may be worth putting this data on computer so you can run analysis on the data. You could, for example, identify which period of the day or week is the busiest for online orders.

Eavesdropping on Conversations

Conversations are increasingly leaving a digital record – either through the text you write in an email, blog, SMS (text) message or social media post, or as an audio recording of a telephone, teleconference or Skype call. This is known as *conversation data*.

IACP Center for Social Media: Fun facts on conversation data

From Twitter to Tumblr to Instagram to Facebook, people share reams of data, as these statistics show:

✔ The ten billionth tweet was posted in March 2010.

✔ More than one billion tweets are sent every 48 hours.

✔ Fifty thousand links are shared every minute on Facebook.

✔ Each minute, 150,000 messages are sent on Facebook.

✔ LinkedIn has over three million company pages with over one billion endorsements.

✔ Eight per cent of world leaders use Twitter.

✔ Every 60 seconds 293,000 status updates are posted on Facebook.

✔ People in New York received tweets about the August 2011 earthquake in Mineral, Virginia 30 seconds before they felt it.

✔ Twenty million emails were written in the time it took to read this sentence.

✔ Every minute Tumblr owners publish approximately 27,778 new blog posts.

When you call a customer service department, it's not unusual to be told that the conversation *may* be recorded for training purposes. Often that data is being mined for content and context. In other words, big data analytics can analyse what is actually said from the words used *and* the mood of the person engaged in the conversation. Companies can now figure out how angry or irritated a customer is just from the stress levels in that person's voice and this information can be used to improve service delivery.

Pros and cons of conversation data

Conversation data can be extremely useful for small business owners because it provides insights into how happy or otherwise your customers, clients and suppliers are.

The main advantages of conversation data for small business are:

- ✔ It provides you with real-time access to customers and what those customers think and feel about your products and services.
- ✔ It allows you to react quickly to changing customer requirements and improve customer service.
- ✔ It allows you to handle customer upset more quickly so that the upset or dissatisfaction doesn't escalate and damage the business or the brand.

The main disadvantages of conversation data for small business are:

- ✔ Most conversation data is unstructured, which can make it more difficult to analyse.
- ✔ The vast amount of conversation data in any business can be potentially confusing with regard to what conversation data is the best to collect and analyse.
- ✔ Legal ramifications affect recording conversations, and you need to be aware of these in your country.

Legally, in most parts of the world, you can't just record customer or client conversations willy-nilly – the recording must be relevant to your business. Additionally, you must make every effort to inform those parties that the conversation is being recorded and give them the opportunity to opt out.

Using conversation data

Conversation data allows you to know what is being said about your business in conversations between your business and your customers, clients and suppliers.

This information can shed valuable light on shifting buying patterns and changing requirements, highlight service or performance issues in the business or indicate new product or service development ideas.

Sentiment analysis

Sentiment analysis or *opinion mining* seeks to extract subjective opinion or sentiment from text or audio files. In any language, some words are neutral, others are considered positive and others still are more negative in tone and meaning. These variations in sentiment or meaning can be identified by text-based sentiment analytics. *Audio-based sentiment analysis* considers the pitch, tone and stress levels in a person's voice to determine how he's feeling and reacting to the conversation he's currently involved in.

The basic purpose of sentiment analysis is to establish the *polarity* of any conversation – positive, negative or neutral. This type of text-based analytics seeks to determine whether the person writing the text is positive, negative or neutral.

A number of software tools (such as Social Mention, Twitter Sentiment, Yacktracker and Twitrratr) can help you measure the sentiment around your product or service. Tools like Twitrratr allow you to separate the positive tweets about your company, brand, product or service from the negative and neutral tweets so you can see how well you are doing in the Twitterverse.

Beyond polarity sentiment analysis goes farther than ordinary sentiment analysis further by classifying the emotional state of the person writing the text, such as 'frustrated', 'angry', or 'happy'. This type of analytics is becoming increasingly popular with the rise of social media, blogs and social networks where people share their thoughts and feelings about all sorts of things – including companies, brands, products and services.

When you consider that according to social media commentator Eric Qualman 53 per cent of people on Twitter recommend products in their tweets, 93 per cent of buyers' decisions are influenced by social media, and 90 per cent of customers trust peer recommendations as opposed to just 14 per cent that trust advertising, you can see why measuring sentiment is so important for businesses big and small.

Millions of people are leaving reviews, rating products, making recommendations and expressing their opinions about businesses, products and services. Your customers or potential customers are using those opinions to influence and direct their purchasing decisions. It follows, therefore, that you absolutely need to know what people are saying about you and sentiment analytics can help you do that.

Large companies like Gatorade and Dell recognise the importance of tracking conversation as a way to market their products, identify new opportunities and manage their reputations. As a result, they have invested heavily in social media command centres.

Sports drink company Gatorade has had a social media Mission Control inside its marketing department since 2010. Gatorade measures blog conversations across a variety of topics and shows how hot those conversations are across the blogosphere. The company also runs detailed sentiment analysis around key topics and product and campaign launches. It also tracks terms relating to its brand, including competitors, as well as its athletes and sports nutrition-related topics. Basically, Gatorade knows what people are saying about the company and its products almost as fast as they've said it!

This sort of activity isn't just for big corporations. Even the smallest of businesses should be monitoring what people say about it and engage with its customers on social media platforms.

Keeping customers happy on social media

Clearly, having happy customers has always been important for business success, whatever the size of the business. But in days gone by, a few unhappy customers were not going to bring the house down. By the time they got through to someone to shout at or fired off a terse email or letter, most of the fire was gone and everyone just moved on. Not today. An angry customer can post social media updates about his experience in seconds, and it's available for the world to see. Measuring and analysing conversation data can help to manage your company's reputation, fix service issues quickly and protect your brand. Plus, putting something right, saying sorry and solving the issue efficiently can actually increase brand loyalty and customer satisfaction, so getting ahead of the curve and understanding what your customers are feeling and thinking can give your small business a huge commercial advantage.

By embracing social media, retail organisations are engaging brand advocates, changing the perception of brand antagonists, and even enabling enthusiastic customers to sell its products. They are also monitoring social media platforms like Facebook and Twitter to get an unprecedented view into customer behaviour, preferences and product perception. And manufacturers are monitoring social networks to detect aftermarket support issues before a warranty failure becomes publicly detrimental.

With the myriad of applications, it's easy to see why more and more companies are investing in social media and seeking to tap into real-time sentiment and opinion around their products, services and brands.

Getting your hands on conversation data

Wherever you are currently having conversations there is an opportunity to collect conversation data.

If you operate a telephone sales department or customer service department where customers call in to purchase or follow up on order delivery then you could record those conversations. Text-based conversation data also exists in the emails you receive from your customers and in any conversations that take place on any of your social media platforms.

Clearly social media platforms are critical for conversation data, and they provide a wealth of information that can then be analysed for future improvements. A good way to start might be some simple sentiment analysis (perhaps using the software mentioned in this chapter) to find out what your customers are saying about your product or service online.

Making one person or team responsible for communicating with your customers online and quickly responding to any complaints or issues is a good idea. If you don't yet have active social media platforms then you need to create those as the first step. Without them, you're missing out on a wealth of data.

Picturing Images and Photos

The volume of photo and video image data generated today is staggering. The explosion of content largely comes down to digital cameras and, more recently, smartphones coupled with our ever-increasing connectivity and our insatiable desire to share content on social media platforms.

In addition to all the photo and video data created and shared via smartphones, there is also all the CCTV camera footage. In days gone by, companies may have recorded their retail or storage premises for security purposes, but the recordings were never stored long term. The recording was made to tape and then after a week or so the tape would be used again and new recordings would be made over the old ones.

Now some of the more data-savvy stores are keeping all the CCTV camera footage and analysing it to study how people walk through the shops, where they stop, what they look at and for how long so they can make alterations to offers and boost sales. Some are even using face recognition software, so it probably won't be long before a combination of data sources such as CCTV camera footage, loyalty card information and face recognition software will have you being welcomed to a store on your smartphone and directed to particular special offers or promotions that may be of interest based on your previous buying habits!

IACP Center for Social Media: Fun facts on photo and video image data

Images of people are uploaded all the time, and people access images at ever-increasing rates. Check out the information on image data:

- Eighty per cent of Pinterest users are women.

- Each day 350,000,000 photos are uploaded to Facebook, which equates to 4,000 photos per second.

- Five million photos are uploaded to Instagram daily.

- Instagram has already had more than 16 billion photos uploaded since debuting in 2010.

- Flickr users upload 3.5 million photos to the site each day.

- YouTube reaches more adults in the United States between the ages of 18 and 34 than any cable network.

- Facebook users watch more than 500 years worth of YouTube videos every day.

- Approximately 100 hours of video is uploaded to YouTube every minute.

Pros and cons of photo and video image data

The main advantages of photo and video image data for small business are:

- The data may already be collected via security footage, and finding better ways to use that data may not be very expensive.

- Photo data contains embedded information such as when the picture was taken. GPS (global positioning system) tracks where it was taken too.

- Photo and video data can be processed using face- and shape-recognition software.

The main disadvantages of photo and video image data for small business are:

- Video footage alone can create huge files, so it's important you have a defined and relevant purpose for collecting and storing the data.

- Photo and video data can be used to recognise individuals without them knowing, causing a concern about invasion of privacy.

Using photo and video image data

The applications for photo and video image data are endless and they already impact crime prevention and health – as well as business.

Photo and video image data can be extremely useful for small business owners because it provides insights into what people – especially in a retail environment – are actually doing.

If your business doesn't have retail premises, then the applications for video data may be limited for you. Photos can provide useful information for many different types of businesses – photo metadata, for example, tells you who took the picture and when and where it was taken. But brands can now use photos and video data to detect where it is used. For example, a clothing brand can start searching for photos that show someone wearing its brand logo or restaurants can search for photographs taken inside or outside their premises. This allows them to identify and potentially engage those individuals.

In 2013, typhoon Hiayan hit the Philippines and killed over 6,000 people and damaged or destroyed over 1.1 million homes within a matter of hours. Almost immediately, a team of UK volunteers started to create a vital map of the damaged areas using just social media – drawing largely on photo and video image data. In today's world, people share their experiences as they're happening in almost real time, so photos, tweets (#Hiayan) and video about the disaster were posted on social media at a rate of about a million a day! Those million data points were then filtered using artificial intelligence to pick out the ones that could be important. The team of volunteers then made an assessment of what they saw. For example, in a photograph they would ask, 'How much damage is visible?' and they simply needed to click the appropriate button: 'none', 'mild' or 'severe'. For text-based messages such as tweets or Facebook updates, the volunteer was asked to decide if the text was 'not relevant', 'request for help', 'infrastructure damage', 'population displacement', 'relevant but other' and so on. Each piece of data (picture, video or message) was then assessed by between three to five different people to make sure the assessment was consistently and therefore probably accurate.

By pinpointing where the data was coming from in the Philippines (using GPS sensors in the photos or through the text) the work of the volunteers then creates an online map, not just of the disaster zone but of the needs in each area.

The result was that when the disaster relief effort arrived in the Philippines they didn't need to waste days working out what was happening and where the worst hit areas were. From the map created by people halfway around the world, relief providers already know who needed water, who needed food, where the dead bodies were, where people had been displaced, where the most damage was and what hospitals were least damaged and therefore more able to help the injured.

Getting your hands on photo and video image data

Video and photo data can be obtained by simply starting to collect it using digital cameras.

In many cases, companies are already using video recording for security reasons. If you're already doing this, consider whether that video data can be used and trailed for analysis.

If more advanced analytics are required, it often means installing purpose-built systems. For example, if a small shop already has a network of CCTV cameras installed then the data can be brought together for an analysis of how customers walk through the shop, where they stop and which parts they avoid. Testing the existing data shows any gaps where new cameras or systems need to be added to improve the analysis.

Photos can often be collected and analysed from the vast amount of photos shared on social media sites such as Twitter, Facebook, Pinterest and many others.

Sensing Your Way to New Data

A vast amount of data is generated and transmitted from sensors that are increasingly being built into products. This is known as *sensor data*. For example, your smartphone is smart because of the inclusion of various sensors that capture data. Your smartphone contains:

- GPS sensor – this lets you and others know where you are.
- Accelerometer sensor – this measures how quickly the phone is moving, and helps you to take better photos because it triggers the shutter when the phone is stationary.
- Gyroscope – this measures and maintains orientation and rotates the screen.
- Proximity sensor – this measures how close you are to other people, locations or objects. In a car, the proximity sensor beeps at you when you reverse your car too close to the kerb.
- Ambient sensor – this measures the surrounding ambience and adjusts the backlight on your phone to save power.
- Near Field Communication (NFC) sensor – when enabled, this allows you to transfer funds just by bumping or waving your phone close to an appropriate payment machine.

There are also sensors in the natural environment. For example, there are sensors in the oceans for measuring the health, temperature and changes in the oceans in real time. In Japan, there are sensors in the soil to collect data on how healthy the soil is. Companies are combining that data with weather data; farmers can then subscribe to the service to get information to optimise yield, including when to put fertiliser on the crop and how much.

Pros and cons of sensor data

Sensor data can be extremely useful for small business owners because it can help to answer some important strategic questions. For information on how to identify your key strategic questions, see Chapter 11.

The main advantages of sensor data for small businesses are:

- ✔ It doesn't have to be expensive and can provide really useful insights for increasingly sales and influence.
- ✔ Once installed, the data is self-generating.
- ✔ Sensor data can radically improve productivity and maintenance when installed.
- ✔ Many devices, such as smartphones, already contain very sophisticated, ready-to-use sensors.

The main disadvantages of sensor data for small business are:

- ✔ You may not have access to sensor data.
- ✔ Sensor data often lacks context and only measures a very small part of reality.
- ✔ Sensor data most likely needs to be combined with another dataset (such as transaction data) to get the best results.

I worked with a small fashion retail company that wanted to increase sales but had no data other than its traditional sales data. After establishing what questions it needed answers to, we installed a small, discreet device into the shop windows that tracked mobile phone signals as people walked past the shop. Everyone, at least everyone passing these particular stores, had a mobile phone which the sensor in the device would pick up and count. The sensors would also measure how many people stopped to look at the window and for how long and how many people then walked into the store. Sales data would then record who actually bought something. By combing the data from inexpensive, readily available sensors placed in the window with transaction data, we were able to measure conversion ratio and test window displays and various offers to see which ones increased conversion rate – the conversion of customers' money to the store's coffers.

Not only did this fashion retailer massively increase sales by getting smart about its data requirements and combing small traditional data with untraditional big data, it used the insights to make a significant saving by closing one of the stores. The sensors were able to tell them the store owner that the foot traffic reported by the market research company prior to opening in that location was wrong and the passing traffic was insufficient to justify keeping the store open.

Using sensor data

Increasingly, more and more machines are equipped with sensors to monitor performance and provide information on when best to service or repair the machines.

For example, modern cars are full of sensors that measure everything from fuel consumption to engine performance. These sensors allow for dynamic servicing and better long-term performance. On-board sensors also alert the driver if he gets too close to another car or object and can even parallel park the car without the driver doing anything!

In retail, data has long been collected via bar code – however, the sensors known as radio frequency identification (RFID) systems increasingly used by retailers and others are generating 100 to 1,000 times more data than the conventional bar code system.

Rolls-Royce is one manufacturer that has transformed its business through sensor data. You may not realise it, but Rolls-Royce manufactures nearly half the world's passenger jet engines, including the Trent 1000 – the engine that powers many transatlantic flights. When in operation, these engines reach incredibly high temperatures – half the temperature of the surface of the sun and 200 degrees *above* the temperature at which the metal used to make the engine melts! The only reason it doesn't melt is because the engines are cooled through special passageways and channels that keep the heat away from the metal. Needless to say, it's vital to know that everything is working and doing its job! The engine is full of vital components all engineered with absolute precision, including an on-board computer that collects and monitors data from sensors buried deep within the engine, measuring 40 parameters 40 times per second, including temperatures, pressures and turbine speeds.

All the measurements are stored in the computer and streamed via satellite back to Rolls-Royce headquarters (HQ) in Derby, England. And that's true for the entire fleet of Rolls-Royce engines – which is a lot of data when you consider that a Rolls-Royce-powered engine takes off or lands somewhere in the world every two and a half seconds.

Whenever those thousands of engines are in the air, they're gathering data that's constantly sent back to HQ and constantly monitored using clever data analytics that look for anything unusual occurring in the engine or any sign that it may need to be serviced early or repaired. In Derby, computers then sift through the data to look for anomalies. If any are found, they're immediately flagged and a human being checks the results and, if necessary, telephones the airline and works out what needs to be done – often before the issue escalates into an actual problem.

These sensors therefore allow for dynamic maintenance based on actual engine-by-engine performance rather than some automatic rota system based on time alone. Instead of pulling an expensive piece of equipment out of service every three or six months, these sensors allow the airlines to maintain their fleet much more cost effectively, and, more importantly, these sensors make the planes much safer.

A similar (if smaller scale!) application could benefit your business. For example, a haulage company could use sensors to monitor vehicle wear-and-tear, thereby maintaining its fleet in the most efficient way. Alternatively, a manufacturing company may use sensor data to monitor machinery on its assembly lines, identifying potential faults before they occur.

Getting your hands on sensor data

Sensor data may be accessed either by using sensors inbuilt in devices you already have or by installing new sensors.

The world is filling up with sensors. Smartphones can contain GPS sensors, accelerometer sensors, light sensors, fingerprint readers and so on, all readily used by any small company. Smart watches contain all these features as well as heart-rate sensors. Soon, most devices, from diapers to clothing, sports equipment to cars and thermostats, will generate sensor data you can use for business purposes.

Sensor technology is developing very rapidly, so often these sensors, like the ones I used with the fashion retailer (see 'Pros and cons of sensor data' earlier in the chapter), are significantly less expensive than people may imagine.

Discovering the Internet of Things

The Internet of Things (IoT) is coming about as a direct result of more objects being manufactured with embedded sensors *and* perhaps more importantly the ability of those objects to communicate with each other.

International Data Corporation describes the *Internet of Things* as 'a network connecting – either wired or wireless – devices (things) that are characterised by automatic provisioning, management and monitoring. It is innately analytical and integrated, and includes not just intelligent systems and devices, but connectivity enablement, platforms for device, network and application enablement, analytics and social business and applications and vertical industry solutions. It is more than traditional machine-to-machine communication. Indeed, it is more than the traditional Information and Communications Technology (ICT) industry itself.'

Essentially, the Internet of Things explores what is and will be possible as a result of advances in smart, sensor-based technology and massive advances in connectivity between devices, systems and services that go way beyond business as usual. For example, according to estimates from research groups such as Gartner and ABI Research, by 2020 there will be between 26 and 30 billion devices wirelessly connected to the IoT. And the resulting information networks promise to create new business models, improve business processes and performance while also reducing cost and, potentially, risk.

The day will come, not far from now, when your alarm will be synced to your email account and if an early meeting is cancelled, your alarm will automatically reset to a later time which will also postpone the coffee machine to the new wake-up time. Your fridge will know what's in it and place online orders to replenish stocks without you having to do anything. When you come home from work, your fridge will tell you what you can make for dinner based on what you currently have in stock.

The wired and wireless networks that connect the Internet of Things often use the same Internet Protocol (IP) that connects the Internet – hence the name. These vast networks create huge volumes of data that's then available for analysis. When objects use sensors to sense the environment and communicate with each other, they become tools for understanding complexity and responding to it quickly. The resulting physical information systems are now beginning to be deployed, and some of them operate without human intervention.

Ever-smaller silicon chips are gaining new capabilities, while costs are falling. Massive increases in storage and computing power, some of it available via cloud computing, make number crunching possible on a very large scale and at declining cost.

One day soon, businesses of all sizes will be taking advantage of the Internet of Things, building sensors into products and learning a whole lot more about their customers in the process.

Chapter 6

Understanding the Technology Changes that Underpin Big Data

In This Chapter

▶ Delving into cloud technology and how it has revolutionised data

▶ Looking at the storage and analytic developments that make big data possible

▶ Understanding recent advances in text, speech, video and image analytics

*I*t may seem like big data has exploded onto the business and tech scene out of nowhere. In fact, the ability to store and analyse information has been a gradual evolution: from paper records and dusty archive rooms to the microfiche, from disks to big mainframe computers to data centres. We humans are continually searching for ways to better understand what's going on around us, which means we gather and store information and try to extract some sort of meaning from that information – in whatever way current technology allows.

This evolution, however, certainly sped up at the end of the last century, with the invention of digital storage and the Internet. Huge advances in computing, storage and analytic technology came together to create the phenomenon that is *big* (circle back to Chapter 2 for a breakdown of what defines big data).

In this chapter, I look at these technology changes and how they make big data possible. I also delve into recent advances in analytic capabilities that have revolutionised how we can extract meaning from data.

The Perfect Storm: Developments that Make Big Data Possible

Three advances in particular have really made big data possible: cloud computing, digital storage and better analytics. I look at each of them in turn in the next sections.

Introducing the cloud

The *cloud,* or cloud computing, basically refers to two things:

- Storing data outside your computer, or outside your smart device such as a phone.

- Performing computing tasks using software and applications that aren't installed on your computer or smart device.

Cloud computing, or computing in the cloud, simply means using software or data that runs on remote servers rather than locally. Anything stored in the cloud is typically accessible over the Internet, wherever in the world the owner of that data might be. So instead of storing or computing things on your own machine, you can use other computers that are connected to your computer via a network (such as the Internet).

If you back up your documents and photos over the Internet using services such as Dropbox or Google Drive, then they're stored in the cloud – meaning they're sent via a network to a server (which can be anywhere in the world) for storage. If you're an iPhone user and enable iCloud, then your photos, apps and music are backed up to a computer managed by Apple. The data is transferred to that outside computer using the Internet. If you're using services such as Gmail, Yahoo! or Microsoft Exchange Online for your emails, then you're a cloud-computing user. The same goes for Facebook, Twitter and LinkedIn. These services are all provided via the Internet rather than being installed on your computer.

Cloud computing isn't exactly new – the notion of networked computers has been around since the 1960s. But the term *cloud computing* really took off around 2006 when companies like Google began using it to describe the increasing shift to storing files online rather than on individual computers.

Before the cloud, computers could still be linked together on a company network, but the storage capacity and computing power was limited to the company's in-house hardware. If you wanted to store more stuff, you had to delete a load of files or buy new hardware.

Now, if a company wants to increase its storage, it can simply move its data to the cloud. This is often a more cost-effective solution than buying and maintaining its own data storage facilities. The same principle applies to software, too. Instead of purchasing software licences and loading hefty programs onto company computers, companies can use SAAS providers. SAAS stands for *Software as a Service,* and in principle works in the same way as online email providers. Instead of selling the software to clients, vendors provide access to software via the Internet. Examples include Salesforce.com, a cloud-based customer-relationship management software, and Xero.com, a cloud-based accounting program.

What does the cloud have to do with big data? Well, cloud computing enables you to massively increase your storage capacity without having to buy new hardware to store stuff on. This means that large volumes of data can be stored and analysed using many different computers, often in completely different locations, which are connected via a network (the Internet). The cloud is all about using the power of lots of different computers to perform tasks. This and the increasing connectivity of a vast range of devices (your phones, your televisions, sensors, videos, and so on) laid the foundation for big data.

Some people worry that the cloud is less secure than storing data on a private company server. I'd argue the opposite is often true. Years ago a friend of mine worked for a small company that was burgled. All the computing equipment was stolen and, with it, all work currently in progress. It was a small publishing company that did its own editing and typesetting in house, so you can imagine how crucial those files were to the business. It took months to get all projects back to the stage they'd been at before the burglary. This was before cloud computing had taken off but imagine how different things would have been if all the files were in the cloud.

With cloud computing, the data is replicated in more than one place. Not only is this often more secure than keeping it all in house, it's often cheaper than buying and maintaining your own storage systems. With your key operational software and data in the cloud, you're effectively outsourcing the maintenance and security of a large part of your infrastructure – for many small businesses this reduces a huge burden.

Transforming data storage

Closely related to cloud computing is *distributed computing,* which makes use of connected computers (not necessarily via the Internet, but usually) to perform actions. In the case of data storage, the data is stored on many different computers and the computing task is broken up so that individual computers perform small parts of the overall task. This spreads the load and makes storing huge amounts of data cheaper, easier and much more efficient.

A *distributed file system* is a data storage system designed to store large volumes of data across multiple storage devices (often cloud-based commodity servers), to decrease the cost and complexity of storing large amounts of data.

Thanks to distributed systems, you can store data anywhere and still find and access it really quickly. Connected computers and the links between the computers are now so fast that you can store and analyse data pretty much anywhere. This has had a dramatic impact on how much data you can work with. It also means you can now store and use more types of data than ever before. (Video, for instance, used to be too large to store in large quantities, but not anymore.) And, distributed computing also makes analysing data much easier – but more about that in the next section.

Diving into data lakes

You've probably already heard of data warehouses or data centres but there's a new term doing the rounds in data storage: data lakes.

In a warehouse, everything is archived and ordered in a defined way – the products are inside containers, the containers are on shelves, the shelves are in rows and so on. This is the way data is stored in a traditional data ware-house or even in a database.

In a *data lake,* information is just poured in, in an unstructured way. A data lake contains data in its rawest form – fresh from capture and unadulterated by processing or analysis. This means that data in a lake has a great deal of agility, in that it can be configured or reconfigured as necessary, depending on the job you want to do with it.

Data lakes use what is known as *object-based storage,* in which each individual piece of data is treated as an object, made up of the information packaged together with its associated metadata and a unique identifier. No piece of information is higher level than any other, because it's not a hierarchically archived system, like a warehouse – it's basically a big free-for-all, just like water molecules in a lake.

At the time of writing, a lot of the talk about data lakes is theoretical because very few organisations are ready to make the move to keeping all of their data in a lake. Many are bogged down in data swamps – hard-to-navigate mishmashes of land and water where their data has been stored in various, uncoordinated ways over the years. Data lakes are expected to become more popular in the future, as more organisations become aware of the increased agility afforded by storing data in data lakes rather than strict hierarchical databases.

Like all advances, there are pros and cons to data lakes. The advan-tages include:

- ✔ Data stored without structure can be more quickly shaped into whatever form is needed.

- ✔ The data is available to anyone in the organisation and can be analysed and interrogated via different tools and interfaces as appropriate for each job.

- ✔ All of an organisation's data can be kept in one place – rather than having separate data stores for individual departments or applications, as is often the case.

- ✔ Having all your data in one place makes auditing and compliancy simpler, with only one store to manage.

It's not all roses and fine wine though, as the disadvantages include:

✔ You have obvious security implications if you're keeping all your eggs in one basket. Data security needs to catch up if data lakes are going to become the mainstream data storage option for businesses.

✔ Some say that the name itself is a problem (and I'm inclined to agree) as it implies a lack of architectural awareness. It kind of implies simply dumping data in one place with little thought or planning, when planning, strategy and careful consideration are vital parts of making big data work for you.

For better or worse, data lakes is a term that you'll probably be hearing more of in the near future.

Revolutionising analytic technology

I believe analytics is something any business leader should know about – not only because analytics is one of the biggest buzzwords around at the moment but also because it can be a game changer for businesses of all sizes. From the examples in Chapters 4 and 5, it's clear that we're in the middle of a data explosion and all this new data is fuelling huge leaps in analytic technology.

Analytics is the process of collecting, processing and analysing data to generate insights that inform fact-based decision making. In many cases it involves software-based analysis using algorithms.

Recognising that SQL is not the only way

In the past if you wanted access to data or to understand what the data was telling you, that data needed to be contained in a database, and you needed to use SQL tools (see Chapter 4) to understand the data. And this worked brilliantly for many years. Businesses could manage orders and stock levels, log customer information and understand where their sales and revenue were coming from. Databases can easily tell you how many units of Product A you sold in December last year, so you can ensure you have enough stock for the pre-Christmas period this year. You can understand what you sold, when and to whom.

So, you've been able to work with structured, neat, hierarchical data for a long time. But if the data wasn't structured, it was virtually impossible (or very expensive and time consuming) to extract information from it.

Advances in analytic technology mean it's now possible to work with data in just about any form. It can be structured or unstructured (see Chapter 4), it can be in a neat database, or it can be in the form of messy, unstructured Facebook updates. You no longer need database technology to understand data. You no longer need structure to get insights.

Harnessing the cloud and better storage to improve analytics

Analytics is closely tied in with cloud computing and increased storage since, without the extra storage and computing power, you're much more limited in the amount and types of data you can store and analyse.

We're generating vastly more data than ever before, which gives you more data to work with and extract insights from. Every minute, humans generate 1.8 million Facebook Likes and 278,000 Tweets – that's data that wasn't being generated at all ten years ago. This data is a goldmine of information for your company, telling you everything from what customers think of your products to who is likely to buy what and when.

Your ability to extract insights from all this new data has also improved massively over recent years. You can now analyse large volumes of fast-moving data from different data sources to gain insights that were never possible before. Systems like Hadoop (which I talk about in more detail in Chapter 9) make it possible for businesses to store and analyse datasets far larger than can practically be stored and accessed on one physical storage device (such as a hard disk). Like distributed storage, the analysis of large amounts of data can be spread across many different computers (each taking on a small chunk of the overall analytic load). By breaking up the analysis this way, it can be done in a faster and more efficient way – and it's much more cost effective too.

Breaking Down the Analytic Possibilities

In the last couple of years lots of new analytics tools have come onto the market, greatly improving your ability to analyse data. These new advances in analytics allow you to analyse numbers, text, photos and even voice and video sequences.

New companies are springing up everywhere that offer businesses the ability to analyse data in one way or another. It's no exaggeration to say that data analytics as a field is growing every single day. A data consultant can help you identify which type (or types) of analytics best suits your needs and which provider to go for.

In Chapters 8 and 9 I look at how you can tap into analytic providers and build your own big data infrastructure (including some of the software involved). In this section I introduce some of the changes in analytics over the last couple of years and what is now possible. For an idea of how these technologies are already being put to use, check out the nearby sidebar 'Five fantastic examples of big data technology in action'.

Text analytics

Text analytics is basically extracting information from large quantities of text data. This text is usually unstructured or semi-structured and may include documents, Tweets, Facebook posts, emails and websites.

In your business you no doubt have a lot of text data floating around. Until recently, it has been very difficult to mine large amounts of text for insights. You could, for instance, search on Twitter for Tweets mentioning certain key words or hashtags, but that's pretty time consuming – not to mention the fact that you'd need to have a very good idea of what it is you wanted to search *for* in the first place.

Now analytic programs can extract information quickly and easily from text, over and above what the text actually says. In a way, not only can text analytics tell you what you didn't already know, it can tell you what you didn't even realise you didn't know. For example, in the case of Tweets about your product, text analytics allows you to understand much more than the words written in the Tweet. It can tell you whether the tone of the content is positive, negative or neutral (this is called *sentiment analysis,* which I cover in Chapter 5). And it can also detect patterns, such as whether there has been an increase in other positive comments or more negative comments recently. Pretty soon, you'll even be able to tell if what's written is true or false.

In a European Union-funded project, an international group of researchers have come together to build a social media lie detector. The project, named Pheme, after the Greek goddess of fame and rumours, brings together experts in the fields of natural language processing and text mining, web science, social network analysis and information visualisation. The goal is to develop algorithms that analyse what people are saying on social media, assess how authoritative a source is, review what that source has said in the past, compare what's being said with facts already known and plot how conversations evolve – and then conclude whether information is true or false. How could this technology be used? During the 2011 London riots, rumours quickly spread on social media that a tiger had been let loose from London Zoo. With this technology, officials would be able to quickly detect that this information was false, therefore reassuring the public and directing resources where they're really needed. Businesses will be able to separate fact from industry rumours and misinformation and even analyse whether what their own people are writing is accurate.

Some of the ways you can now analyse text include:

- ✔ **Text categorisation:** Applying some structure to a text so that it can be classified by features such as author, subject, date and so on.

- ✔ **Text clustering:** Grouping text into topics or categories to make filtering easier. Search engines, for example, use this technology all the time.

> ✔ **Concept extraction:** Honing in on the text that is most relevant to the task at hand.
>
> ✔ **Sentiment analysis:** Extracting opinion or sentiment from text and categorising it as positive, negative or neutral.
>
> ✔ **Document summarisation:** Distilling documents down to the key points.

Text analytics helps you get more out of text, so that you can understand more than just the words on the page or screen. It's especially helpful for understanding more about your customers but could also easily be applied internally to analyse what your own people are saying.

Speech analytics

Speech analytics, also known as *voice analytics,* is the process of analysing audio data (such as conversation recordings) for insights.

The latest speech analytics software can not only detect what is being said, but can also analyse the way it is said, largely by analysing the tone of voice, in order to understand the emotional content.

This isn't a particularly new notion – think of how investigative interviewers pick up on changes in voice to detect whether a suspect is lying. But what's especially exciting is the way businesses can use this technology (without hiring a *Cracker*-style expert!) to understand more about their customers, products and services and employees.

Ever told a fib? Be warned: linguistic analysis can now pick up on those signals in your voice and identify possible lies. One example is computer voice stress analysis (CVSA) that detects changes in your voice pitch to detect lies. Approved by a US federal court ruling, this technology can be used to monitor sex offenders as part of their post-release supervision. It won't take long for this technology to find its way into call centres and helpdesk centres to help companies detect lies customers might tell their service providers.

Speech analytics can be especially useful in any business with a call centre at its heart – not just for policing the ne'er-do-wells and catching out liars, but to detect common complaints or phrases that keep coming up in conversations so that you can make positive changes to your products or service. And you know the old disclaimer 'this call may be recorded for training purposes'? One of my clients does just that and uses speech analytics to analyse how well call centre operatives relate to customers (by detecting certain words and monitoring tone of voice). This information is used to help train new staff and to help identify existing employees who might need a little extra training.

There are a number of commercial speech analytics tools available to purchase or license such as CallMiner or Nice Speech Analytics. These tools can help you get to the bottom of what customers really think about your company, products and services, and they can also help you understand more about how your people are performing.

Image analytics

Image analytics is the process of extracting information from images, particularly photographs, although it could apply to graphics and other images, such as medical scans.

Until recently, the only way to analyse images was by eye – a human being looking at an image in order to make sense of it. Certain tags or data can be added to the image automatically (such as date the photo was taken and, in some cases, the location). And some need to be added by humans, such as descriptive tags or keywords. For example, when you search online for an image of a bear catching a salmon, the search engine isn't sifting through the photos themselves to find an image of a bear catching a salmon; it's searching an index of photo metadata for the tags 'bear' and 'salmon'. The metadata tags (key words and descriptors) were added by the person who uploaded the photo. Computers simply couldn't tell what was in a photo . . . until now.

Now it's possible to teach a computer what a bear and a fish look like so that it can find them in other photos, without needing humans meticulously tagging photos with key descriptive phrases (see the Metamind example in Chapter 2 for more on this technology).

Then there's the whole issue of face recognition – a technology that's terrifically exciting and more than a little creepy at the same time. Facial recognition has been around for a little while now but recent analytic advances are taking it to a whole new level. It used to work by using algorithms to pick out facial features and analyse their position, size, shape and so on. Thanks to 3-D face recognition, this technology is now way more accurate. In fact, Facebook believes that its DeepFace face recognition system is becoming as accurate at recognising faces as the human eye!

Some companies are already using image analytics to analyse photos of their products online and on social media platforms to find out more about who's using their products. You could, for example, get software that searches social media for images that contain your product or logo. Right now perhaps this is a little too Big Brother for the average business, but as the technology advances, it may well become a more regular feature of business life.

Video analytics

Closely related to image analytics, *video analytics* is the process of extracting information from videos. This type of analytics involves much of the same technology as image analytics (such as face recognition) but because the images are not static, they can tell you more – such as how people behave or move around a space or whether a person being filmed is telling the truth.

Much like image analytics, in order to extract meaning from a video, you used to have to physically watch the video and see what happened in it. Now though, you have the technology to automate much of this process. For example, CCTV (closed-circuit television) might once have been used to track who enters and exits a building for security purposes. You'd still need someone to monitor the video for activity (or, in the event of a break-in, someone to review it to see what happened). With face recognition software, a security system could detect whether the person approaching the building is authorised to enter or not, allowing automatic entry only to authorised personnel. This increases security and reduces the risk of a break-in. Or a retailer could use video analytics to understand how customers move around the shop floor and which displays draw the most interest.

Video analytics can detect accuracy just as well as speech and text analytics. With video analytics, it's possible to detect spikes in your language, fidgeting body movements and pupil dilation – all physical indicators of lying that are difficult to consciously control. Biometric data such as pupil dilation is one of the factors analysed to detect whether interviewees entering the country are telling the truth. While humans can be trained to look for signs that someone is lying (body language being a key example), computers are more accurate and consistent. The possibilities that this technology offers are both fascinating and, if I'm being honest (because a computer is analysing me) a little scary. And this is just what you're capable of now. Imagine what might be possible in ten years' time.

Increased storage capacity has played a crucial role in the development of video analytics. Before advances like cloud computing and digital video files, it was just too difficult for the average business to store masses of video. Now, for example, you could easily upload and store all your CCTV footage in the cloud without buying any special in-house hardware. In theory, you'd be able to store years and years worth of video and have quick and easy access for analysing that footage. Of course, whether five-year-old CCTV footage is useful to you is another matter but at least the days of taping over last week's CCTV video are long gone. Now you can compare video footage of this month's key retail display with another month (or the same month last year) to see if it's drawing more customers.

Five fantastic examples of big data technology in action

Big data is being put to use in a range of ways, from the indispensably useful to the weird and wonderful. Here I look at five creative examples of big data in action:

✔ **Big data billboards:** Outdoor marketing company Route is using big data to define and justify its pricing model for advertising space on billboards, benches and the sides of busses. Traditionally, outdoor media pricing was priced *per impression*, based on an estimate of how many eyes would see the ad in a given day. No more! Now companies use sophisticated GPS, eye-tracking software and analysis of traffic patterns to have a much more realistic idea of which advertisements are seen the most – and therefore are the most effective.

✔ **iPhone's ResearchKit:** Apple's new health app, called ResearchKit, effectively turns your phone into a biomedical research device. Researchers can now create studies through which they collect data and input from users' phones to compile data for health studies. Your phone might track how many steps you take in a day, or prompt you to answer questions about how you feel after your chemo, or how your Parkinson's disease is progressing. It's hoped that making the process easier and more automatic will dramatically increase the number of participants a study can attract as well as the fidelity of the data.

✔ **Big data on the slopes:** Ski resorts are even getting into the data game. RFID (radio frequency identification) tags (see Chapter 5) inserted into lift tickets can cut back on fraud and wait times at the lifts. They help ski resorts understand traffic patterns, which lifts and runs are most popular at which times of day and can even help track the movements of a lost individual skier. They've also taken the data to the people, providing websites and apps that display your day's stats, from how many runs you slalomed to how many vertical feet you traversed. You can then share this information on social media or use it to compete with family and friends.

✔ **Big data weather forecasting:** Applications have long used data from phones to populate traffic maps, but an app called WeatherSignal taps into sensors already built into Android phones to crowdsource real-time weather data as well. The phones contain a barometer, hygrometer (humidity), ambient thermometer and light meter, all of which can collect data relevant to weather forecasting and be fed into predictive models.

✔ **Yelp hipster watch:** Whether you want to hang with the hipsters or avoid them, Yelp has you covered. With a nifty little search trick they call the Wordmap, you can search major cities by words used in reviews – like hipster. The map then plots the locations for the reviews in red. The darker the red, the higher the concentration of that word used in reviews – and when it comes to hipsters, ironic tee shirts and handlebar moustaches.

Data mining

You might have heard of data mining as another buzzword thrown in with the big data hype. It's often used as a catchall to describe any kind of information processing on a large scale. But I prefer a more precise definition – one that emphasises the *insights* that data can give you, not just the process of extracting the data itself.

Data mining is the process of exploring large amounts of data in order to gather commercially relevant insights, patterns or relationships that can improve business performance. It is the automatic (or semi-automatic) analysis of data to spot previously unknown but useful patterns that can be exploited. The technology itself is a hybrid of statistics, database systems, machine learning (see Chapter 7) and artificial intelligence.

For most businesses, data mining boils down to two main uses: predicting what might happen and making better decisions. I talk more about these uses in Chapter 3 and the chapters in Part 4.

Specific examples of using data mining include:

- ✔ Identifying factors that your customers have in common, so that you can target others who meet that criteria.

- ✔ Spotting patterns that show you how customers move around your website, so that you can make improvements to the site.

- ✔ Understanding which products are most commonly bought together or identifying external factors (such as weather changes) that boost sales of certain items.

Three of the four Vs of big data that I mentioned in Chapter 2 – volume, velocity and variety – are what really make data mining possible. The sheer volume of data being generated every day gives you the potential to spot patterns and relationships that would have been very hard (or impossible) to spot before. The same goes for the variety and velocity of data, without which you wouldn't have access to the types of data you do or the ability to access and analyse that data so quickly.

Data mining is great for identifying patterns, anomalies or relationships that you weren't aware of, but it will not necessarily tell you the reason for those patterns, anomalies or relationships. It helps you understand the who, what, where and when, without shedding any light on the *why*. If the *why* is a critical insight for your business, you'll need to look at combining data mining with other types of analysis to get a fuller picture. Which brings me on to . . .

Combined analytics

This is an area that's really interesting to me, and it's something I always emphasise when I'm working with clients. More often than not, the value of big data is not in any one flashy data set, rather it's in the insights that can be gained from combining different types of data.

If one dataset will help you answer your strategic business questions (which I talk about in Chapter 11), and that's all you need to move your business forward, then great. Go for it! In reality though, most businesses need a combination of datasets, perhaps two or three, to get a full picture.

The idea is to base your decision making on as clear a picture as possible, not just what one dataset is telling you. For instance, you may have sold 20 per cent more units of a particular product last month through your website. Based on just that information, you might be tempted to make it a key part of your upcoming marketing campaign, or bump it up to the front of your website or increase the amount of stock you order. But what if there's more to it than what that data tells you? What if the increase was related to particular weather conditions that don't apply this month? What if a trending topic on Twitter led to a one-off spike in sales of that product for other companies too, not just yours? Combining information from more than one source (ideally three sources, in my opinion), allows you to triangulate the information and verify insights from more than one angle. This can especially important in smaller businesses where resources are scarce.

One of my clients is a supermarket chain. It's now collecting data from a wide range of sources, including external sources like social media and internal sources like their stock control systems. Social media text, for instance, is monitored for positive and negative feedback from shoppers. And products have RFID chips (see Chapter 5) so their exact location is known at all times, whether they're in the warehouse, on the shop floor or in a delivery truck. These sources came together to solve a curious case of missing cookies. The chain found that a certain type of cookie was a bestseller across all stores, regardless of location. Well, almost all stores. One of the company's data analysts flagged that the cookie wasn't selling at all in one particular location. Not a single unit. The analyst first noticed this because people on social media were saying they couldn't find it in their local store and were asking why. The company found from the RFID data that the cookies were hidden on a pallet in the back of that store's warehouse and were never put out on the shop floor. Case solved – and all thanks to a combination of data.

All the examples in this chapter show only a tiny fraction of the possibilities big data offers. Just a few years ago, none of this was possible; you couldn't do sentiment analysis on text, computers couldn't tell an image of a bear from any other image, facial recognition software was in its infancy and a long way from being as accurate as the human eye. All of this is now possible and we're on the cusp of much, much more. Although the technology I've mentioned has come a long way, we're really only just at the start of the big data and analytics journey. Analytics in particular has undergone such a dramatic transformation that no one really knows what's going to be possible in five years' time. Not even me. That's an exciting position to be in.

Part III
A Brave New World for Small Business

Top Five Tips for Partnering with an External Big Data Contractor

- It's a good idea to already have a draft data strategy before you approach contractors. It helps you identify what you're trying to achieve and informs your initial discussions with providers.

- If you really don't know where to start, a big data consultant can help you devise your big data strategy and find the right company to carry out the data capture and analysis.

- You need a provider who understands exactly what you're trying to achieve in your business. A contractor with a good understanding of your goals and challenges is much more likely to get you the data and insights you really need.

- Ask for very specific examples of who the provider has worked with, how the projects unfolded and, crucially, what results those clients saw as a result.

- Focus on the six key big data skills that I set out in Chapter 8. I also provide a list of recruitment questions which can easily be adapted to vet external contractors.

Find out more about overcoming the big data skills shortage at www.dummies.com/extras/bigdataforsmallbusiness.

In this part . . .

- ✔ Move from data to insights to action.
- ✔ Find out how to tap into big data skills and competencies.
- ✔ Understand how demand for big data skills outstrips supply.
- ✔ Create the necessary big data infrastructure in your business.

Chapter 7

Focusing on the Value of Insights

· ·

In This Chapter

▶ Understanding the differences among data, insights and knowledge

▶ Getting insights to your key people in a way they'll understand

▶ Linking data with your machines and processes

· ·

*B*usinesses have access to more data than ever before. In fact, many organisations are now drowning in data, but that doesn't mean they're necessarily gaining useful insights – the kind of insights that can support decision making and help a business develop. In the data era, I believe the success of a business rests on the ability to gain fact-based insights and turn those into smart decisions.

Data is worth very little unless you can turn it into insights and actionable knowledge.

Focusing on the data itself rather than insights is a bit like attempting to bake a cake with just a list of ingredients. You may have gathered the right ingredients in front of you – 250 grams each of flour, butter and sugar, plus three eggs – but that doesn't mean you can turn that into a successful cake. You need a recipe that tells you to first beat the sugar and butter together, then add the eggs one at a time, then slowly fold in the flour. You need to know which size tin to put the batter in, how hot the oven should be and how long it needs to bake. You also need to know not to open the oven door for a peek! Likewise, having the right data doesn't automatically translate into success – it's how you use it that counts.

In this chapter, I look at how to move from data to insights to actionable knowledge, as well as how to present insights in a way that facilitates action. I also look at how some companies are feeding data directly into machines and processes.

Moving from Data to Insights to Knowledge

First, let me clarify what I mean by insights and knowledge. Insights are basically just information – information that tells you something about your company, employees, customers, products and so on. An insight could be how many units of a product you sold last month or whether your customers are generally happy with your product or service (based, for instance, on the volume of calls to your customer service team).

But those insights aren't the same as actionable knowledge. Interesting though those insights are, you can't directly *act* on them. For that you'd need to know what makes your customers happy and unhappy so that you can do more or less of it. This is the difference between insights and actionable knowledge.

Actionable knowledge is gained by understanding the insights and information in context that help you to make better decisions. Crucially, you then need to *act* on those decisions. It's this process that provides the fifth V of big data: value. (I talk about the Vs in Chapter 2.)

In today's competitive business world, success often comes down to a company's ability to learn faster than the competition and act on what it learns faster than the competition. The process of turning data into insights and actionable knowledge is the key to that success.

Turning data into insights

Research shows that many organisations are still focused on simply collecting as much data as they can rather than analysing it to extract meaningful insights. This is a big mistake.

By analysing the data, you should arrive at various insights. Presenting these insights in a helpful way is a key step in turning them into actionable knowledge. I believe the ultimate goal in businesses of any size should be to have data inform decision making across the business – as opposed to gut-based decisions leading the way. To make this a reality, the key decision makers need easy access to data-based insights that are clear and easy to understand. I talk more about getting insights to the key people in your organisation later in the chapter.

How do you help make sure your data leads to insights and actionable knowledge? The answer lies in your strategic business questions, which I cover in detail in Chapters 10 and 11.

It's important to clearly set out your key strategic business questions before embarking on any data project. Understanding exactly what it is you want to know leads you to better, sharper insights and to the information you need to make decisions. I set out a process for identifying your strategic questions in Chapter 11 but examples of these questions include:

- ✔ How should we redesign our website in order to maximise online sales?
- ✔ Which customer groups should we focus our marketing efforts on?
- ✔ What is the best location for a new store?
- ✔ What is the most efficient route for our delivery truck?

Sadly, in business, decisions are often made based on the information available at the time rather than the information that is really needed to make those decisions. By starting with your key strategic questions – defining what it is you really want to know – you can then gather the information needed to answer those questions and make decisions.

Setting out your strategic business questions leads you to the best data. In order to turn that data into insights that help you answer your questions, you need to analyse the data (see Chapters 6 and 9).

Translating insights into actionable knowledge

You know that interesting insights don't automatically result in action. But, if you set out your key strategic questions in advance, then the insights you gather should help you answer those questions.

The knowledge you gain from answering your strategic questions then needs to be turned into action. You (and your people) need to make decisions based on that knowledge – and then follow those decisions through. If the knowledge gained is not turned into action then the whole thing is pretty much a waste of time and resources.

In their book *The Knowing-Doing Gap: How Smart Companies Turn Knowledge into Action*, Jeffrey Pfeffer and Robert Sutton (Harvard Business Review Press) explain why many companies fail to turn knowledge into action. They argue the knowing-doing gap (where knowledge is not implemented) is the most menacing phenomenon most organisations face today, costing billions of dollars and leading to a wide array of failures. One reason for this gap is what the authors call the *smart talk trap*, in which talk becomes a substitute for action and decisions don't actually result in any changes.

Closing the knowing-doing gap requires a number of changes in an organisation. It's partly about changing processes and technology so that you can gather and analyse data. But it also requires something of a cultural shift to one that emphasises insights and action. I talk more about shifting to a culture of data-based decision making in Chapter 13.

Here are my top tips for translating insights into action:

✔ Try not to get distracted by interesting insights that have nothing to do with answering your strategic business questions. There may be scope to revisit those insights in future (they may, for instance, lead to new strategic questions to explore) but, for now, focus on what you set out to achieve.

✔ Gather all the information you need to answer your strategic goals. Avoid the trap of making decisions based on the information you have to hand. If you don't have everything you need, see if you can revisit the data capture process to get exactly you what you need.

✔ Arrive at an answer (or a set of insights) related to each question you set at the start of the process. Depending on your questions, you may need to distribute those insights to key people in your organisation. These insights should be presented in a clear, accessible and easy-to-understand way, not buried in lengthy reports. I talk more about this later in the chapter.

✔ Together with the relevant people in your organisation, you need to take each of those questions/answers and decide how best to move forward based on the knowledge gained. It's a good idea to break the actions into specific tasks and milestones so everyone is clear who needs to do what and when.

✔ Revisit the whole process after a few months (three to six months usually makes sense but you may need to do it sooner in your business) to see if the actions you decided upon have been carried out and led to the results you expected.

Here's an example of moving from data to insights to action. Sociometric Solutions produces employee name badges with built-in sensors that detect social dynamics in the workplace. The sensors measure how employees move around the workplace, whom they speak to and even the tone of voice they use when communicating. Bank of America used these name badges to collect data on its employees. By analysing this data, Bank of America found that their top performing call centre staff were those that took breaks together. They turned this insight into action by instituting group breaks as standard. As a result, performance improved 23 per cent.

Feeding humans and machines

Data can be fed to your people through dashboards (which I talk about in Chapter 11) or simple reports. The goal is to help them make better decisions that lead to improved business performance.

Or data can feed into any machines that form part of your business operations. Often, this process of feeding data to machines and the machines making decisions based on the data can be automatic, without any human intervention. You can find out more about this later in the chapter.

Getting Insights to the People Who Need Them

Who needs access to the insights? In a very small business, the decision makers may be you (as the owner) and perhaps one or two key members of staff. In larger companies, you may need to share insights with various people throughout the business so that they can be involved in the decisions that drive the business forward. Or you may need to present insights to board members. In any case, it's important to involve all the key players that relate to the business's goals and strategic questions.

However you decide to disseminate the information, keep in mind that the format in which it's presented plays a big role in how useful that information is. People are less likely to act if they have to work hard to understand what the information is telling them. Present your insights in a clear, concise and interesting way, and you make it easy for your people to turn them into action.

Businesses gain competitive advantage when the right information is delivered to the right people at the right time.

What's the best way to disseminate insights to decision makers? It depends on what you're measuring, who needs to know about it and how you usually communicate across the company. You could for instance have an indicator (such as sales, revenue or employee performance) included in a monthly report that's distributed to your managers. Or, you may need more sophisticated, real-time information in the form of a dashboard that allows decision makers to access information whenever and wherever they want. I talk more about presenting insights in Chapter 9 (in terms of infrastructure requirements) and Chapter 11 (in terms of how it fits into the step-by-step decision-making process).

Grabbing attention

Data can be presented as a number, a written narrative, a table, a graph or a chart. The best approach may actually involve a combination of these formats.

Think about the front page of a newspaper. What makes you stop and pick it up when you actually only came into the shop to pay for petrol or buy milk? First of all there's the headline: a short, snappy, attention-grabbing description that makes you want to find out more. Then there's usually a picture that puts the headline into context and adds interest. And underneath there's a short narrative that introduces the story and gives the key information.

Unfortunately, I rarely see this approach in the material that organisations distribute to their people. There's usually complicated graphs or charts that no one understands and the key takeaway points are buried in lengthy narrative that few people read all the way through. It might look snazzy or impressive, but the key messages are hidden. And if the messages are hidden, people aren't likely to act on them.

Try to present your information as a newspaper would. Start with an interesting and informative headline that summarises the main finding. Include a useful visual (such as an image, graph or chart) along with a short narrative that sets out the key messages and supports the visual. Use colour where appropriate, but don't get lost in style over substance.

Making the insights easy to access and digest

Visuals are great for conveying information because they're quick and direct, they're (usually) easy to understand, they're memorable, and they add interest (being much more likely to hold the reader's attention than a full page of text).

Narrative is also important because it, without it, people can interpret the data differently. With a short narrative you can ensure everyone understands the data in the same way. It also gives managers a story that they can easily share or filter down as appropriate.

Using visuals and narrative together is much more powerful than using either on its own. For instance, a graph detailing sales history is extremely useful for analysing trends over time, but a narrative can put that information into context – explaining what might be behind that trend.

Big data and barbecue – A surprising flavour combination

Barbecue and big data probably don't seem like the most natural of bedfellows – but one US restaurant chain, Dickey's Barbecue Pit, threw them together to increase sales and its understanding of the customer. The company implemented a system called Smoke Stack that crunches data from point-of-sale systems, marketing promotions, loyalty programs, customer surveys and inventory systems to provide near real-time feedback on sales and other key performance indicators. Operational behaviour can then be manipulated on the fly to respond to supply and demand issues.

All of the data is examined every 20 minutes to enable immediate decisions, as well as during a daily morning briefing at corporate headquarters, where higher level strategies can be planned and executed.

Chief information officer Laura Rea Dickey says: 'We look at where we want to be on a tactical basis – we are expecting sales to be at a certain baseline at a certain store in a certain region, and if we are not where we want to be, it lets us deploy training or operations directly to contact that store and react to the information. For example, if we've seen lower than expected sales one lunchtime, and know we have an amount of ribs there, we can put out a text invitation to people in the local area for a ribs special – to both equalise the inventory and catch up on sales.'

One challenge for the chain has been end-user adoption. 'We have folks in very different, vertically integrated positions within the company,' explains Laura. 'Those folks in the corporate office are based in a traditional office setting working around the reality of the business, all the way down to the folks in our stores on the front line who are running a barbecue pit and interacting with customers. Having a platform that can integrate with all of those different user types is probably our biggest challenge.'

The solution comes in the form of the dashboard that helps staff make those key decisions on the fly by presenting them with the information they need in a way they can easily understand. 'The interface makes it much easier – it's excellent, particularly for people who you might traditionally think of as more analogue than digital – they came to work for us because they wanted to be barbecue artisans, not analysts.'

Following a trial involving 175 users, the chain planned to roll the system out across 350 of its restaurants. As Laura puts it, 'We've really been fortunate in finding an excellent partner and being able to pull together technology that's really met our needs – we've made barbecue and big data a kind of strange reality.'

In terms of access, it's important that your decision makers can get at the information they need when they need it in order to make the best decisions. It's no good disseminating monthly reports if key decisions need to be made on a daily or weekly basis. Restaurant chain Dickey's Barbecue Pit offers an excellent example of getting the right information to the right people at the right time, in the sidebar 'Big data and barbecue – A surprising flavour combination'.

Getting the Insights to the Machines that Need Them

As well as going to the people in your business, data and insights can also feed into the machines in your company. This applies to any machine or technology that's a key part of how the business operates on a day-to-day basis. This could be the equipment on your manufacturing line, it could be your security system or it could even be your website.

Data can also feed into processes just as well as machines. For instance, in the nearby 'Big data and barbecue – A surprising flavour combination' sidebar, the data gathered from the chain's restaurants is analysed to see if any changes are needed to the way staff in various locations are trained to deal with customers.

I look at both machines and processes in turn in the next sections and you can find more about using data to improve your operations and processes in Chapter 12.

Understanding machine learning

Machine learning involves feeding data into machines, which then determine the best course of action based on that data.

Machine learning refers to the fast growing field of creating self-learning algorithms that can adapt themselves based on given data without any human intervention. In a nutshell, the machines *learn* from the data they're given and decide what to do next.

Sometimes the course of action decided by the machine may need human intervention (for instance, if something needs repairing or replacing). But increasingly computers are able to carry out the intervention themselves. An example of this can be seen in what Rolls-Royce refers to as its Ship Intelligence Initiative – see the nearby sidebar, 'Rolls-Royce's space-age initiative', for an insight into how this works.

Connecting data with machines

The potential for machine learning and data is all very exciting. But how are businesses already using this technology? Here I set out some great examples of how businesses are already connecting their machines with data, allowing access to a whole range of useful insights that we haven't had before, even just a few years ago.

Rolls-Royce's space-age initiative

Prestige manufacturer Rolls-Royce has implemented a Ship Intelligence Initiative. This not only provides captains and crews with a remarkably _Star Trek_-like experience: Personnel are automatically scanned for security clearance and then personally greeted by the computer when they enter the bridge. Ship Intelligence Initiative also provides sophisticated big data-driven automatic piloting and operating systems. Hazards detected by sensors can be highlighted to the crew right in front of their eyes by augmented reality (AR) displays, and should the crew ignore them for some reason, the ship can automatically plot a safe path.

Taking the concept a step further, Rolls-Royce is also proposing _drone ships_ – autonomous cargo ships that would carry thousands of tons of goods across the oceans without a single human being on board, controlled instead from a single nerve centre control room. Without the need to sustain humans in comfort during long sea voyages, cargo vessels could be built far more cheaply and be more environmentally friendly. Fuel use would be cut by 15 per cent. The company already has many of the building blocks that could make this concept a reality, such as remote equipment monitoring and highly reliable propulsion systems, and expects to have a small-scale demonstrator vessel at sea within a few years.

This vision of a future where ships operate with minimal human interaction – with humans placing trust in machines' superior speed and ability to process huge amounts of data far more quickly than we can ourselves – might seem like science fiction, but we're likely to see more and more of it appearing in the real world in the near future.

By connecting data and machines, the insights you gain can help you increase efficiency, improve product quality, provide a better service to your customers, cut costs, make your employees happier and much more.

I should clarify here that you don't need to be running a manufacturing business with big, expensive machinery to care about connecting data with machines. _Machines_ can, in fact, refer to your website infrastructure, for example, using algorithms to tailor your website based on the visitor's IP address (perhaps by flashing up an offer on overseas shipping).

It could even refer to office equipment! Humanscale builds sensors into its line of office chairs, standing desks and work stations and offers its OfficeIQ system to monitor workplace activity such as how much time individuals spend sitting or standing at their desks as well as how long they're away from their desks.

In Ireland, grocery chain Tesco has its warehouse employees wear armbands that track the goods they take from the shelves, distribute tasks, and even forecast completion time for a job. In other sectors, including healthcare and the military, wearables can detect fatigue that could be dangerous to the employee and the job they perform.

I mention Rolls-Royce a few times in this chapter because it's one of the foremost examples of sensor technology and machine learning in action – and a great example of a relatively traditional company embracing big data. The company is already connecting data with machines in order to improve the way the business operates. Rolls-Royce manufactures enormous engines that generate huge amounts of power as they propel airplanes and ships across skies and oceans. These engines and propulsion systems are all fitted with hundreds of sensors that record every tiny detail about their operations and report any changes in data in real-time to engineers who decide the best course of action. In addition, the company's manufacturing systems are increasingly becoming networked and communicating with each other. At its factories, the innovation is not just in the way machines bash and shape metal – it's in the way the company automatically measures aspects of the manufacturing process and monitors quality control of the components being made. At its Singapore factory, Rolls-Royce generates half a terabyte of manufacturing data on each individual fan blade. With 6,000 fan blades being produced each year, that's three petabytes of data from the manufacture of just one component. And these concepts are creeping into all manner of manufacturing areas: check out the nearby sidebar 'After smartphones comes smart . . . shirts' if you need to be convinced!

Connecting data with processes

Big data is about so much more than how much data you can generate. It's about analysing that data in order to draw out insights that drive efficiency and progress in your business.

Your processes and systems can also be connected with data, so that you can improve how you do things based on what the data shows.

Big data analytics helps Rolls-Royce identify maintenance actions days or weeks ahead of time, so airlines can schedule the work without passengers experiencing any disruption. This idea can be scaled down and applied to any company with machinery or vehicles that require regular maintenance. So, if you run a delivery fleet, your servicing schedule could be connected with data that monitors wear and tear on the vehicles, enabling you to service or repair vehicles when they need it rather than when an arbitrary timetable says they need it. Maintenance can be scheduled in advance to avoid vehicles being off the road at inconvenient times.

After smartphones comes smart . . . shirts

The world that we live in is becoming increasingly digitally connected. This trend is having an impact on everything, and fashion is no exception. Wearable technology, often referred to simply as *wearables,* is expected to become increasingly popular as the Internet of Things (see Chapter 5) takes off.

Among the big names in high-end consumer fashion that have shown they're keen to embrace this new market is Ralph Lauren, which unveiled its connected polo tech shirt at the 2014 US Open tennis tournament.

Sensors attached to silver threads inside the shirt pick up the wearer's movement data as well as heart and breathing rates, which can be monitored on the accompanying smartphone app. Potentially, the data could be uploaded to the cloud for analysis, although the company has not yet released details of exactly how this will work. For those who are wondering, yes, you can wash the polo tech shirt, but you have to remove the slightly-larger-than-credit-card-sized Bluetooth transmitter first. The company currently is looking into ways that the device can be shrunk — perhaps eventually ending up the size of a button — or incorporated inside the fabric in a way that makes removing it unnecessary.

And although the polo tech shirt is firmly in the realm of sportswear, Ralph Lauren has plans beyond that. Ralph Lauren made its name with ties, so perhaps the Smart Tie is on the drawing board and will be featured across both fashion and tech blogs in the near future? According to David Lauren, the son of founder Ralph and in charge of global marketing for the company, 'A lot will come in the next few months. We are a lifestyle brand, a major fashion luxury brand. I want to be able to gather this (biometric) information in a boardroom or from a baby in a crib. We'll find new needs and we're just at the beginning.'

If you think about it, a wealth of data is generated in the average board meeting — not just in what is said, but who says it and the manner and tone of voice in which they say it. Biometric readings of meeting participants could deliver useful information about how people perform under pressure in corporate situations. Solutions such as Hitachi's Business Microscope offer opportunities to capture some of this information, and integrating this functionality into clothing seems like a logical step.

The development of smart clothing is a clear sign that every industry is waking up to the potential benefits of smart, data-driven innovation, and no one wants to be left out. Effectively, all businesses are becoming data businesses — even the ones you'd least expect.

Not only do approaches like this help you run your business in a more efficient way, they also reduce costs, especially when you're able to fix things before they go wrong.

Connecting data with processes also helps you offer a better service to your customers. For example, monitoring your stock control system helps you ensure items stay in stock at peak ordering times and allows you to run dynamic promotions based on stock levels. It allows you to measure data from your customer service team and make changes that improve your service or product based on what the data tells you. It's about much more than machinery and metal and cables – it's about making your business more competitive and securing its future.

Transport for London (TfL) oversees a network of buses, trains, taxis, roads, cycle paths, footpaths and even ferries used by millions every day. Running these vast networks, so integral to so many people's lives in one of the world's busiest cities, gives TfL access to huge amounts of data. This is collected through ticketing systems as well as sensors attached to vehicles and traffic signals, surveys and focus groups and of course social media. This data feeds into TfL's processes in two ways: planning services and providing information to customers.

The data is made anonymous and used to produce maps showing when and where people are traveling, giving a far more accurate overall picture, as well as allowing more granular analysis at the level of individual journeys, than was possible before. This allows TfL to understand *load profiles* (how crowded a particular bus or tube line is at certain times) and to plan interchanges, minimise walk times and plan other related services, such as retail.

In this chapter I share some very impressive examples of how companies are acting on insights from big data. At present, a lot of this innovation is driven by larger corporations who have the manpower and resources to generate and analyse huge volumes of data. But that doesn't mean this is all beyond the scope of smaller businesses. In fact, I'd say the opposite is true.

Smaller businesses are often much more nimble than larger corporations, making them better equipped to quickly act upon what data tells them. You may not be generating petabytes of data in your daily operations but that doesn't mean your data is any less valid. The key is to focus on the insights that the data throws up, communicate those insights to the people who need to know, make informed decisions and follow through with action.

As all areas of business become more data-driven, this process of turning data into action becomes a core factor in success – and that's true whether you manufacture aeroplane engines or run a small organic grocery shop.

Chapter 8

Developing and Accessing Big Data Competencies

*D*emand for big data expertise is growing every day, as more and more companies become aware of the benefits of collecting and analysing data. Unfortunately, the number of people trained to analyse this data isn't growing in line with the demand. This creates a challenge for companies looking to hire expert people.

For companies of all sizes looking to unlock big data's potential, there's one big hurdle to overcome: stiff competition in hiring the necessary staff.

However, hiring in-house staff isn't the only way to access big data skills. You can train up your existing people, work with external providers or partner with other interested parties. In this chapter, I look at all the options for tapping into big data skills. But first, I explore the skills shortage in a little more detail to see why it's such a big deal.

Big Data and the Skills Shortage Challenge

At the end of 2015 there were expected to be 4.4 million big data jobs globally in governments and every sector of industry. Combine this with a shortage of people trained to carry out the analysis needed and that's a lot of unfilled vacancies.

Big data skills are in high demand, which drives up wages and makes it difficult to attract good people without breaking the bank. Small and medium-sized companies are usually unable to compete with the big corporations when it comes to wages and benefits. This means you may need to get creative in order to access the skills you need – more on this in the section, 'Thinking outside the box' later in the chapter.

Data scientists are currently such hot property that the *Harvard Business Review* even called it the sexiest job of the 21st century! Perhaps this means kids will grow up with dreams of becoming data scientists instead of pilots or astronauts?

Unfortunately the role of a data scientist is often ill-defined within the field and even within a single company. People throw the term around to mean everything from a *data engineer* (the person responsible for creating the software that collects and stores the data) to statisticians who merely crunch the numbers.

Because there aren't enough true data scientists out there to fill the need, less qualified (or unqualified!) candidates make it into the ranks. Many calling themselves data scientists are lacking the full skill set I'd expect.

For example, I've seen people who don't have any understanding of big data technology or big data programming languages call themselves data scientists. At the opposite end of the spectrum are programmers from the information technology (IT) function who understand programming but lack the business skills, analytics skills or creativity needed to be a true data scientist. I believe a really valuable data scientist should possess the six skills set out in the next section.

Six Key Big Data Skills Any Business Needs

One question I get asked a lot is: What are the key skills required to work with big data? Usually my clients are asking me this question so they can select the right candidates for their organisation. I believe there are six key skills required so, ideally, you're looking for data scientists who offer these skills.

Keep in mind that, rather than hiring people with these skills, you may be able to build on your existing employees and their skills. For example, an IT person who already covers the computer science side of things may be super keen to learn about analytics. Pair her up with a creative, strategic thinker who understands the business's needs (this might be you), and you're well on your way to having the skills you need without hiring anyone new. In smaller businesses on a tight budget, it's a good idea to try to develop your existing people wherever possible.

Analysing data

Perhaps the most obvious skill needed is to be able to make sense of the reams of data that your newly deployed data collection strategy (see Chapter 10 for more on this) is piling up for you. Analytics involves the ability to determine which data is relevant to the question that you're hoping to answer and interpreting the data in order to derive those answers.

You may have some of these abilities in-house already – business analysts, accountants and IT people are usually skilled at making sense of data in one way or another. This is a great starting point, but you really need people who have (or are willing to develop) a strong understanding of big data.

Key analytical skills include:

- A knack for spotting patterns and establishing links between cause and effect

- A thorough understanding of interpreting reports and being able to make sense of masses of data, both structured and unstructured

- The ability to build simulated models that can be warped and tweaked until they produce the desired results, such as answers to your strategic questions (see Chapter 11)

- A sound knowledge of industry-standard analytics packages, such as SAS Analytics, IBM Predictive Analytics and Oracle Data Mining, and a firm idea of how to use them to spot the answers to the questions you're asking

Being creative

Creativity is vital when working with big data. After all, it's an emerging science and there are no hard-and-fast rules about what a company should use big data for.

In this sense, *creativity* is the ability to apply technical skills and use them to produce something of value (such as an insight) in a way other than following a pre-determined formula. Anyone can be formulaic – you should be aiming for innovation that will set your business apart from the pack.

Creativity is especially important for any business hoping to make sense of *unstructured data* – data that doesn't fit comfortably into tables and charts, such as human speech and writing.

Valuable creative skills include:

- ✔ The ability to look beyond a particular set of numbers, beyond even the company's own datasets to discover answers to questions – and perhaps even pose new questions.

- ✔ A knack for pulling out key insights and solving problems. This may include solving problems the company doesn't even know it has – for example, the insights spotted can highlight bottlenecks or inefficiencies in the production, marketing or delivery processes that the company was unaware of.

- ✔ The ability to come up with new methods of gathering, interpreting, analysing and – crucially – profiting from data. This is especially important in smaller companies where first-choice options may not be possible due to budget constraints.

Applying mathematics and statistics

Ah, good old-fashioned number crunching. It may not be sexy, but it's still got a big role to play. Despite the growing amount of unstructured data available, much of the information being gathered and stored for analysis still takes the form of numbers.

And even when dealing exclusively with unstructured data like emails, social media messages and so forth, the objective of the exercise is often to reduce that data into easily quantifiable information: Hard numbers are good. This means a person with a strong background in maths or statistics has a good grounding for big data-related work.

The following maths and analytic skills are particularly important:

- ✔ At least a basic grasp of statistics. For data scientists involved with operational data science as opposed to strategic data science (I explain the difference later in the chapter, in the section 'Understanding Two Very Different Types of Data Scientist'), a more in-depth knowledge of statistics and mathematics is desirable.

- ✔ The ability to define appropriate populations and sample sizes at the start of a project, based on the goals set out in the data strategy and to clearly report the results at the end.

- ✔ The ability to wrangle messy, unstructured data into figures that can be quantified, so that definite conclusions can be drawn from them.

Understanding computer science

Computers are the workhorses behind every big data strategy. If an eager, fresh-faced graduate from university had any exposure to the world of data science before throwing herself into the workforce, it probably was in the university's computer science lab.

Such a broad category covers a whole range of subfields, such as machine learning, databases and cloud computing. It could cover everything from plugging together the cables to creating sophisticated machine learning and natural language processing algorithms.

The core computer science skills that relate to big data are:

- ✔ A solid understand of database technology, cloud computing and distributed computing

- ✔ A firm grasp of key open-source technologies such as Hadoop, Spark, Java and Python, which make up the foundations of most big data enterprises

- ✔ The ability to design and program the algorithms that process data into insights

Grasping the business side of things

The idea that a company hires an egghead data scientist, who's then locked away in a basement lab to work her magic on data fed to her through a slot in the door, is flat-out wrong and should occur only in television sitcoms.

Instead, a good data scientist should have a firm grasp of the company's goals and objectives as well as an understanding of whether the business is heading in the right direction.

I think the following business skills are especially important:

- ✔ An understanding of business objectives and the underlying processes which drive profit and business growth (for example, what makes the business tick and what makes it grow).

- ✔ A thorough appreciation of the key performance indicators (KPIs) and metrics used to evaluate every aspect of the company, from financial measurements to people and performance.

- ✔ The ability to evaluate what it is that makes the business thrive and stand out from its competitors. If the business doesn't stand out, then you need an understanding of why it doesn't and what needs to improve.

If you're looking to hire a data scientist and your best candidate doesn't have much business experience, you can always pair her with someone in the company who does.

Communicating insights

Of course, communication skills are important across all disciplines, but they're especially important in extracting the maximum amount of value from big data.

You can have the best analytical skills in the world, but unless you're able to present findings in a clear way and demonstrate how they will help to improve performance and drive success, all that analysis will go to waste.

The following communication skills are absolutely vital:

- ✓ Great interpersonal and written communication skills. It's important to be able to clearly communicate the results of the analysis to other people in the company, including key decision makers. Those people need to be able to understand the key messages quickly and easily.

- ✓ The ability to add significant value to data. Simply presenting the data is what a statistician does. You need someone who can add value to that data through insights and analysis.

- ✓ A good working knowledge of data visualisation and reporting data. Anyone can make a chart or graph; it takes someone who understands visual communications to create a representation of data that tells the story the audience needs to hear (see the next point).

- ✓ A knack for storytelling. Because, in the end, data is useless without context – you need to tell the story behind the data in order to make it really valuable. For example, if your data shows an increase in sales over a five-month period, the underlying story is what caused that increase and what other factors were at play.

There's more in Chapter 7 on focusing on insights and adding value to data.

Understanding Two Very Different Types of Data Scientist

In reality, of course, there are as many types of data scientist as there are people working in data science. I've worked with a lot and have yet to meet two who are identical.

But when I think about the similar skills, methods, outlooks and responsibilities required of data scientists, then group those together, I'm left with two quite distinct groups. I call them strategic data scientists and operational data scientists.

Just to be clear, individuals who fall into either of these groups doubtless have a lot in common. But in order to best examine whom these two types of data scientists are, and how they bring value to an organisation, it's obviously useful to focus on the differences.

Broadly speaking, a *strategic data scientist* has a firm understanding of business performance and growth, strategic thinking and communication skills, but is less well versed in the technical, nitty-gritty of setting up database systems and defining or selecting algorithms.

On the other hand, the *operational data scientist* is more likely to come from a background of programming, statistics or mathematics and can use these skills to implement systems to probe and interpret the data and draw out the most relevant results.

In other words – and here you get to the crux of the difference and see why both are essential – the strategic data scientist sets the questions (or works with management to set the questions), and the operational data scientist provides the answers. Asking the right questions and arriving at the correct answers are both essential parts of the process. Both are equally worthless without the other.

Pair a great strategic data scientist with a great operational data scientist and you have an unstoppable team, capable of crunching its way to the most useful and innovative insights. You might occasionally stumble into someone who has the qualities to fill both roles exceptionally well – but in my experience this is rare!

Of course, it isn't always essential to break down data scientists into these two types. Especially in smaller companies looking to employ just one data scientist, the distinctions become much harder to make. Here it's particularly important to ensure any data scientist has the strategic business understanding as well as the data crunching skills. If she doesn't, she needs to work closely with someone in the company who does.

Building Big Data Skills In-House

You may be thinking, 'Crikey, wherever do I find someone with all these skills?' It's not as impossible as it may at first seem.

I think developing your existing people is a brilliant place to start. So, the first thing to consider is whether your existing people have the potential to meet some or all of these needs, with a little extra training and knowledge, of course. Over the past couple of years, a raft of big data-related courses have sprung up and some are even available for free. I give plenty of examples in the next sections.

If you're heading down a recruitment path, then hiring a data scientist can seem daunting if you don't have any experience in the tech field. But, with the advice and questions I set out in these sections, you'll be better equipped for the task.

Developing the people you already have

Not every business can afford to spend a fortune retraining its staff. Luckily, there are alternatives.

Increasingly colleges and universities are putting courses online where they can be studied for free. Some of the courses offer certificates of completion or other forms of accreditation; some don't. But the skills learned should be more important than a piece of paper.

If you're a very small business, you could take one of these courses yourself. There's no reason you couldn't use that knowledge to develop your own data strategy and reap insights.

The next sections provide an overview of what's available online from various schools, colleges and universities.

Data science

The University of Washington's Introduction to Data Science is available online at Coursera (`www.coursera.org/course/datasci`). The course can be completed in 8 weeks if you put in 10 to 12 hours' study per week, and covers the history of data science, key techniques and technologies such as MapReduce and Hadoop as well as traditional relational databases, designing experiments using statistical modelling and visualising results. Some basic programming knowledge is needed, but don't worry, there are plenty of free courses where you can pick that up too, if you don't already have it (read on).

Coursera's courses usually run between set dates – if you want accreditation or certificates, you have to register before a set date and complete the course before a final deadline. However, if you're just interested in the knowledge, you can download all the course materials – which come as videos and reading material – to browse at your leisure.

Harvard also makes its Data Science course available for free online. All lectures are uploaded as videos shortly after they take place, and materials and homework assignments are uploaded to the open source knowledge repository, Github (http://cs109.github.io/2014/). Some basic Python knowledge is required.

Statistics

Stanford has a Statistics One course, which is also available on Coursera (www.coursera.org/course/stats1). The course assumes very little background knowledge and describes itself as 'a comprehensive yet friendly' introduction to the subject.

Those looking for slightly more in-depth or specialist knowledge may be interested in Stanford's Algorithms: Design and Analysis course (www.coursera.org/course/algo). The course covers the fundamental principles behind algorithmic design – design paradigms, randomised algorithms and probability, graph algorithms and data structures. Programming knowledge is essential – you'll be expected to know at least one language, such as C, Java or Python.

Programming

Speaking of programming, a basic level of familiarity with at least one language is recommended for anyone really interested in data. Python is a good choice as it's designed for very fast processing of very large datasets and is widely used in big data enterprise.

The following all offer free courses in Python designed for absolute beginners with no programming experience. There's also a *Beginning Programming with Python For Dummies* by John Paul Mueller (Wiley) if you're looking for a little bedtime reading!

- Codecademy (www.codecademy.com/en/tracks/python)
- Coursera (www.coursera.org/course/pythonlearn)
- MIT (http://ocw.mit.edu/courses/electrical-engineering-and-computer-science/6-00sc-introduction-to-computer-science-and-programming-spring-2011/)

Visualisation

University of California, Berkeley offers its Visualization course available for free online, which covers the techniques and algorithms used to create effective and well-designed graphical representations of data. You'll need some familiarity with one popular graphics program (such as OpenGL or GDI+) as well as one data application (Excel will do). Whichever you choose is up to you as the assignments can be submitted in any format. The course is available at http://vis.berkeley.edu/courses/cs294-10-sp11/wiki/index.php/CS294-10_Visualization.

Recruiting new talent

If data is going to be a core part of your business and you have a little wiggle room in your recruitment budget, then hiring a data scientist is a worthwhile investment.

The skills I set out in 'Six Key Big Data Skills Any Business Needs' earlier in the chapter can help you put together a list of what sort of person you should be looking for. If you can find a candidate with all six traits – or someone who has most of them along with the ability and desire to grow – then you've found someone who can deliver incredible value to your company. You may also want to partner a data scientist with other employees who really excel in certain skills (such as communication or business acumen).

Data scientists are in high demand, so when your company is ready to make the leap into hiring one, it pays to make sure you get a good one, not someone piggybacking on the hype. The following questions (which loosely tie in with the key big data skills) can help you make sure you get the right person for the job:

✔ Does the candidate have solid programming skills? A data scientist needs the skills to not just view and analyse the data, but to manipulate it as well. A statistician who reviews and interprets a set of data is very different from a data scientist who can change the code that collects the data in the first place.

✔ Does the candidate excel at producing analytics for computers or humans? (And which do you need?) If your end result is a machine learning algorithm to, for example, choose which ads to show on a website or automatically top up your stock when it reaches certain levels, your analytics are for computers. There's more on using data this way in Chapter 12. If, on the other hand, a human will make a choice based on the analytics, your analyst needs a different set of skills – chiefly, being able to tell a story through data and providing good visualisation of that data. Chapter 11 gives more information on using data to make better decisions.

✔ Can the candidate provide concrete examples of when she's improved a business process through her work? As with any position, you hope to see real-world examples of successfully implemented improvements to a business process.

✔ Is the candidate a good communicator? Stereotypes would have you believe that it's okay for scientists and techy types to be introverts with poor communication skills, but that's not really an option with a data scientist. She needs to be able to communicate effectively with people who don't speak the same language, tell a story through data and use visual communications effectively.

✔ Can the candidate be creative and open-minded? Big data is a rapidly changing and expanding field that requires a certain open-mindedness. To innovate, a good data scientist must be able to look beyond what came before. If a candidate has implemented the same processes or procedures at multiple companies, ask yourself seriously if she's able to innovate and try something new.

✔ Does the candidate have a scientific mind-set? As the name suggests, data scientists should be scientists that apply the scientific model to data. This means being able to experiment with data to find models and algorithms that are useful for businesses and can be used to predict future events.

✔ Does the candidate have a solid business understanding? It's one thing to understand the science and mathematics behind analysing huge data-sets; it's another thing entirely to truly understand how that data affects profitability, user experience and employee retention – or any other factors important to the business. Someone with a background in business will be better at spotting trends that will benefit your business.

I've seen many companies try to narrow their recruiting by searching for only candidates who have a PhD in mathematics, but, in truth, a good data scientist could come from a variety of backgrounds – and may not necessarily have an advanced degree in any of them. Focusing on these questions and the six core skills will help you find someone who can help you turn data into actionable results for your business.

Thinking outside the box

Because supply outstrips demand (for the time being at least), it can be hard for smaller businesses to find good data scientists. This means you may need to consider alternative ways of tapping into big data skills.

Consider unusual sources where you might be able to recruit help, either on a permanent basis (for example, recruiting talent) or on a temporary basis (such as getting help to analyse data for a one-off project).

A university with a data science department, or any kind of data institute for that matter, is a good place to start. You could offer an internship, taking on some students to help with an analysis project, or you could see if the university is open to a joint project of some kind. If you have data to crunch, the university may very well be up for crunching it! In return you could mentor students on the key skills needed to survive in business or offer interview training and practice.

Remember too that your focus should always be on the skills I outline in 'Six Key Big Data Skills Any Business Needs' earlier in the chapter. It may be easy to find someone with statistical and analytical skills who falls short on business insights, but your own people could help supplement those skills. Thinking outside the box is about finding creative ways to pull the necessary skills together in whichever way works for you.

Sourcing External Skills

If training your staff or hiring new people aren't viable options, you can still make the leap into big data. A great way to supplement missing skills – particularly when it comes to the statistical, analytical and computer science aspects – is to turn to external providers who can handle your data and analytics needs.

When it comes to third-party providers, hiring a big data contractor is usually the most common option. But there are alternatives, such as partnering with other interested parties or crowdsourcing analytic work. I look at each of these options in turn in the next sections.

Tapping into service providers

There are more and more big data providers and contractors springing up who are able to source or capture data on your behalf and analyse it (or work with data you already have). Some big data providers are household names, like Facebook and IBM, but you certainly aren't limited to big blue-chip companies. There are tons of smaller providers out there adept at working with small and medium-sized firms.

Unfortunately finding a big data service provider is nothing like finding a plumber; you can't just go on Checkatrade.com for a list of big data tradespeople in your area. Nor are there any real professional accreditations to look out for, like the Gas Safe accreditation for plumbers.

So, how do you find a good provider? Like many things in business, networks and contacts can be a huge help. If you have contacts who have worked with a data firm, ask your contact whom she worked with and whether she'd recommend the firm. If not, it's a good idea to look at some big data case studies online and in books like this to get a feel for who's doing excellent, innovative work in the field. Failing that, take a look online and start sifting through big data company websites to find one that piques your interest.

You may prefer a provider who has knowledge and experience of working with similar companies in your specific industry. In fact, I'd say industry-specific providers are becoming the norm as opposed to generalists. While the big blue-chip providers may have enormous datasets and impressive armies of analysts, they aren't necessarily the best option if you're looking for very specific information. In the last couple of years lots of smaller, more affordable providers have popped up and many of them have in-depth, industry-specific knowledge.

The six key big data skills and the recruitment questions I set out in 'Six Key Big Data Skills Any Business Needs' earlier in the chapter are just as helpful in finding external contractors as in-house staff. They'll give you a good grounding for discussions with potential contractors and should help you narrow down your choice. But here are some extra tips to help you find the ideal firm for you:

- Wherever possible, it's a good idea to already have a draft data strategy (see Chapter 10) before you approach contractors. This helps you identify what you're trying to achieve, which in turn feeds into your initial discussions with providers.

- If you really don't know where to start, either in terms of developing a strategy or finding providers, then a big data consultant like me will be able to help you devise your big data strategy and find the right company to carry out the data capture and analysis.

- You need to work with someone who understands exactly what you're trying to achieve in the business. A contractor with a good understanding of your goals, your unanswered questions and the challenges you're facing is much more likely to get you the data and insights you really need.

- Ask for very specific examples of whom a contactor has worked with, how the projects unfolded and, crucially, what results those clients saw as a result.

Dickey's Barbecue Pit restaurant provides a useful example of an excellent partnership between a business and its big data contractor. (I talk about Dickey's in more depth in Chapter 7, and if you've not read that chapter yet, take a quick trip there to grab some food from the barby!) The company has a full-time IT staff of 11 people, including two dedicated analytical staff, but also works closely with a data partner, iOLAP. iOLAP delivered the data infrastructure behind Dickey's big data operation, which runs on a Yellowfin business intelligence platform combined with Syncsort's DMX data integration software, hosted on Amazon Redshift servers. Dickey's CIO Laura Rea Dickey explains: 'Even though our team is probably a bit larger than the traditional in-house team for a restaurant business – because it's where our focus is – it requires a partner. We have been very lucky in choosing the right partner. We have an account contact in our office at least 20 hours a week and we're working very closely with them at all times – it's closed the gap of what would have been a skills shortage for us if we didn't have a partnership like this.' The nearby sidebar on women's cycling offers a completely different spin on setting up analytics.

How the US Olympic women's cycling team competes on analytics

At first glance, you might think an Olympic sports team has little to do with a small business. In this case, you'd be wrong. The US women's cycling team were, before the 2012 London Olympics, complete underdogs with little funding and precious few resources. But a new coach with a data-based approach to training changed everything . . . culminating in a silver medal.

The struggling team turned to Sky Christopherson for help when they read that he, himself a former Olympic cycling team member, had broken a world record (in the over 35 s 200-metre velodrome sprint) – a decade after retiring as a professional athlete. He'd done this using a training regime called Optimized Athlete that he designed himself, based on data analytics and originally inspired by the works of Dr Erik Topol.

Working with the team, Christopherson implemented sophisticated data capture and monitoring techniques to record every aspect affecting the athletes' performances, including diet, sleep patterns, environment and training intensity. However, he soon realised the data was growing at an unmanageable rate. This prompted him to contact San Francisco-based big data analytics and visualisation specialists Datameer.

Christopherson said, 'They came back with some really exciting results – some connections that we hadn't seen before. How diet, training and environment all influence each other – everything is interconnected, and you can really see that in the data.'

What big data enables high-performance sports to do is to quantify the many factors that influence performance, such as training load, recovery and how the human body regenerates. Teams can finally measure these and establish early warning signals that stop them from pushing athletes into overtraining, which often results in injury and illness.

The depth of the analytics meant that tailored programs could be tweaked for each athlete to get the best out of every member of the team. One insight that came up was that one cyclist – Jenny Reed – performed much better in training if she had slept at a lower temperature the night before. So she was provided with a temperature water-cooled mattress to keep her body at an exact temperature throughout the night.

Big data analytics, if sophisticated enough, can provide detailed information on exactly how hard and how often the body can be pushed to its limits during training without causing injury. 'It's manipulating the training, based on the data you have recorded, so that you are never pushing into that danger zone, but also never backing off and under-utilising your talent. It's a very fine line and that's what big data is enabling us to finally do.'

When used accurately and efficiently, big data could vastly extend the career viability of professional athletes and sportsmen. Instead of retiring at 30, with the right balance of diet and exercise and avoiding injury through over-exertion, athletes could potentially continue to compete at highest levels for years or even decades longer than is expected today.

The Optimized Athlete program has now been turned into an app, OAthlete. The aim of the app is to make this data-driven approach to performance improvement available to a much wider audience outside the world of elite sports.

Partnering to succeed

Earlier in the chapter I mention that universities as a great source of big data talent. There are other ways to creatively partner with third parties.

When it comes to big data, budget is usually the number one sticking point – the thing that stops companies from embarking on a big data strategy. Partnering can offer ways around the budget/resources issue and still help you achieve your goals.

Consider whether there's an opportunity to create an industry group with other companies facing similar challenges to your own. You may not be keen to share detailed data with these companies (nor would they want to with you in all likelihood), but you can certainly pool resources to get data analysis done on a large scale without necessarily sharing your private data with competitors. Remember that data can always be aggregated or made anonymous to remove specifics that you don't want shared.

Crowdsourcing talent

If none of the options in the preceding sections work for you, then you might consider crowdsourcing your big data project. *Crowdsourcing* is a way of using the power of a crowd to complete a task. (If you haven't heard of crowdsourcing before, you've probably heard of crowdfunding platforms, like Kickstarter, which operate on a similar basis – using the power of a crowd to achieve a funding goal.)

A few crowdsourcing platforms now allow thousands of data scientists to sign up for big data projects. Businesses can then upload the data they have, say what problem they need solving and set a budget for the project. It's a great option for companies with a small amount to spend or those that want to test the waters. But it's also a regular resource for big firms like Facebook and Google. Some firms are even known to recruit full-time analysts from crowdsourcing platforms. This gives you an idea of the quality of talent you could tap into.

Kaggle is one such crowdsourcing platform. The San Francisco-based business awards cash prizes to its teams of citizen scientists that competes to untangle big data challenges of all shapes and sizes. Chief scientist at Google and Kaggle investor Hal Varian describes it as 'a way to organise the brainpower of the world's most talented data scientists and make it accessible to organisations of every size.'

At a time when demand for data scientists far outstrips supply, Kaggle has an estimated 150,000 data scientists ready to go to work for businesses like yours. They also offer the Kaggle In Class service – an academic spin-off of the main brand that offers free data processing tools and simulated challenges. It's intended for use in schools and colleges struggling to meet the challenges of training the first generations of professional data scientists.

As it stands today, Kaggle is one of the more forward-thinking innovations in big data and has done much to raise awareness of the power that crowd-sourcing data analysis can bring to businesses and organisations of all sizes.

Chapter 9

Building a Big Data Infrastructure

*B*ig data can bring huge benefits to businesses, whether small, medium or large. However, as with any project, proper preparation and planning is essential, especially when it comes to infrastructure.

You'll need to invest in some tools or services in order to achieve the ultimate objective: gleaning insights that lead to better decision making and improved performance.

Until recently it was hard for companies to get into big data without making heavy infrastructure investments – expensive data warehouses, software, analytic staff, and so on. But times have changed. Cloud computing in particular has opened up a lot of options for using big data, as it means businesses can tap into big data without having to invest in massive on-site storage facilities. Other developments, such as big data as a service and the ever-increasing range of big data providers, also make big data a possibility for even the smallest company, allowing you to harness external resources and skills very easily.

In this chapter I look at the key infrastructure considerations and set out the main options for small businesses, including a few ideas for those on a budget.

Making Big Data Infrastructure Decisions

You may think a traditional data warehouse would be a good place to start and, up until a few years ago, you'd have been spot on. But today you have more options than ever, including distributed storage and data lakes (see Chapter 6 for more about these). Besides, data storage isn't the only element you need to consider.

Understanding the key infrastructure elements

When I talk about infrastructure, I mean the software or hardware necessary to take big data and turn it into insights and action (see Chapter 7 for more about insights and action). There's no point having masses of data at your disposal if you don't have the capability to learn something from that data, take action based on what you've learned and grow your business as a result.

In order to turn big data into insights and business growth, it's likely you'll need to make investments in the following key infrastructure elements:

- Data collection
- Data storage
- Data analysis/processing
- Data visualisation/communication

These are generally known as the layers of big data, and I look at each layer in more detail later in the chapter.

Evaluating your existing infrastructure

Before you splash out on any new technology, it's worth looking at what you're already using in your business. Some of your existing infrastructure could have a role to play.

Go through each of the four key infrastructure elements listed in the preceding section and note what related technology or skills you already have in house. For example, you may already be collecting useful customer data through your website or customer service department. Or you very likely have a wealth of financial and sales data that could provide insights. Just be aware that you may already have some very useful data that could help answer your strategic business questions (see Chapter 11).

In terms of data storage, you probably already have some data storage capabilities, even if you're just storing company information on a server or desktop. If you're a bigger operation, you may already have a data warehouse. Now, what you have may not be enough storage for the data you intend to use, but you need to be aware of what you have now so that you can decide how it can be improved or supplemented to cope with more data.

Your data processing infrastructure may be limited or non-existent at present. Maybe you have systems in place to make sense of sales and financial data, but not much beyond that. That's okay. The beauty of big data is the ever-increasing range of analytic options opening up for businesses. Even if you're starting from scratch, the right analytic option is within reach.

Your existing data visualisation and communication basically comes down to how you communicate information across your company at present. If your people are already well versed in communicating information and making decisions based on that information then you have a great starting point for using big data in your business.

If you're accessing someone else's data (like Facebook or Twitter, for instance), then the data capture, storage and processing elements may not apply to you – or they may apply to a lesser degree (you may want to partner someone else's data with some of your own internal data). Data as a service, for example, which I talk about in the next section, allows you to sign up to use someone else's data. This means you have no need to store or process that data, as you simply access it through the service provider's web interface. This is a great option if you're looking to understand more about customers, markets and trends, but it gets trickier if you want to use your own data to improve your processes (see Chapters 7 and 12 for more on this). In that case, it's much more likely you'll need to invest in the technology to capture your own data, which then means you'll need somewhere to store it and a way to analyse that data.

Big Data on a Budget: Introducing Big Data as a Service

The good news is that big data doesn't have to cost the Earth – although as with most things in life, you usually get what you pay for. Some of the platforms involved can be quite expensive, but there are ways to keep your costs down.

Open source (free) software exists for most of the essential big data tasks (which I talk about in 'Introducing the Four Layers of Big Data' later in the chapter). And distributed storage systems are designed to run on cheap, off-the-shelf hardware. The popularity of Hadoop has really opened big data up to the masses – it allows anyone to use cheap off-the-shelf hardware and open source software to analyse data, providing you invest time learning how. That's the trade-off: it will take some time and technical skill to get free software set up and working the way you want. So unless you have the expertise (or are willing to spend time developing it) it might be worth paying for professional technical help, or 'enterprise' versions of the software. These are generally customised versions of the free packages, designed to be easier to use, or specifically targeted at various industries.

Then there's another, often simpler option for businesses: big data as a service (or BDaaS, which is a fun acronym to say out loud!). In the last few years many businesses have sprung up offering cloud-based big data services to help other companies and organisations solve their data dilemmas. At the moment, BDaaS is a somewhat vague term used to describe a wide variety of outsourcing of various big data functions to the cloud. This can range from the supply of data, to the supply of analytical tools that interrogate the data (often through a web dashboard or control panel) to carrying out the actual analysis and providing reports. Some BDaaS providers also include consulting and advisory services within their BDaaS packages.

BDaaS removes many of the hurdles associated with implementing a big data strategy and vastly lowers the barrier of entry. When you use BDaaS, all of the techy nuts and bolts are, in theory, out of sight and out of mind, leaving you free to concentrate on business issues. BDaaS providers generally take this on for the customer – they have everything set up and ready to go – and you simply rent the use of their cloud-based storage and analytics engines and pay either for the time you use them or the amount of data crunched.

Another great advantage is that BDaaS providers often take on the cost of compliance and data protection – something that can be a real burden for small businesses. When the data is stored on the BDaaS's servers, generally, the provider is responsible for compliance and protection.

It's not just new BDaaS companies that are getting in on the act; some of the big corporations like IBM and HP are also offering their own versions of BDaaS. HP has made its big data analytics platform, Haven, available entirely through the cloud. This means that everything from storage to analytics and reporting is handled on HP systems that are leased to the customer via a monthly subscription – entirely eliminating infrastructure costs. And IBM's Analytics for Twitter service provides businesses with access to data and analytics on Twitter's 500 million tweets per day and 280 million monthly active users. The service provides analytical tools and applications for making sense of that messy, unstructured data and has trained 4,000 consultants to help businesses put plans into action to profit from them.

As more and more companies realise the value of big data, more services will emerge to support them. And competition between suppliers should help keep subscription prices low, which is another advantage for smaller businesses. I've already seen BDaaS making big data projects viable for many businesses that previously would have considered them out of reach – and I think it's something you'll see and hear a lot more about in the near future.

Introducing the Four Layers of Big Data

Big data systems are usually made up of what's called *layers,* which are the different stages the data has to pass through on its journey from raw statistic or snippet of unstructured data (for example, social media post) to actionable insight. There are four layers that you need to consider, and I give a brief overview of each in the following sections.

Data source layer

This is the data that arrives at your company. It includes everything from your sales records, customer database, feedback, social media channels, marketing lists, email archives and any data gleaned from monitoring or measuring aspects of your operations. One of the steps in setting up a data strategy (Chapter 10 has more on this) is assessing what you have and measuring it against what you need to answer the critical questions you want help with. You might have everything you need already, or you might need to establish new sources.

Data storage layer

This is where you keep your data after it's gathered from your sources. As the volume of data generated and stored by companies has started to explode, sophisticated but accessible systems and tools have been developed to help with this task.

Data processing/analysis layer

When you want to use the data you have stored to find out something useful, you need to process and analyse it. So, this layer is all about turning data into insights. This is where programing languages and platforms come into play. I set out the key analytics platforms in 'Turning Data into Insights' later in the chapter.

Data output layer

This is how the insights gleaned through the analysis are passed on to the people who can take action to benefit from them. Clear and concise communication is essential, and this output can take the form of reports, charts, figures and key recommendations. Ultimately, at this layer, you need a system (however fancy or simple) that shows how decisions and actions based on your analysis can lead to business improvement and growth.

Sourcing Your Data

You may already have the data you need to answer your strategic questions. (If so, lucky you!) But chances are you need to source some or all of the data required.

If you need to source new data, this may require new infrastructure investments. Ask yourself, 'What do I need to access this data?' The answer depends on the type of data you need but may include sensors, cameras or systems to collect text or audio data. For example, if you want to collect machine data from your factory operations or vehicles, you need to invest in sensors to collect the data.

Collecting your own

Options for collecting your own data include:

✔ **Created data:** Asking questions and capturing the answers – from customer surveys, focus groups and/or capturing details when customers are registering for something. This data can be structured or semi-structured and can be internal and external. (I talk about the different types of data in Chapter 1.)

- ✔ **Provoked data:** Asking people to express a view, such as rating a product. The data can be structured or semi-structured, internal or external.

- ✔ **Transaction data:** Data created every time someone buys something, online or offline, including what he bought and when. It's usually internal and structured.

- ✔ **Compiled data:** Data that comes from giant databases that companies like Experian, a credit-rating agency, hold. This type of data is usually external and structured.

- ✔ **Experimental data:** This is a hybrid of created and transaction data. For example, running a marketing campaign and observing the results. It can be structured or semi-structured and can be internal or external.

- ✔ **Captured data:** Information gathered from individuals' behaviour, for example, search terms, GPS (global positioning system) data and so on. It can be structured or unstructured, internal or external and often includes data generated by machines.

- ✔ **User-generated data:** Information generated consciously by a person – for example, Facebook posts, tweets, comments on a blog. It's usually unstructured and can be internal or external.

Infrastructure requirements for capturing data depend on the type or types of data you're collecting. Key options might include:

- ✔ Sensors that could sit in devices, machines, buildings, or on vehicles, packaging, or anywhere else you would like to capture data from.

- ✔ Apps that generate user data – for example, a customer app that allows customers to order more easily.

- ✔ CCTV (closed-circuit television) video.

- ✔ Beacons, such as iBeacons from Apple, that allow you to capture and transmit data to and from mobile phones.

- ✔ Changes to your website that prompt customers for more information.

- ✔ Social media profiles, if you don't have them in place already for your business.

I provide a list of the top ten data collection tools in Chapter 16. With a little technical knowledge, you can set many of these systems up yourself, or you can partner with a data company to set up the systems and capture the data on your behalf.

Accessing external sources

There are thousands upon thousands of options for accessing external sources of data, and the options are growing every day. I list my favourite free sources in Chapter 15. Other sources include big players like HP and IBM, as well as smaller, more industry-focused providers.

Accessing external data sources may require little or no infrastructure changes on your part, since you're accessing data that someone else is capturing and managing. If you have a computer (or a smartphone) and an Internet connection, you're pretty much good to go.

Keep in mind that you're looking for the right data for you – the data that best answers your strategic questions. If a provider's data doesn't help you do that, then it doesn't matter how big or impressive its dataset is, it's not the right one for you.

Storing Big Data

After you have your data, you need to think about where to store it. The main storage options include:

- A traditional data warehouse
- A data lake (see Chapter 6)
- A distributed/cloud-based storage system (Chapter 6, again)
- Your company server or a computer hard disk

Regular hard disks are available at very high capacities and for very little cost these days and, if you're a small business, this may be all you need. But when you start to deal with storing (and analysing) a large amount of data, or if data is going to be a key part of your business going forward, a more sophisticated, distributed (usually cloud-based) system like Hadoop is called for.

Distributed storage is a method of using cheap, off-the-shelf components to rig up your own high-capacity storage solutions, which are then controlled by software that keeps track of where everything is and finds it for you when you need it. *Cloud storage* really just means that your data is stored, usually remotely, but connected to the Internet and accessible from anywhere you can get online. So you don't have to worry about physically holding onto it yourself at all. Most distributed storage systems make use of cloud technology and the terms are often used interchangeably.

I think cloud-based storage is a brilliant option for most small businesses. It's flexible, you don't need physical systems on-site and it reduces your data security burden. It's also considerably cheaper than investing in expensive dedicated systems and data warehouses.

As well as a system for storing data that your computer system can understand (the file system) you need a system for organising and categorising it in a way that people can understand (the database). Hadoop has its own database, known as HBase, but other popular options include Amazon's DynamoDB, MongoDB and Cassandra (used by Facebook).

Understanding Hadoop and MapReduce

Hadoop can be thought of as a set of open source programs and procedures (essentially meaning they're free for anyone to use or modify, with a few exceptions), which anyone can use as the backbone of his big data operations.

Development of Hadoop began when forward-thinking software engineers realised that it was becoming useful to be able to store and analyse datasets far larger than can practically be stored and accessed on one physical storage device (such as a hard disk). The idea behind it is that many smaller devices working in parallel are more efficient than one large one.

Hadoop was released in 2005 by the Apache Software Foundation, a non-profit organisation that produces open source software that powers much of the Internet behind the scenes. (If you're wondering where the odd name came from, it was the name given to a toy elephant belonging to the son of one of the original creators!)

Looking under the Hadoop hood

Hadoop is made up of modules, each of which carries out a particular task essential for a computer system designed for big data analytics. The first two are the most important:

✔ **Distributed file system:** This allows data to be stored in an easily accessible format. A *file system* is the method used by a computer to store data so that it can be found and used. Normally, the file system is determined by the computer's operating system; however a Hadoop system uses its own file system that sits 'above' the file system of the host computer – meaning it can be accessed using any computer running any supported OS.

- ✔ **Map Reduce:** This provides the basic tools for poking around in the data. It's named after the two basic operations this module carries out – reading data from the database, putting that data into a format suitable for analysis (map) and performing mathematical operations – for example, counting the number of males aged 30 and over in a customer database (reduce).

- ✔ **Hadoop Common:** This provides the tools (in Java) needed for the user's computer systems (Windows, Unix or whatever) to read data stored under the Hadoop file system.

- ✔ **YARN:** This manages resources of the systems storing the data and running the analysis.

What makes Hadoop so popular?

The flexible nature of a Hadoop system means companies can add to or modify their data system as their needs change, using cheap and readily-available parts from any IT (information technology) vendor.

Today, Hadoop is the most widely used system for providing data storage and processing across *commodity hardware* – relatively inexpensive, off-the-shelf systems linked together, as opposed to expensive, bespoke systems custom-made for the job in hand. Thanks to the flexible nature of the system, companies can expand and adjust their data analysis operations as their business expands.

It's estimated that more than half of the companies in the Fortune 500 make use of Hadoop. Just about all of the big online names use it, and as anyone is free to alter it for his own purposes, modifications made to the software by expert engineers at, for example, Amazon and Google, are fed back to the development community, where they are often used to improve the official product. This form of collaborative development between volunteer and commercial users is a key feature of open source software.

In its raw state, using the basic modules supplied by Apache, Hadoop can be very complex, even for IT professionals, which is why various commercial versions, such as Cloudera, have been developed to simplify the task of installing and running a Hadoop system, as well as offering training and support services.

Understanding Spark

Spark is a framework – in the same way that Hadoop is – that provides a number of interconnected platforms, systems and standards for big data projects.

Like Hadoop, Spark is open source and under the wing of the Apache Software Foundation. It's seen by techies in the industry as a more advanced product than Hadoop – it's newer and designed to work by processing data in chunks *in memory,* which means it transfers data from the physical, magnetic hard disks into far faster electronic memory where processing can be carried out far more quickly – up to 100 times faster in some operations.

Spark has proven very popular and is used by many large companies for huge, multi-petabyte data storage and analysis. This is partly because of its speed. Last year, Spark set a world record by completing a benchmark test involving sorting 100 terabytes of data in 23 minutes – beating the previous world record of 71 minutes that was held by Hadoop.

Additionally, Spark has proven itself to be highly suited to machine learning applications (which I explore in Chapter 7), where computers are being taught to spot patterns in data and adapt their behaviour accordingly.

Spark is designed to be easy to install and use – if you have a background in computer science! In order to make it accessible to more businesses, many vendors provide their own versions geared towards particular industries, or custom-configured for individual clients' projects, as well as associated consultancy services to get it up and running.

Spark uses cluster computing for its computational (analytics) power as well as its storage. This means it can use resources from many computer processors linked together for its analytics. It's also a scalable solution, meaning that if more oomph is needed, you can simply introduce more processors into the system. You can also add more storage when needed, and the fact that it uses commonly available commodity hardware (any standard computer hard disks) keeps down infrastructure costs.

Unlike Hadoop, Spark does not come with its own file system – instead it can be integrated with many file systems, including Hadoop's HDFS, MongoDB and Amazon's S3 system.

Another element of the framework is Spark Streaming, which allows applications to be developed that perform analytics on streaming, real-time data – such as automatically analysing video or social media data on the fly. In fast-changing industries such as marketing, real-time analytics has huge advantages; for example, ads can be served based on a user's behaviour at a particular time, rather than on historical behaviour, increasing the chance of prompting an impulse purchase.

Other considerations: Data ownership and security

Remember that if the data is going to form a key part of your ongoing operations, then it's really important that you own that particular data. If you're reliant on another party's data in order to performs key business functions, and the supplier ups its prices or denies access for any reason, you're scuppered.

There are also some big things to consider in terms of data security. Depending on the sort of data you're storing, there may well be security and privacy regulations to follow, particularly when it comes to personal data. Wherever possible, try to use *anonymised* data that doesn't identify individuals' details. When this isn't possible, you need to ensure that data is kept safe and secure. Even if this isn't a legal requirement in your country, there are reputational and moral reasons to ensure your customers' data is kept safe. I talk more about big data ethics and the need for being transparent with your customers in Chapter 2.

People used to worry about the security of data stored in the cloud but, these days, it's often safer there than with companies that store their own data in-house. Often the cloud security systems are much more up to date and the fact that the data is stored in more than one place provides an extra safety net. Personally, I recommend cloud storage as a safe and secure option for small businesses.

Turning Data into Insights

After you have your data, the next step is to analyse it. By analysing data you can extract the insights you need to answer your strategic questions and meet your business goals. The chapters in Part IV set out the strategic process in more detail.

Processing and analysing data

There are three basic steps in processing and analysing data:

1. **Preparing the data.**

   Preparation includes identifying the data crucial to the task at hand, cleaning it to get rid of unnecessary background noise and putting it into a format that's accessible to the software or people who need to understand it.

2. **Building models and validating data.**

   You need to adjust variables and see how this impacts on the data. Then you need to assess how the changes you're making work towards achieving the goals you set yourself at the start.

3. **Drawing a conclusion.**

   You assess the insights you gleaned during Step 2 and decide what changes you're going to make as a result.

Software from vendors such as IBM, Oracle and Google is designed to help you do all of this: turn raw data into insights. Google has BigQuery, which is designed to let anyone with a bit of data science knowledge run queries against vast datasets. And many start-ups are piling into the market, offering simple solutions that claim to let you simply feed it with all of your data and sit back while it highlights the most important insights and suggests actions for you to take.

A common method for analysing data is using a MapReduce tool (see 'Looking under the Hadoop hood' earlier in the chapter). Essentially, this is used to select the elements of the data that you want to analyse and put them into a format from which insights can be gleaned.

Understanding Python

Python is a programming language frequently used to create algorithms for sorting through and analysing large amounts of data. It's another open source program so it integrates very well with other open source technologies like Hadoop and Spark.

Python is a high-level language – meaning that the code that the programmer types in to create the program is more like natural human language than code written to control machines. This not only makes things simpler for the programmer, it means others are more likely to understand the code if they want to use it themselves. The high-level, human-like code can be converted into machine code through a piece of software known as an interpreter.

This means that programs written in Python can be run on any computer operating system that has an interpreter for it – which is pretty much all of the operating systems you're ever likely to come across! It also means that code can be ported between projects and organisations even if the people running it are using completely different hardware.

Aside from its ease of use and portability, one of the features that has made Python particularly popular is the powerful libraries available for it, which basically means it's great at manipulating very large amounts of data.

It's also great for creating scalable systems – in fact it's used for creating much of the back-end, data-processing functions of Google, YouTube and Facebook. As well as constantly increasing in size, these services need to be constantly updating and adding to their functionality. With giant operations such as these, programmers need an environment where new code (features) can be integrated on the fly without disruption of the service to users. Python is ideal for this as it's designed for use in agile environments where new features need to be added all the time.

Popular data analytics platforms

The past few years have seen an explosion in the number of platforms available for big data analytical tasks. These platforms are commercial offerings, meaning you pay an ongoing service charge. Most use the Hadoop framework as the basis and build on it for analysis.

The following sections contain a rundown, in no particular order, of the best and most widely used of these services. Like any commercial product in a competitive market, each has its advantages and disadvantages, so what's best for one company may not be best for another.

Cloudera CDH

Cloudera was formed by former employees of Google, Yahoo!, Facebook and Oracle and offers open source as well as commercial Hadoop-based big data solutions. Its distributions make use of its Impala analytics engine that has also been adopted and included in packages offered by competitors such as Amazon and MapR.

Hortonworks Data Platform (HDP)

Unlike every other big analytics platform, HDP is entirely comprised of open source code, with all of its elements built through the Apache Software Foundation. HDP makes its money offering services and support for getting it running and providing the results you're after.

Microsoft HDInsight

Microsoft's flagship analytical offering, HDInsight is based on Hortonworks Data Platform but is tailored to work with its own Azure cloud services and SQL Server database management system. A big advantage for businesses is that it integrates with Excel, meaning even staff with only basic IT skills can dip their toes into big data analytics.

IBM Big Data Platform

IBM offers a range of products and services designed to make complex big data analysis more accessible to businesses. IBM offers its own Hadoop distribution known as InfoSphere BigInsights.

Splunk Enterprise

This platform is specifically geared to businesses that generate a lot of their own data through their own machinery. Splunk Enterprise's stated goal is 'machine data to operational intelligence' and the Internet of Things (which I talk about in Chapter 5) is key to this strategy. Its analytics drive Dominos Pizza's US coupon campaigns.

Amazon Web Services

Although everyone thinks of Amazon as an online store, it also makes money by selling the magic that makes its business run so smoothly to other companies. The Amazon business model was based on big data from the start – using personal information to offer a personalised shopping experience. Amazon Web Services includes its Elastic Cloud Compute and Elastic MapReduce services to offer large-scale data storage and analysis in the cloud.

Pivotal Big Data Suite

Pivotal's big data package is comprised of its own Hadoop distribution, Pivotal HD, and its analytics platform, Pivotal Analytics. It's business model allows consumers to store an unlimited amount of data and pay a subscription fee that varies according to how much Pivotal analyses. The company is strongly invested in the data lake philosophy of a unified, object-based storage repository for all of an organisation's data.

Infobright

This is another database management system that's available as both an open source, free edition and a paid-for proprietary version. This product is geared towards users looking to get involved with the Internet of Things. It offers three levels of service for paid users, with higher-tier customers given access to the helpdesk and quicker email support response times.

MapR

MapR offers its own distribution of Hadoop, notably different from others as it replaces the commonly used Hadoop File System with its alternative MapR Data Platform, which it claims offers better performance and ease of use.

Kognito Analytical Platform

Like many of the other systems here, this takes data from your Hadoop or cloud-based storage network and gives users access to a range of advanced analytical functions. Kognito is used by British Telecom to help set call charges and by loyalty program Nectar for its customer analytics.

Presenting the Insights

All too often I see businesses bury the nuggets of information that could really impact strategy in a 50-page report or a complicated graphic that no one understands. It's clearly unrealistic to expect busy people to wade through mountains of data with endless spreadsheet appendices and extract the key messages.

If the key insights aren't clearly presented, they won't result in action.

In these sections, I set out the main data output options in terms of the tools required. You can find more on communicating data in Chapter 7 (for honing in on insights) and Chapter 11 (for advice on communicating data).

Getting to grips with the main data output options

There are a range of methods for getting data to the people or machines that need them. The key options are:

- ✔ Algorithms that help machines perform certain functions. For example, an algorithm that tells your website that if someone buys X to recommend Y.
- ✔ Dashboards that provide your people with the information they require, whenever they require it.
- ✔ Commercial data visualisation platforms that make the data attractive and easy to understand.
- ✔ Simple graphics (like bar charts, for instance) and reports that communicate key insights.

In my experience, for most small businesses looking to improve their decision making, simple graphics or visualisation platforms are more than enough to present insights from data. Therefore, I focus on the best visualisation tools in the next section.

Looking at the visualisation tools available

Big data analytics have created a wave of new visualisation tools capable of making the outputs of the analytics look pretty, and improving understanding and speed of comprehension. Many of these tools are open source, free applications that can be used independently or alongside your existing design applications, often using simple drag-and-drop functionality.

There are enough data visualisation tools to warrant a book on their own, but as the technology is evolving and developing all the time, I just want to give you a flavour of what exists right now.

 Many of the analytics platforms mentioned earlier in the chapter have some sort of visualisation function included. If a platform doesn't meet your needs, some excellent cloud-based visualisation tools are relatively easy to use. Two of my favourites are QlikView and Tableau (which is free).

Some other tools and ideas you might like to check out:

- **D3 charts:** D3.js is a JavaScript library for manipulating documents based on data and helps to bring that data to life. This free software can manipulate data in a mind-boggling array of ways, including box plots and dendrograms.

- **Word clouds:** These offer a great way to illustrate sentiment or weighted opinion in text without getting into the nitty-gritty of what individual people or sub-sets said. This can be particularly useful for illustrating the qualitative information contained within a customer survey or employee engagement survey. The weighting (for example, most popular words and phrases in bigger type) allows you to see what people think about your product, service, brand or company, without reading every response. Many free software programs convert text data into word clouds, including Wordle and Tagul.

- **Maps:** These can be presented in a variety of different ways with additional information overlaid across the map. Google Maps offers a range of tools that enable developers to build interactive visual mapping programs for any application or website.

- **Displaying emotions and behaviour:** There are ways to display behaviour or emotion data that weren't possible a few years ago. Crazy Egg allows you to track visitor clicks on your website, see where visitors stop scrolling down the page, connect clicks with traffic types and pinpoint hotspots using their heat map tool. This type of tool can easily and very quickly illustrate user or customer behaviour online.

Now you have an understanding of the infrastructure elements required, you're ready to start putting these building blocks in place and put data to work in your business (I delve into this in Part IV). As with any aspect of big data, if you're still unsure where to start, then I recommend working with a big data consultant. A consultant can help you identify your data strategy and narrow down the infrastructure elements so you can ensure you have the technology that's right for you.

Part IV
Show Time! Making Big Data Work for Small Business

Five Tips for Making a Solid Big Data Business Case

- Summarise or outline your big data project in brief.
- Define your goals – what are you aiming to find out?
- List the tangible benefits to the business – how will data help you improve or transform your business?
- Describe the capabilities needed and whether any skill gaps will be filled through training or bringing in external help.
- Discuss timeframe, likely disruption to the business and costs. It's important not to gloss over this part, otherwise your business case will not be as robust as it should be.

Find out more about why a big data strategy is so important at www.dummies.com/extras/bigdataforsmallbusiness.

In this part . . .

- ✔ Start with creating a big data strategy.
- ✔ Make a solid business case for using big data.
- ✔ Enhance your business decision making with data.
- ✔ Transform your business operations with data.
- ✔ Build a culture that emphasises data-based decision making in your business.

Chapter 10

Creating a Big Data Strategy

- -

In This Chapter

▶ Understanding the importance of starting with strategy

▶ Breaking your big data strategy down into six manageable steps

▶ Making a robust case for using big data in your business

- -

We now live in a world in which the amount of data being generated each second is staggering. While some companies are leveraging data very well to generate mouth-watering competitive advantages, many are barely scratching the surface, dipping into data in an arbitrary way without any real underlying strategy.

The truth is, those companies that can turn big data into valuable insights are the ones that will thrive. The companies that continue to merely dip their toes in the big data and analytics pond will be left behind. And those that ignore big data altogether will wither away.

Whether you're a big data giant like Facebook or Google, or a small, family-run business, all smart business starts with strategy. Therefore, every company, big or small, in any industry, needs a solid big data strategy. I find that many companies are either raring to get started and want to dive straight in or they're so overwhelmed that they just don't know where to start. Wherever you sit on the spectrum, you can start thinking strategically about big data by following some very simple steps.

In this chapter, I look at what you need to consider when creating your big data strategy. If you're not yet up to speed on the big data basics, circle back to Part II for more information before you tackle your big data strategy.

Deciding How to Use Big Data

The really good news is that, initially, it really doesn't matter what data you have access to already, what you have the potential to generate and collect or even what data is available out there in the universe. Whether your business has tons of analysis-ready data or not is unimportant at this stage. It doesn't change the fact that you need to start with strategy. And your strategy shouldn't be determined by what you have or can get your hands on – it's about what you want to achieve in your business.

So, for now, set aside the data itself and focus on how using data could help you achieve your business goals. There are millions of ways data can help a business but, broadly speaking, they fall into two categories: one is using data to improve your existing business and how you make business decisions; the second is using data to transform your whole business operations or business model. I look at each in turn in the next sections.

You might want to focus on decision making for now and see if the data leads to any operational opportunities farther down the line. Not too many companies set out with the definitive focus on the second (operational) aim but if that's your goal then it's perhaps wise to skip the decision-making aspect for now – transforming your operations is a bigger and trickier exercise, so you'll need to focus fully on that if it's what you really want to do. In practice, most companies start out wanting to improve their decision making and take it from there.

Using big data to improve your business decisions

This is the goal for most clients I work with, and I think it's something that all business should be working towards. Whatever you want to do – whether you want to better understand your customers, target new customers, make your supply chain more efficient or so on – you need to make smarter business decisions. Data provides the insights needed to make those decisions.

Even if you run a very traditional company and can't yet imagine how data can help you improve your business, that doesn't mean it can't. I firmly believe data can help businesses of all sizes and across all industries.

I am working with a bus and coach company that had very traditional views and didn't think data mattered to it. Now it's collecting and analysing telematics data from its vehicles to improve driving behaviour as well as to optimise routes and maintenance intervals. It has also started to better understand its customers by collecting and analysing time and location stamped data on ticket purchases. All this new data is helping the company make better decisions for the future.

To ensure your decision making becomes more fact based, you need to identify your company's priorities and unanswered business questions. You then use data to help you answer those questions, gather insights and communicate insights across the company – thereby helping everyone in the company make better decisions.

At first, you may choose to focus on one very specific area of your business, such as understanding the customer response to a particular product, but the very idea of basing decisions and ongoing business strategy on what data tells you should become a company-wide thing. So, even if you run a short, neat data project to find an answer to a specific question, it's likely the data possibilities will extend far beyond that initial question to other areas of the business. Having a clear big data strategy helps you identify your key questions and prioritise them, so that you're using your time and resources in the best way possible.

I talk through the detailed process of using data to improve decision making in Chapter 11. For information on building a company culture that supports data-based decision making, turn to Chapter 13.

Using big data to transform your business operations

This is a bigger step than improving business decisions and therefore not something that all businesses do. In this process, you use data to challenge your whole business model: not how you do business and how well you do it, but the very nature of *what* you do. Data can throw up some surprising insights that can have big ramifications for what your business does.

Here's an example of a company that changed its business model thanks to data, moving from a manufacturer to a big data company. Jawbone is the company that manufactures the fitness tracking band that I wear every day. It tracks my activity levels, calorie consumption and sleep levels. With millions of users, Jawbone gathers an incredible amount of data. The company soon realised that all the data it collected was more valuable than the device itself! It's no wonder the company is now transitioning to a big data company. It still manufactures the products, as they're the vehicle for continuing to collect data, but the data itself is now the company's primary focus. Analysing the collective data brings insights that can be fed back to users and sold to interested parties.

In Chapter 12, I talk through the detailed steps involved in using data to transform your business operations.

If you feel this stage isn't relevant to your business, that's fine, but it's a good idea to stay open to operational opportunities that your data may point to. You may be surprised at what you find: You may spot exciting new business opportunities, or ideas for new products and revenue streams or the data may lead to a fundamental change in your business model.

Transforming your business operations is a big step, and it's likely to require a total mindset shift. For it to work, you need to build a company culture that's open to opportunities that data highlights. For more on how to build such a culture in your business, check out Chapter 13.

Small Can be Beautiful: How Not to Collect Everything

Remember being a kid and desperately wanting that piece of cake or pie that was far too big? You either couldn't finish it or you felt sick from squeezing it in. In my family we called this having eyes bigger than your belly. A similar thing applies to big data. You need to remember what your business can, well, stomach.

It's easy to get dazzled by big data opportunities. The sheer volume of data available and the amazing things that companies are doing can be overwhelming. But trying to replicate what the big companies are doing in your own business is stressful, expensive and completely unhelpful.

Or maybe you're so dazzled that you feel almost paralysed by the possibilities. The same advice applies: Don't worry about what the big guys are doing; focus on what's best for your business.

Big data giants never throw data away; every tiny piece of data may be valuable to them to some extent or other. Everything is captured and analysed because it can potentially offer unique and powerful insights for business development. Even errors are captured and analysed. Take misspelled words and names in Internet search queries – you'd think those could be discarded, but you'd be wrong. Instead of discounting incorrect entries, Google captures that data and uses it to create the world's best spell checker!

For big data giants like Google, Tesco and Amazon, every tiny piece of data may well be valuable. But that's because they have the expertise, money and technology to cope with massive datasets. They have the storage capacity, manpower, analytical know-how and software to mine all that data for insights. Also, they have the best talent gagging to work for them. (Each year, a staggering two million people apply to work at Google but only around 5,000 get hired!)

I'd guess that 99.9 per cent of all the companies in the world will never be in that position, nor do they need to be. For most business leaders, the idea of collecting and storing everything is terrifying. They already have a mountain of dusty archive material lying around, let alone dealing with all the new data that is generated every day.

Most businesses will never have the time, money, expertise or even inclination to collect and crunch data like the big guys do. And that's a good thing. Rather than trying to collect as much data as possible, your aim should be to collect *only* the data that you really need to meet your goals. Aim for the smallest, most focused dataset that you can possibly get away with in order to answer your key business questions. To keep your dataset small and focused, you need a really clear strategy.

Merits and pitfalls of data discovery

When you start with strategy, you work out what you need to know and what data you need to collect to provide the answers you're looking for. *Data discovery* (sometimes called *data mining*) is the process of looking at data from the other direction.

In data discovery you just look at the data with no questions or agenda to see what the data tells you about your business. This process can be a useful addition to a more structured, strategic big data approach and can potentially unearth some interesting data gems. Note that I said *addition* to the process; it should never be a substitute for a properly planned and executed big data strategy.

I always advise my clients to focus on the important things first, for example, crafting a proper big data strategy and following that through. However, if you're interested in data discovery then keep the ratio 90/10 in mind: 90 per cent of your time should be focused on following your big data strategy and maybe 10 per cent of your time and budget can be devoted to data discovery – and even then *only* if you can afford it. If your business has access to a huge amount of data that can be mined and analysed then it may well be worth spending ten per cent of your analytics efforts on data discovery.

For example, Facebook looked at all the data it had via millions of status updates and was able to decipher a pattern around relationships from that chaos. So much so that Facebook can now predict when you will change your status from *Single* to *In a relationship* – and presumably vice versa. For now, this may just seem like a quirky insight, but there may come a day when Facebook could license that data to companies who make products that might be of interest to someone embarking on a new relationship (romantic minibreaks in the country, for instance). Likewise, I bet Kleenex and Ben & Jerry's would be very interested in targeting the recently dumped! But remember, Facebook invests in data discovery because it *can* – it has a huge amount of data not to mention the time, talent, technological capabilities and money to make it worthwhile.

In the future these types of data discovery insights could certainly revolutionize business and could even end up changing your entire business model. But it's absolutely not the place for most businesses to start, and it should only ever be considered as an addition to your big data strategy.

The Key Steps in Creating Your Big Data Strategy

After you have an idea of how you want to use big data (improve business decisions, transform operations or both), you're ready to create your big data strategy. Before embarking on any big data project, you must start with strategy. For example, what data you gather and how you analyse it depends entirely on what you're looking to achieve – so you need to have considered this at the outset. A good, strong strategy helps the whole process run more smoothly and prepares you and your people for the journey ahead.

In the next sections, I break down the big data strategy into six components or steps. There's more of the nitty-gritty on how to implement these steps in Chapters 11 and 12, but here the focus is on understanding what you want to do. I also look at why it's so important to make a good case for data in your business.

Keep in mind that, like any business improvement process, things may shift or evolve along the way. While it's important to know what you want to achieve at the outset, nothing in business is ever set in stone. Some strategic questions lead to neat and tidy one-time data projects that do exactly what they say on the tin. Others need to be monitored over time and strategies tweaked depending on what the data indicates.

You may find that your data points to interesting new questions that you want to explore or leads to modifications to your existing data strategy. If that happens, simply revisit your strategy, re-evaluating each of the points in the next sections in turn.

The six components of your big data strategy

These components form the basis of your big data strategy, helping you understand and focus on what you want to do. They should be considered in the order set out in the next sections.

While I don't expect you to carve your big data strategy in stone and swear blood allegiance to it, it's a good idea to create a formal strategy document. It doesn't have to be a masterpiece, but it will be helpful to have your goals and requirements on paper – that way, the strategy can be shared, referred back to and updated as necessary.

Be sure to involve the important people in your big data strategy. Getting the key company players and decision makers involved now can help you create a more robust strategy overall. Getting key people to buy in at this crucial early stage means they'll be more likely to put all that data to good use later on.

What do I need to know or what business problem do I need to solve?

Many of the companies I work with tend to ask for as much data as possible – not because they plan to do incredibly detailed analytics, but because they don't know what to ask for, so they ask for everything. Rather than starting with the data (for example, what you already have, what you might be able to get access to, or what you would love to have), it's much better to start with company strategy. After all, why bother collecting data that won't help you achieve your business goals?

Think about the strategic priorities you have laid out for the coming months or years. Define what it is you want to achieve and then think about the big unanswered questions you need to answer to deliver that strategy. Throughout the book, you'll often see me refer to these as *strategic questions*. Work out what it is you need to achieve through the analysis of data. Are you looking to reach more customers, better understand your current ones or determine the best locations to provide your service?

Defining these questions helps you identify exactly what you need to know. And by making sure your questions are linked to your company's priorities, you can ensure they're the most strategically important questions, rather than asking every little 'nice to know but not essential' question.

For more detailed information on how to identify your questions, turn to Chapter 11. Once you've identified your business priorities and strategic questions, then you can look at the data you need to solve those problems.

What data do I need to answer my questions?

Most companies get caught up in collecting data on everything that walks and moves, simply because they can, rather than collecting the data that really matters.

This might sound paradoxical, but when it comes to big data is it even more important to think small. I recently worked with one of the world's largest retailers and, after my session with the leadership group, the CEO went to his data team and told them to stop building the biggest database in the world and instead create the smallest database that helps the company to answer its most important questions. This is a great way of looking at big data.

Stay focussed. Don't get lost in the background noise from all the data out there that isn't relevant to your business goals.

Look at each question you've identified and then think about the ideal data you want or need to answer that question. You may be able to find the data from within the company, but you could also look to the millions of new sources out there: structured and unstructured, conversation data, video data and so on (I talk about the different kinds of data in Chapters 4 and 5.)

After you define the ideal data, look inside the organisation to see what data you already have. Then look outside and establish what data you may have access to. At this point you can then decide whether you can use existing internal data, bring in existing external data or create new data collection mechanisms. But remember, only by knowing what data you need will you know where to look for it and how to collect it.

How will I analyse that data?

When you're clear about your information needs and the data required, you need to define your analytics requirements. For example, how you will turn that data into insights. Here you define how the data will be analysed to ensure the raw data is turned into valuable insights that help you answer your questions and achieve your business goals.

Traditional data collection and analysis is one thing – like point of sale trans-actions, website clicks and so on – but where much of the promise of big data lies is in unstructured data, like email conversations, social media posts, video content, photos, voice recordings, sounds and so on. Combining this messy and complex data with other more traditional data, like transactions, is where a lot of the value lies, but you must have a plan for the analysis.

How will I report and present insights?

All the fancy datasets and cool analytics don't mean anything if they aren't presented to the right people in the right way in order to help decision making. Making good use of data visualisation techniques and taking pains to highlight and display key information in a user-friendly way will help ensure that your data gets put to good use.

So, in this step you need to define how the insights will be communicated to the information consumer or decision maker. You need to think about which format is best and how to make the insights as visual as possible. You also need to consider whether interactivity is a requirement. For example, do the key decision makers in your business need access to interactive self-service reports and dashboards?

Keeping your target audience in mind is perhaps the most important thing to remember at this stage. The target audience may be you as the business owner or manager, or it may well be other key decision makers in your busi-ness, depending on what your strategic questions are.

Why do you need to think about this before you've even gathered a scrap of data? Well, quite simply, it may impact your overall strategy and big data infrastructure. For instance, if you know that the managers in your company will need access to real-time reports and dashboards, then that is going to have a big impact on your software and hardware requirements.

What software and hardware do I need?

Following on from defining what data is needed, how it will be turned into value and how it will be communicated to the end user, you need to define your software and hardware requirements.

Is your current data storage technology adequate? Should it be supplemented with cloud solutions? What current analytic and reporting capabilities do you have and what do you need to get? There's more on building a big data infrastructure in Chapter 9 but, for now, you need to consider the overall requirements that will help you meet your goals.

What's the plan of action?

Having identified the various needs, you're now ready to define an action plan that turns your big data strategy into reality. Like any action plan, this will include key milestones, participants and responsibilities. After creating your strategy, one of your first steps will be to make a robust business case for big data to the people in your organisation – effectively convincing them of the merits of using big data.

Importantly, you should also identify training and development needs within the company and identify where you might need external help. Chapter 8 has more information on key big data competencies that your company is likely to need.

Making a solid big data business case

Like any major business project, you need to make a strong case (a business plan, if you like) for your big data project. These days, no sane person starts a business without first drawing up a business plan. It's a process that has filtered down to any key business activity – for example, a company is unlikely to embark on a major expansion project without first making a clear business case for doing so, weighing up the costs and benefits. Setting off without such a plan is a recipe for disaster. It's the same with big data.

Treat your big data project as any other major business project: Build a robust written business plan and communicate the key elements of that plan to all areas of the business. This is an essential step but one that's pretty easy to do once you have your completed your data strategy.

Attitudes that kill a big data project in its early days

When getting any business project off the ground, you're likely to encounter some negative attitudes. In my experience, people have a lot of misconceptions about big data, so here are the main attitudes I've come across and my counter-arguments for each.

- **We're not a data company.** Every company is now a data company. Data is everywhere and a part of everything, and I cannot think of a single industry or business that couldn't benefit from understanding more about its customers, its sales cycles, or its production inefficiencies. Just because you don't yet know how big data could benefit your company, doesn't mean it won't.

- **Big data is too expensive for us.** This is a flat-out myth, because you can get started by using relatively cheap cloud services and open-source software. People also believe that in order to start using big data, they need to employ expensive full-time data scientists. A good consultant can get you set up and an analyst can help you understand your data long before you need to bring in a full-time data scientist.

- **We have to collect as much data as possible.** This attitude simply leads to data obesity. In fact, in my experience, when clients ask for more data it's because they don't know what they need. Instead of a 'lets collect everything we can' attitude, most companies should only collect data if there is a clear business reason to do so.

- **We already have loads of data.** It is true that most companies are already overwhelmed by the amount of data in their businesses.

However, the proliferation of data means that there are so many new data sources you can use and what's more, many of those datasets can be accessed for free. Smart business people should always be on the lookout for additional information that can help solve business problems.

- **Big data is only for the Silicon Valley tech companies.** Even the most traditional of companies is turning to big data. Take Midwest farm machinery manufacturer John Deere as an example: The business is now collecting data from sensors on its machines and probes in the soil to give farm managers insights about how much fertilizer to use, how to save money on fuel and the level of crop they can expect.

- **Everyone else is already way ahead of us.** Putting your head in the sand now is not going to make it any better in the future. It's true that more and more companies are joining the big data movement. But even though the adoption curve of big data is growing steeper by the day, the majority of companies are still in pre-implementation or pilot stages. In other words, you might not be as far behind you think.

- **Our customers aren't asking for it.** Well, they are if they're looking for things like a more personalised service, comparative pricing or optimised supply chains. While they may not be using the phrase 'big data', they're asking for the things that only data can help you deliver. These days, customers are demanding smarter products and services, and the hard truth is that if you don't provide them, someone else will.

Covering the key elements of a business plan

Business leaders, managers and decision makers always want to know up front what a project is going to cost, how it will benefit the business and, basically, whether the benefits outweigh the costs. That's what you're looking to set out in your big data business plan.

Your big data business plan should aim to cover the following elements:

- ✔ Summarise or outline the project in brief.

- ✔ Define your goals – what are you aiming to find out?

- ✔ List the tangible benefits to the business. How will data help you improve or transform your business?

- ✔ Describe the capabilities needed and whether any skill gaps will be filled through training or bringing in external help.

- ✔ Discuss timeframe and likely disruption to the business.

- ✔ Be very clear on costs. Most of the costs will be related to getting the right talent on board, storing and maintaining the data and, crucially, keeping it safe. It's important not to gloss over this; otherwise your business case will not be as robust as it should be.

Shouting it from the rooftops

You've built a solid argument for using big data in your business. Now you need to promote the idea and evangelise it across the whole company. I can't stress enough how important this is – *selling* big data to your colleagues is a crucial early step on your big data journey.

Communicating your business case effectively instils confidence in your big data project and helps you get buy-in across the company early in the process.

Ensuring your colleagues understand the value of big data in the organisation means they're much more likely to incorporate data into their decision making further down the line. By making the business case early, you're sowing the seeds for data-driven decision making in future. There's more on building a culture of data-driven decision making in Chapter 13, along with some helpful tips on facilitating company-wide buy-in.

How you communicate your plan across the company depends on a number of factors, such as the size of your company and your usual processes for kicking off new initiatives. You may simply want to share your business plan document with colleagues and have an informal discussion. But I think a good way to go about this process is by distilling your big data plan into key points that can be communicated in a short presentation. Not everyone in the company will need to know the ins and outs of big data capabilities and costs, but you want everyone to be in love with the general idea of using data in the business. Distilling the plan down into the key nuggets is a good way to get broader buy-in.

Here are my tips for communicating your ideas:

- ✔ Keep the information simple and brief.

- ✔ Enthusiasm is infectious, so evangelise data and emphasise the positives.

- ✔ Focus on tangible benefits, for example ,what questions the data will hopefully answer and how these insights will add value to your business. Explain how data can help your company gain competitive advantage.

- ✔ Use examples to demonstrate the power of big data. It's particularly helpful if these are related to your industry and demonstrate how others in your field are already using data.

Ultimately, starting with strategy and making a proper business case gives you the best chance of successfully using data in your business – no matter what your goals are or the scale of your ambitions, this is always the place to start.

The steps in this chapter are designed to get you thinking about what you want to achieve with the help of big data. I've used this approach with companies and government organisations of all sorts of sizes, across many sectors. I find it a simple and intuitive approach to creating a big data strategy and one that engages the key decision makers in an organisation.

When you're ready, Chapters 11 and 12 can help you nail down your strategic questions and implement your big data strategy in detail.

Chapter 11

Applying Data in Your Business: Decision Making

In This Chapter

▶ Identifying strategic business questions to improve your business

▶ Finding and analysing the data to help answer those questions

▶ Communicating and acting upon what the data tells you

I believe data should be at the heart of strategic decision making in businesses, whether those businesses are huge multinationals or small family-run operations. Data can provide insights that help you answer your key business questions such as 'How can I improve customer satisfaction?' Data leads to insights; business owners and managers can turn those insights into decisions and actions that improve the business. This is the power of data.

In this chapter I look at the process for applying data to your decision making – from identifying your key business questions to finding data, analysing it and incorporating insights from the data into the business.

This process is broken down into ten steps and I explore each step. Don't be tempted to skip steps or jump ahead to juicier parts – the strategic steps are as important (if not more) than the data itself. It's best to follow the steps in order. This ten-step process of applying data to business decision making is one that I have used with clients time and time again. I find it's a simple blue-print to follow and I hope it helps you navigate your big data journey.

Unless you're a tech wizard (or someone in your company is), it's likely you will need some expert help at some or all of these stages, such as a data consultant and data analyst. While there is some financial outlay involved, in most cases this is earned back via the long-term business improvements gained from data insights.

Starting with Strategy

If you've read any other chapter in this book already (or read anything anywhere about data), you can probably understand that it's easy to get overwhelmed by the possibilities that big data provides. It's easy to get lost in the noise and hype surrounding data. Starting with strategy helps you ignore the hype and cut to what's going to make a difference for *your* business.

Instead of starting with what data you could or should access (which is a recipe for failure and instant overwhelm), start by working out what your business is looking to achieve. In a nutshell, you need to work out what your strategic goals are – for example, increasing your customer base.

I recommend you read Chapter 10 before embarking on defining your strategic goals as it underlines the importance of strategy and gets you thinking about what it is you want to achieve.

Introducing the SMART strategy board

To help my clients take a step back and identify their strategic goals, I developed the SMART strategy board, shown in Figure 11-1. You can use the SMART strategy board to consider your strategic objectives for each key area of your business. Once you understand your objectives, you can then highlight key strategic questions that will help you achieve those objectives. (I get to that in 'Identifying Your Unanswered Questions' a bit later in the chapter.)

There are six panels in the SMART strategy board:

- ✔ The purpose panel
- ✔ The customer panel
- ✔ The finance panel
- ✔ The operations panel
- ✔ The resource panel
- ✔ The competition and risk panel

You can't identify what data you need if you're not clear about your strategy. The value of data is not the data itself – it's what you do with the data. Having really clear objectives helps you get the most out of data.

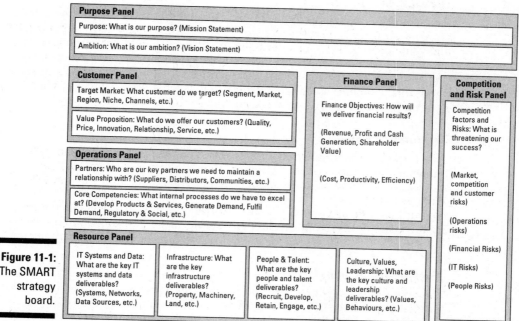

SMART Strategy Board

Purpose Panel

Purpose: What is our purpose? (Mission Statement)

Ambition: What is our ambition? (Vision Statement)

Customer Panel

Target Market: What customer do we target? (Segment, Market, Region, Niche, Channels, etc.)

Value Proposition: What do we offer our customers? (Quality, Price, Innovation, Relationship, Service, etc.)

Operations Panel

Partners: Who are our key partners we need to maintain a relationship with? (Suppliers, Distributors, Communities, etc.)

Core Competencies: What internal processes do we have to excel at? (Develop Products & Services, Generate Demand, Fulfil Demand, Regulatory & Social, etc.)

Finance Panel

Finance Objectives: How will we deliver financial results?

(Revenue, Profit and Cash Generation, Shareholder Value)

(Cost, Productivity, Efficiency)

Competition and Risk Panel

Competition factors and Risks: What is threatening our success?

(Market, competition and customer risks)

(Operations risks)

(Financial Risks)

(IT Risks)

(People Risks)

Resource Panel

IT Systems and Data: What are the key IT systems and data deliverables? (Systems, Networks, Data Sources, etc.)

Infrastructure: What are the key infrastructure deliverables? (Property, Machinery, Land, etc.)

People & Talent: What are the key people and talent deliverables? (Recruit, Develop, Retain, Engage, etc.)

Culture, Values, Leadership: What are the key culture and leadership deliverables? (Values, Behaviours, etc.)

Figure 11-1: The SMART strategy board.

© Bernard Marr

Completing the SMART strategy board

So that you can complete the board, look at each of the individual panels in turn.

The purpose panel

This sets the scene and provides an inspiring framework or overall context regarding your *corporate strategy,* or what your business is aiming for or seeking to achieve. You can do this by detailing your mission and vision statement – each doing a distinctly different job. Your *mission statement* is a clear, concise statement of purpose setting out why your organisation exists. It should include your target audience, what products or services you provide to that audience and what makes your product or service unique. Your *vision statement* also defines purpose, but from the perspective of what you want your business to be in the future.

The customer panel

Here you need to consider how much you currently know about the customers your strategy is targeting. There are two parts to consider – target market and value proposition. Considering your strategy (including your mission and vision), you ask questions including: what is your target market? Are you planning to appeal to a particular segment? If so, why, and what do you know about that segment? Your value proposition is what you're going to offer your target market. Why are these customers going to buy from you?

The finance panel

This prompts you to think about how much you currently know about the financial implications of your strategy. How does your strategy generate money? What is the business model and are you confident it's accurate? What assumptions have you made about the revenue, profit and growth of your business as you implement the strategy? How much will it cost to produce and deliver your product and services? Do you know for sure or is it a guess?

The operations panel

The operations panel prompts you to consider what you actually need to do internally to deliver your strategy. There are two components: partners and core competencies. First you need to consider which suppliers, distributers, partners or other intermediaries are crucial in delivering your strategy. Do you currently work with these people or will you need to create the relationships? If the relationships already exist, how healthy are they right now? You also need to consider what core competencies you need to excel in if you're going to execute your chosen strategy. Are there any gaps? If so, how easy is it going to be to fill those gaps?

The resource panel

There are four components of the resources panel: IT (information technology) systems and data; infrastructure; people, talent and cultures; and values and leadership. For each, you should consider what resources you need in order to deliver your strategy.

The competition and risk panel

Here you consider what competition you will be up against as you seek to deliver your strategy and what risks you may face along the way. Considering your aspirations, who is your main competition and why? What is potentially threatening your success? Are there any specific market, customer, competition or regulatory risks that could derail your strategy? What are the operational, financial or talent risks you face?

Honing in on the Business Area

Having looked at each area of the strategy board, you now need to identify which areas are most important to achieving your overall strategy. If you could only work on improving one or two of these areas, which would you choose?

For most businesses, the customer, finance and operations panels are the key areas. Often these are the core of the business, so it's important to consider how they impact on each other and how they work together. So, if you identify the customer panel as being your most important, you'll need to consider the financial and operational implications of any decision.

Identifying Your Unanswered Questions

After you identify your objectives and consider each area of the strategy board, you need to identify the unanswered questions that relate to each panel. For example, what do you need to know in each area of the business to be able to achieve your goals? Throughout the book, I use the phrase *strategic questions*. What I really mean is *SMART questions*.

You need to know what questions you need answers to before you dive into data – big or otherwise. Focusing on SMART questions allows you to forget about big data and focus on SMART data. By working out exactly what you need to know, you can hone in on the data that you really need.

For each panel on the board, except the purpose panel, identify a few SMART (or strategic) questions. When you know the questions you need answered, it's much easier to identify the data you need to access in order to answer those key questions (I get to data in the next section). Your data requirements, cost and stress levels are massively reduced when you move from 'collect everything just in case' to 'collect and measure x and y to answer question z'. Check out the nearby sidebar for a few sample questions.

Choosing SMART questions

I worked with a small fashion retail company that wanted to increase sales. Together we worked out that the SMART questions it needed answers to included:

✔ How many people actually pass our shops?

✔ How many stop to look in the window and for how long?

✔ How many of them then come into the shop?

✔ How many then buy?

Understanding the power of questions

When you start with a simple question and seek to find and analyse only the data that can directly answer that question, then you move away from the overwhelming idea that you have to have all the data and the panic that you're going to need to collect and analyse everything, to a much more manageable and sensible enquiry. That's the power of SMART questions.

SMART questions help you and your people to:

- ✔ See the wood from the trees regarding what's important and what's not.
- ✔ Understand the relevance of the data sought because SMART questions indicate to everyone what your company's biggest concerns are.
- ✔ Open communication and guide discussion.
- ✔ Make better evidence-based decisions.

The do's and don'ts of SMART questions

When identifying your questions, do:

- ✔ Identify a small number of SMART questions for each panel (between two and five).
- ✔ Engage key personnel from each panel in the creation of the SMART questions to facilitate buy-in.
- ✔ Make your SMART questions clear and concise.
- ✔ Use your SMART questions to guide your data needs. Focus only on the data that answers your questions.

Here are some common pitfalls to avoid:

- ✔ Getting carried away and listing everything it would be vaguely interesting to know. Not only is this expensive data-wise, but it's unlikely to help you achieve your strategic goals.
- ✔ Lumping unrelated questions in together (maybe so it looks like you've got fewer questions!). Instead, keep each question really tightly focused.
- ✔ Asking certain questions because you know you have the data already. This is a false economy if those questions aren't going to help achieve your goals. Don't think about the data until you set out your questions.

Google's Project Oxygen and the power of great questions

One of the Google myths or opinions that emerged from the early days of the company was that managers didn't matter that much. As a tech company, the jobs with the highest status that everyone wanted were the tech jobs, not the people-management jobs. In fact, Google was so sure that managers didn't matter that much to the business that it decided to get rid of them all. It didn't work well, and managers were brought back into the company. But the stigma remained, and the managers were not nearly as valued as the tech people. The assumption at this time was that there really was no proven impact about what the people managers brought to the table as opposed to the tech professionals.

So Google set out to establish whether the stigma was justified or not. And to do that it started with a question: Do managers actually make a positive impact at Google? The first thing researchers did was to look at data sources that already existed: performance reviews and employee surveys. Plotting the results on a graph, all the managers appeared to be pretty tightly clustered and it looked like they were doing well. But the graph didn't answer the question, 'Do managers actually make a positive impact at Google?' In order to answer the question, they needed to look more closely at the data and cut it into sections, looking specifically at the top quartile (best managers) and the bottom quartile (worst managers).

Further analysis was made on how the best and worst managers performed in terms of team productivity, how happy their employees were, how likely their employees were to stay with the company and so on. And the results were astonishing. Even though most of the managers

appeared to be tightly clustered together on the graph, further investigation highlighted statistically significant differences between the best and worst managers in the cluster. This analysis clearly answered the question. Managers do matter and they can make a positive impact at Google.

But this information alone wasn't really going to change anything. So the researchers came up with a new question they wanted to answer: What makes a great manager at Google? They had no idea how the good managers became good or what made them so effective compared with others. To answer the new question, they started two different qualitative studies, one with direct reports and the other with managers. The data from both studies was coded and analysed. Based on this data, they came up with eight behaviours that made the biggest impact for managers at Google – things like 'is a good coach' and 'has a clear vision for the team.' The data also highlighted three pitfalls that might cause a manager to struggle.

Google went from the opinion 'Managers don't impact performance' to using the data and metrics to prove that great managers had a statistically significant impact. It was then able to identify and articulate what made a great manager at Google. These insights were then embedded into Google culture through ongoing measurement of these factors, which acts as an early warning system to detect both great and struggling managers. And all this was possible because it started with the right question; refining the question until it got to a practical, verifiable hypothesis that has improved management performance across Google.

Finding the Data to Answer Your Questions

The next step is to identify what data you need to access or acquire in order to answer your SMART questions.

It's really important to understand that no type of data is inherently better or more valuable than any other type. The key is to start with your strategy and establish your SMART questions so that those questions guide you to the best data *for you*.

To work out what data you're going to need, you should consider each of your SMART questions separately. Go through the various panels from the SMART strategy board (refer to Figure 11-1) and describe the ideal data sets that would help you answer each SMART question (see Chapter 5 for examples of how businesses are using data). You will probably need to consider more than one data set.

Make a note of which data sets you intend to use or could use. A good data consultant will be able to help you with this. Describe the data for each data set and make a note of its location and who owns it. Consider whether the data you need is internal or external and structured or unstructured (see Chapter 4). If external, who owns it? How much do you need? How would it be analysed? You can then choose the best data options to pursue based on how easy the data is to collect, how quick and how cost effective.

There is a logical hierarchy of where you should first look when identifying the data that will answer your SMART questions:

1. Internal structured data. This is easiest to find and easiest to analyse. It is also probably the least expensive to acquire.

2. Internal semi-structure.

3. Internal unstructured.

4. External structured.

5. External unstructured.

Forgetting what you have or what's out there

What I mean by this is: Don't concern yourself with all the metrics and data that currently exist. Don't worry about what data you can and can't get your hands on at this stage (I get to that in the next sections). The data possibilities are endless . . . and distracting.

What you should be doing at this stage is focusing on identifying the ideal data *for you* – the data that could help you answer your most pressing questions and deliver on your strategic objectives.

Thinking big and small

The trick with data is to focus on finding the exact, specific pieces of data that will benefit your business. Instead of collecting or accessing as much data as possible, your aim should really be to gather as little data as possible while still reaching your objectives. This might mean you don't need much *big* data at all, but can instead gather insights from smaller data like your transaction records or customer feedback surveys.

Many people in business are too focused on external unstructured data – this is the sexy stuff (if any data can be called sexy!). But this is a mistake. If you can effectively answer your SMART questions from internal structured data why on earth would you waste valuable time seeking the answers anywhere else?

In reality, most businesses need a combination of datasets in order to answer their questions – some big, some small, some internal, some external. I've found it's this combination of small, in-house data and external big data that is especially powerful.

Identifying What You Already Have or Have Access To

Internal data accounts for everything your business currently has or could access. A lot of the time this isn't considered very exciting, and people tend to skip over what they have in favour of external data. But I think this is a huge mistake. Internal data can be a gold mine, even if you need to combine it with some external data to get a fuller picture.

Once you've identified the data you need, it makes sense to see if you're already sitting on some of that information, even if it isn't immediately obvious.

Does it exist in some form somewhere?

Internal data includes private or proprietary data that is collected and owned by your business and that you control access to. Examples of internal data include:

- Customer feedback
- Sales data
- Employee or customer survey data
- CCTV (closed-circuit television) video data
- Transactional data
- Customer record data
- Stock control data
- HR (human resources) data

This data may be in a range of formats, some of it neat and tidy and some of it messy. Keep in mind that some work may be needed to tidy the data to make it ready for analysis before you can get started.

Internal doesn't always mean cheap

Internal data is usually less expensive than external data, but that isn't always the case. For example, if all your past customer records are on microfiche, although it's internal and you own it, it would be very costly to get all that data converted to digital format. It may be that there is an alternative external solution that could prove cheaper in the long run.

If you need external data

So you've worked out what you have and haven't got access to. You may find you also need some external data. *External data* is the infinite array of information that exists outside your business (see Chapter 4). External data is either public or private, meaning either it's data that anyone can obtain or it's owned by a third party. Your data consultant will be able to help you identify the best external sources for your needs, but there's a list of the top free external sources in Chapter 15.

Working Out if the Costs and Effort Are Justified

Many business people think big data is simply beyond their budget or it's the domain of multi-million- (or billion-) pound businesses. The answer is yes, of course big businesses have the resources (money and talent) to tackle big data. But that doesn't mean smaller businesses can't. Massive increases in storage and computing power, some of it available via cloud computing, means the costs are declining. Some of the technology used to capture data (such as sensors) is now incredibly cheap and easy to source. Big data has never been cheaper.

Once you have identified your ideal data sets, you need to work out how much it will cost you to work with the data. For each data set, you need to set out how much it will cost you to capture or retrieve the data, how you plan to analyse the data, the costs of that analysis and how much it will cost to store the data safely.

Although the cost of data is falling all the time, it can still add up if you get carried away. This is why it's crucial to focus only on the data that you really need.

Only after you know the costs, can you work out if the tangible benefits outweigh those costs. At this stage it's helpful to make a solid business case (a business plan, if you like) for using data in your business. In this respect, you should treat data like any other key business investment. You need to make a clear case for the investment that outlines the long-term value of data to the business strategy. Making a proper business case gives you the best chance of successfully using data in your business as you can get buy-in from all areas of your business. Turn to Chapter 10 for more information on creating a solid business case for big data.

If you find that the cost of a particular data set is very high, you need to be really sure the answer you will derive from the data is strategically important enough to warrant the time, money and effort. Of course, you also need to weigh up the potential cost to the business if you *don't* go ahead (for example, if you *don't* increase your customer base). If you believe the costs outweigh the benefits, then you may need to look at alternative data sources.

Collecting the Data

Much of this step comes down to building big data competencies and infrastructure, which sounds scary but really just means setting up the processes and people who will gather and manage your data. Here I'm just relating this step to decision making, with a couple of examples on what worked for one of my clients. Circle back to Chapters 8 (competencies) and 9 (infrastructure) for more detailed information on what is required.

Deciding who will collect it

Once you know what data you need, your next step is to identify who will collect it. You may be buying access to an analysis-ready data set, in which case there is no need to collect data as such. But, in reality, most data projects require some amount of data collection.

Who collects this data will depend very much on your questions and what data you're looking to create or capture. In Chapter 9 I explore the various ways of creating and capturing data (such as surveys, asking people to rate products, using transaction data). Some of this can be captured in-house relatively easily – for example by your website or by your customer service people. Some will require external help and you'll find guidance on tapping into external service providers in Chapter 8.

Deciding when it will be collected

Is the data changing rapidly? Is it collected frequently and how recent is it? These are all things you need to consider at this stage. There is no rule of thumb for when to collect data except for when it will best answer your SMART questions.

The retail client in the 'Choosing SMART questions' sidebar earlier in the chapter wanted to increase sales. For that client, the best solution was to collect data continually to understand how many customers pass the shop and to be able to run experiments to see which window displays were most effective in attracting customers into the shop.

Deciding how it will be collected

Data collection tools include sensors, video, GPS (global positioning systems), phone signals, social media platforms . . . the list goes on. What tool or tools you choose depends on your strategic questions and who is collecting the data and when. As a starting point, I set out my top ten data collection tools for small businesses in Chapter 16.

Back to the retail client from the 'Choosing SMART questions' sidebar that was looking to improve sales. What we did was install a small, discreet device into the shop windows that tracked mobile phone signals as people walked past the shop. Everyone, at least everyone passing these particular stores with a mobile phone on them (which nowadays is almost everyone), was picked up by the sensor in the device and counted, thereby answering the first question: How many people actually pass our shops? The sensors also measured how many people stopped to look at the window and for how long, how many people then walked into the store, and the company's internal sales data would record who actually bought something. By combining the data from inexpensive, readily available sensors placed in the window with transaction data, we were able to measure conversion ratio and test window displays and various offers to see which ones increased conversion rate. Not only did this fashion retailer massively increase sales by getting smart about the way it combined small traditional data with untraditional big data, but it used the insights to make a significant saving by closing one of its stores. The sensors were able to finally tell them that the footfall reported by the market research company prior to opening in that location was wrong and that the passing traffic was insufficient to justify keeping the store open.

Analysing the Data

Data and analytics go hand in hand. You need to analyse the data in order to extract meaningful and useful business insights. After all, there's no point coming this far if you don't then learn something new from the data. As such, the field of analytics is growing in line with the growth of data.

In Chapter 2 I explore the four V's of big data: volume, velocity, variety and veracity. Analytics provide the fifth, and perhaps most important, V of big data: value. Analytics allows you to identify patterns and this knowledge is crucial to improving the way you do business.

You need to understand what's possible before you can confidently decide what analytic techniques are best able to deliver answers to your questions. The bottom line is this: data is just information and there are only a set number of ways that information exists and/or can be presented.

There are five key formats in which business data exists (see Chapter 5 for more information):

- ✔ Text data (including numbers)
- ✔ Sound data (audio files and music)
- ✔ Image data (photographs and graphics)
- ✔ Video data (combination of audio and visual)
- ✔ Sensor data

The most common types of analytics are as follows (there's more on analytic technology in Chapter 6):

- ✔ Text analytics
- ✔ Speech analytics
- ✔ Video/image analytics

The past few years has seen an explosion in the number of platforms available for big data analytical tasks. Some are free to use, like Hadoop, but it's very technical to set up and not specialised towards any particular job or industry. To use it well in your business, you need a platform to operate it from, such as Cloudera or Microsoft HDInsight. I recommend getting specialist advice (ideally from a data consultant) on which platform is best for your business.

In-house analysis versus external analysis

Some platforms require nothing more than a working knowledge of Excel, meaning most employees can dip their toes into big data analysis. However, in many cases, data requires a more experienced analytical hand.

Because of this, people often believe that in order to start using big data, they need to bring in expensive data scientists as full-time employees. That's not necessarily true – a good consultant can get you set up and an external analyst can help you understand your data long before you need to bring in a full-time data scientist. But, if data is going to be a core, ongoing part of your business, then it's worth considering employing an in-house analyst or data scientist.

The advantages of in-house analysis include increased control over the project, greater flexibility (for example, if you identify a new strategic question, you can run with it fairly easily) and keeping a tighter rein on the costs of analysis by paying a set salary.

The flip side is that in-house analysis could be a false economy. An external analysis firm may be better set up to provide the analysis you need, meaning it's able to do it more quickly, easily and cheaply. Outsourcing analysis may not be as expensive or difficult as you think. Of course, the downside to using external providers is that you have less overall control than if the analyst is a direct employee.

There's no right or wrong answer here. Talk to your data consultant about what's the best solution for your project.

It's very easy to be seduced by some of the really cool analytic capabilities that currently exist. Don't be led astray by the marketing blurb – your job is to find the best, most accessible and inexpensive technique possible, regardless of how sexy it is.

Chapter 8 has more information on partnering with external providers and recruiting in-house talent.

Combining data to improve and validate insights

Like data itself, the value is not just in one data set over another; the real value comes from the combination of data sets and the combination of analytics tools to analyse that data (like the retailer I worked with who ran analytics on a combination of sensor data, traditional sales data and video data).

I think it's always better to have two data sets than one and, if possible, you should have three. Three data sets allow you to triangulate or verify the data from different perspectives. So if one data set is structured internal (for example, sales data) and another is unstructured internal (for example, customer comments) and another unstructured external (for example, Facebook data), then you will almost certainly get a much richer picture of what's happening so you can answer your SMART questions more effectively and accurately.

Presenting and Distributing the Insights

Big data and analytics may well pave the way to some really cool innovations, greater customer understanding and real-time monitoring of what's actually happening in the business. But unless the results are presented to the right people in a meaningful way, then the size of the data sets or the sophistication of the analytics tools won't really matter and the results will not inform decision making and improve performance.

Big data or any data analytics is only useful if you make sure the right people get the right information, in the right format, so they can make the right decisions more often.

Presenting insights isn't as cool as analytics, but it is important. And anyway, these days there are more interesting ways to present data and exciting tools to help you do it.

Communicating and visualising insights

People don't want to search for the insights locked within the data. They want their insights provided to them, nicely packaged in a way that helps them understand the messages and make decisions that improve the business.

Huge written reports or long-winded verbal explanations are a sure-fire way to bury insights. Instead, wherever possible, present insights from your data using visuals, such as graphs (bar graphs and line graphs) and charts (pie charts and scatter charts). Visualising the data through graphics can not only make the data more accessible and meaningful but also can better illustrate the relationship among the data.

Big data analytics have created a wave of new visualisation tools capable of making the outputs of the analytics look pretty and making them quicker and easier to understand. Many of these tools are open-source, free applications (see Chapter 9 for examples).

Visualisation is not the only goal – beautiful graphics can still be meaningless! Make sure your insights shine through with these top tips:

✔ Where appropriate use *short* narratives to introduce what you're showing and highlight the key insights. Numbers and charts may give only a snapshot; narrative allows you to embellish on key points.

✔ Use clear headings to make the important points stand out. This way, even at a quick glance, the key points will be obvious.

✔ Link the information to your strategy. If your visualisation presents data that answers a SMART question, then include the SMART question in the opening narrative and maybe even the headline.

Keeping in mind the target audience

Too often in business, reports are disseminated to everyone just in case they're useful. Instead, consider who really needs the results in order to make better strategic decisions and tailor your data visualisation to their needs. This is a two-step process:

1. **Identify your target audience.**

   Who your audience is depends on your SMART questions (it could be you if you're the business owner, or it could be your HR team, your marketing team or a combination). Ask yourself who is going to see these results. What do those people already know about the issues being discussed? What do they need and want to know? And, what will they do with the information?

2. **Customise the data visualisation.**

   Based on the answers to your SMART questions, be prepared to customise your data visualisation to meet the specific requirements of each decision maker.

Dashboards and infographics

Some analytics that you run will be one-offs, answering a specific SMART question or questions. The results can then be reported via data visualisation or through the new trend of infographics.

However, you might have other data sources that you want to continuously measure, particularly if they relate to ongoing strategic, tactical or operational issues. If they need to be reported regularly, then the best way to do that is to create a management dashboard or key performance indicator (KPI). Dashboards and KPIs provide a concise visual display of relevant ongoing results, helping your key decision makers to keep the business on track toward its objectives.

There are two kinds of dashboards: operational and strategic. Operational dashboards monitor day-to-day processes and outputs to make sure expectations and performance are met consistently. They provide information that allows you to fix issues before they become problems and incrementally improve performance. Strategic dashboards, on the other hand, look to the future and seek to identify obstacles and challenges that may occur on the way to the strategic destination.

Infographics is an area that has grown alongside big data and analytics. As the ability and opportunity to analyse more and more data has grown, so too has the need to find ways to communicate and report the results in ever-more snazzy ways.

An *infographic* – a hybrid of information and graphics – is a one-page visual representation intended to express a lot of information, data or knowledge quickly and clearly. An infographic of a detailed report, data analysis or employee survey, for example, can tell the whole data story through a one-page visual map. After all, everyone has time to look at one page!

Figure 11-2 is an infographic I created about big data.

There are three distinct parts of a successful infographic:

- ✓ **Visually attractive:** Using colour, graphics and icons
- ✓ **Useful content:** Using time frames, statistics and references
- ✓ **Imparting knowledge:** Using facts and deductions

A good infographic should look good, engage the reader by simplifying content *and* provide meaningful answers and insights into important SMART questions.

Whether you decide to report results through traditional reporting with some data visualisation techniques or whether you opt for management dashboards and/or infographics will very often depend on your in-house expertise. But one thing's for sure, if you want to be a SMART business, you must develop these competencies either in-house or outsource to a trusted provider. Either way, data analysis and data visualisation are two sides of the same coin.

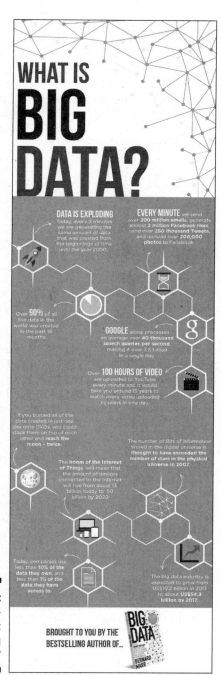

Figure 11-2:
An info-
graphic:
What is big
data?

© Bernard Marr

Incorporating the Learning into the Business

Clearly I find the whole big data process exciting and fascinating, but this step is probably the one I find most rewarding. This is where you get to turn data into action. In this step, you need to apply the insights from the data to your decision making, making the decisions that will transform your business for the better.

All these insights are not worth anything if you don't *use* that knowledge to improve your business.

Making the right decisions

Once you have done all that you can with the data, and you've communicated your insights to the key people in the company, it's time to review the evidence so that everyone in the business can move toward more fact-based decision making and leverage data to meet your objectives.

You can use the insights gained from the SMART process to improve your decision making, your customer experience, your employee brand and your business performance and to gain competitive advantage. You can solve problems, react to opportunities, enhance product quality and improve efficiency. The power of data is in how you use it. For more on building a culture of data-based decision making in your business, check out Chapter 13.

Finding questions for the future

Some of the strategic questions you're asking will be one-offs; some will be ongoing issues that you want to keep an eye on. And some of the answers you discover may lead to entirely new questions that you want to explore in future.

Naturally, your focus in this process should be on your initial strategic questions. But, once you have identified and answered those strategic questions, you may find that the data also points to interesting new opportunities or questions. If you have the appetite and resources to take the data further, then go for it.

The trick is to stay vigilant and be aware of any new questions or opportunities that your data exposes. For some businesses, data even leads to an entirely new business model. There's more on this in Chapter 13.

Twiddy & Company: How a family-run business turned data into action

With its miles of sandy stretches, the Outer Banks in North Carolina is a perfect rustic getaway for stressed-out tourists. Many of those travellers find vacation rentals through Twiddy & Company, a family-owned local enterprise that manages 998 homes on the islands, from simple cottages to 24-bedroom beachfront mansions. Twiddy's dual challenge is to satisfy guests while ensuring homeowners rent their properties as profitably as possible. But don't let the Outer Banks's sleepy feel fool you. Big data has made a difference here.

Like many companies, Twiddy had amassed years of operational data buried inside spreadsheets. 'We kept running into the same obstacles,' says marketing director Ross Twiddy. 'Unless we had a good way of looking at the data, how could we make good decisions?'

Twiddy settled on SAS's business analytics tools, which distilled the company's spreadsheets into a customisable format the company could share with homeowners and contractors. Before, Twiddy could tell homeowners the dates when their property was available to rent. Now, the company can offer pricing recommendations pinpointed down to the week on the basis of market conditions, seasonal trends and the size and location of a home, among other criteria.

'We noticed that the week after the Fourth of July saw a drop off in demand,' says Twiddy. Armed with that knowledge, Twiddy started letting its homeowners tweak prices in January for that week. Since the company began making such recommendations, overall bookings have increased, and more homeowners recommend Twiddy as a property manager. The inventory Twiddy manages has increased more than ten per cent over the past three years. As Twiddy says, 'There's truth in numbers.'

Chapter 12

Applying Data in Your Business: Operations

Although many businesses start by using data to inform their decision making (Chapter 11), you can take your data one step further and integrate it into your daily business operations. This aspect is less focused on extracting insights from the data to make better decisions and more focused on how data can help you run the business more smoothly. Therefore, it's less about your people making better decisions and more about using systems and algorithms that automate and improve processes. Until recently, most applications of data in business have been focused on the decision-making aspect but, thanks to new technologies, we're seeing more businesses successfully integrate data and algorithms into their everyday operational processes.

An *algorithm* is a mathematical formula or statistical process run by software to analyse data. It usually involves multiple calculation steps and can be used to automatically process data or solve problems.

In this chapter, I set out an eight-step process for changing the way you run your business, using data and algorithms. Whether you want to improve your manufacturing process by automatically detecting faults, optimise delivery routes, target the right customers, detect fraud or something else, data can help.

Unless you or someone in your company is very well versed in data and analytics, get some specialist help to integrate data into your business operations. A good data consultant will help you get up and running, but you may also need help from a data analyst and a data security expert.

Understanding the Role of Data

How you use data in your business is up to you; making processes more automatic and efficient is perhaps the most obvious way, but data can also lead to bigger changes in your business, even to reshaping your business model.

To incorporate data really successfully, you need to build a big data culture in your business. I talk more about that in Chapter 13 and give more examples of how businesses are using data every day.

Using data to improve operational processes

Businesses big and small are beginning to use data to refine their processes, reduce waste, increase efficiencies and increase revenue. Retail and sales companies are seeking to collect as much information about their customers' lives as possible so as to fulfil their changing needs more effectively. Manufacturing companies are seeking to streamline operations. Equipment calibration settings can be recorded and refined, and product storage environments monitored to determine the optimum conditions that lead to minimum spoilage and waste.

Of course, in business, once a product has been grown or manufactured, it needs to be sold and distributed. The petabytes of customer data (including data on you and me) already gathered by big retailers tells them who will want to buy what, where and when.

Amazon uses its S3 system to keep track of millions of stock items across dozens of warehouses and distribution centres scattered around the globe. Operatives can track deliveries in real time to see what is where and where it should be going.

At the point of sale, retailers can use data to determine where stock should be displayed, which stores will sell most of which particular product and to track customer movements around stores.

In the US, Macy's has reportedly been able to save 26 hours every time it optimises pricing for its 73 million products through big data, allowing them to change pricing more frequently to follow retail trends.

Loyalty cards are not new, but ever more sophisticated analysis of customer habits will lead to an increase in retailers predicting what customers will buy. This has advanced to the point where Amazon believes it will soon be able to predict what you will buy accurately enough to despatch it to you before you've even bought it!

The connectivity that's now possible, particularly the Internet of Things (which I talk about in Chapter 5), is also changing the way you do business. For a business, the ability to have its production, stock control, distribution and security systems all connected and talking to each other will mean greater efficiency and less waste.

With so many possibilities, it can be difficult to know where to start. If you've already used data to improve your decision making (Chapter 11 talks about this), then you've already identified your strategic priorities and key business questions. That's an excellent starting point as it gets you thinking about your key business goals and what you need in order to get there. Where to start differs from business to business but the operational priority areas for many business include:

- **Manufacturing:** Data uses include monitoring equipment wear and tear to reduce unexpected downtime.

- **Sales and marketing:** For example, monitoring social media and web search trends to predict customer interest, or using weather data to predict sales of a given product at certain times of the year.

- **Warehousing and distribution:** For example, automatic stock control, optimising delivery routes to avoid traffic jams and monitoring delivery vehicles and drivers.

- **Business processes:** For example, automatic diagnostic of tumours from scan images, predicting crime, fraud and cyber attacks and predicting and preventing accidents.

Reshaping your business model

Data has applications beyond your everyday operational processes. For some businesses, it has led to a change (even a complete shift) in their business model. John Deere, for example, is transitioning from its traditional agriculture manufacturing business towards more data-based services that meet modern customers' needs (tractor over to the John Deere sidebar for more information).

How John Deere transformed its operations with big data

US agricultural manufacturer John Deere has always been a pioneering company. Its eponymous founder personally designed, built and sold some of the first commercial steel ploughs.

Often at the forefront of innovation, it's no surprise that John Deere has embraced big data enthusiastically – assisting pioneers with the taming of the virtual wild frontier just as it did with the real one. John Deere has launched several big data-enabled services that let farmers benefit from crowdsourced, real-time monitoring of data collected from its thousands of users.

Myjohndeere.com is an online portal that allows farmers to access data gathered from sensors attached to their own machinery as they work the fields, as well as aggregated data from other users around the world. It's also connected to external datasets including weather and financial data. These services allow farmers to make more informed decisions about how to use their equipment, where they will get the best results and what return on their investment they're realising.

For example, fuel usage of different combines can be monitored and correlated with their productivity levels. By analysing the data from thousands of farms, working with many different crops in many different conditions, it's possible to fine-tune operations for optimum levels of production.

The system also helps to minimise downtime by predicting, based on crowdsourced data, when and where equipment is likely to fail. This data can be shared with engineers who will stand ready to supply new parts and service machinery as and when it's needed – cutting down on waste caused by expensive machinery sitting idle.

Another John Deere service is Farmsight, launched in 2011. It allows farmers to make decisions about what crops to plant where based on information gathered in their own fields and those of other users.

Of course, with all of this data being generated and shared, there's one question that needs answering – who owns it? Deere offers what it calls its Deere Open Data Platform, which lets farmers share data with each other (or choose not to, if they wish) and also with third-party application developers. But this has not stopped many farmers asking why they should effectively pay for their own data and asking why John Deere and other companies providing similar services shouldn't pay *them*. Talks are currently ongoing over how to address these concerns.

Farming is one of the fundamental activities that distinguishes humans from animals. But it's clear that even in this seemingly traditional industry, big data has a huge role to play.

If your company has the potential to generate quite a bit of data (through sensors in your products, for example), you, too, could develop services related to that data. Whether you manufacture huge equipment or tennis rackets, data that tells your customers how they're using your product and how they can use it more efficiently is pretty valuable. This could lead to additional income streams or, for some businesses, a complete change in business model. There's more on identifying new or additional business models in Chapter 13.

Sourcing the Required Data

Sometimes companies look only at what data they have already, such as sales data, customer information, stock records and so on. And that's certainly a good starting point, but it's important to understand that there's lots of data out there and lots that could potentially be captured.

When it comes to sourcing data, there are two basic options: external data and internal data. There's more on the different types of data in Chapters 4 and 5. You may find you need a combination of data sources to fully meet your goals.

Finding external data

External data is all the information about the wide world outside your company that you can turn to your advantage. This could either be self-generated, for example customer surveys, or collected from an external source – either paid or free.

The data economy is booming and many companies exist purely to supply other companies with information. On the other hand, there's a huge amount of information out there available for free – most governments these days make concerted efforts to make as much of their data as possible available to the public free of charge. This can be a great source for information on everything from population to weather and crime statistics. Depending on the human need or desire your company is catering for, you will almost certainly find something useful in external sources. I list my top ten free data sources in Chapter 15.

Using internal data

Internal data is information about your company's performance, activities, wins and losses, which you can generate yourself. This includes sales records, customer databases, employee records and all the day-to-day data that can be captured in the course of your business activities.

In sophisticated industrial operations, internal data may include machine data that allows you to fine-tune the efficiency of your equipment. Data like this can be generated by dedicated devices such as sensors, radio-frequency identification (RFID) or cameras that collect the data in real time. I list my top ten data collection tools for businesses in Chapter 16.

Data has always played a role in how car insurance premiums are calculated: customer postcode, local crime rate, estimated annual mileage, where the car is parked overnight and so on. But insurance companies are now much smarter about this data collection process, using sensors and apps to gather data such as actual annual mileage, the time of day customers do most of their driving and driver speed. All this new data means insurance companies can price policies based on individual driving conditions. Thanks to data and algorithms, dynamic pricing is now a reality.

Weighing up Costs and Benefits

Big data can bring benefits to businesses of any size. However, as with any project, proper preparation and planning is essential. Naturally, implementing data into your operations requires some level of investment. You need to invest in tools – for example, tools to collect, store and analyse data – to help you improve operational performance.

The good news is that big data doesn't have to mean big budgets – although as with most things in life, you usually get what you pay for. *Open source,* or free, software exists for most of the essential tasks. And many systems used by industry are designed to run on cheap, off-the-shelf hardware. The trade-off is that it will take some time and technical skill to get it set up and working the way you want. So unless you have the expertise (or are willing to spend time developing it), it might be worth paying for professional technical help, or enterprise versions of the software. Enterprise software is generally a customised version of the free packages, designed to be easier to use or specifically targeted at various industries.

Studies also show that companies (especially small and medium sized companies) put cost and personnel problems as the top reasons they haven't implemented big data yet. The truth is, data needs to become a priority fast, or companies risk being left behind. When weighing up the costs and benefits, remember to consider the potential costs of *not* integrating data into your business and potentially being left behind.

Making the business case

You wouldn't invest in a new warehousing facility or renting new retail premises without first making a solid business case for doing so. The same is true of any big data project. It's a bit like creating a business plan, but for data.

When making your business case, be sure to consider the following:

- The costs of integrating data into your business, including hiring new talent or getting specialist help as well as the hardware and software requirements for collecting, storing and analysing the data.

- The benefits this data will bring to the organisation – for example, increasing efficiency on the production line, saving time and increasing sales by introducing dynamic online pricing or reducing waste by managing stock more efficiently.

More information on making a solid business case can be found in Chapter 10.

Sourcing alternative data sets

Sometimes the costs just don't stack up, and you can't justify the data you originally wanted. But that doesn't mean your data journey is over before you've even started.

Some tips for sourcing data elsewhere:

- Competition is becoming increasingly fierce between data companies, so be sure to shop around to see if you can get similar data elsewhere for less money.

- Look at your data requirements to see if you really need all the data you're asking for. Many businesses fall into the trap of trying to obtain too much data. The trick is to get the minimum amount of data necessary to achieve your goals. While extra data may be nice to have, it's not essential to what you're trying to do.

- Consider whether you could generate similar data yourself, for example, by implementing a customer survey on your website.

- Instead of commercial data companies, look at other kinds of partnerships, such as partnering with a local organisation or university that might be looking to achieve similar things.

Securing Ownership

When data becomes a part of your everyday operations, the business begins to rely on that data. It becomes a core part of how you do business. As such, it's crucial you own the data and secure it.

Big data as a business asset

The companies that are really going to succeed are those who consider big data as a core business asset. I believe those companies who don't view data as an asset will lose serious competitive advantage.

Data as an operational or business asset means it's essential to how your business operates and makes money, just like your employees, your inventory, your building premises and your intellectual property.

Amazon pioneered e-commerce in many ways, but possibly one of its greatest innovations is the personalised recommendation system – which, of course, is built on the big data it gathers from its millions of customer transactions. In fact, its ability to use data (and indeed, its whole attitude towards data as an asset) is one of the key building blocks of Amazon's success. In the early days, when Amazon was primarily a book retailer, the company was the first to extensively use algorithms so that it could automatically provide recommendations for customers: 'Customers who bought this item, also bought this one . . . .' Today, it uses item-to-item collaborative filtering on many data points such as what users have bought before, what they have on their virtual wish list, the items they have rated and reviewed, as well as what other similar users have bought. This means Amazon can heavily customise the browsing experience using data and algorithms. And having worked out how to use data to get more money out of customers' pockets, Amazon is now setting out on a mission to help other global corporations do the same – by making that data, as well as its own tools for analysing it, available to buy. In my opinion, Amazon is one of the best examples of a company that really values data. As a result, it's even starting to reshape its business model, creating new revenue streams from its data.

Ensuring access rights and ownership

If you consider data as a key business asset, it's very important you secure ownership of that data.

Ownership is becoming a big deal in big data, with many people becoming uneasy about the amount of data companies have on them. As an individual, you don't own your data; the companies you interact with do. Sinister as this may seem (and it's only going to become an even bigger issue in the next few years), it's an important thing for companies to think about.

Make sure that, wherever possible, you own the data that's crucial to your business operations. This is easy if it's your own internal data, but it gets stickier with external data. If you can't own the data, then you need to make sure that you at least aren't going to lose access to it.

Managing the Data

The thing about big data is that sometimes it can be really, well, big. As such, you need to think hard about how you're going to store, manage and secure your data. If you think of data as a key operational asset (and you really should!), then it's important that you avoid storage and security problems. These can be hugely costly, both in terms of money and your company's image.

Finding the right data storage for you

Computer hard disks are still the storage medium of choice because, at higher storage capacities, they're often very cheap. For many small businesses, this may be all that's needed. Of course, you also need computers to house the hard disks, which in turn need a building with an electrical supply.

Distributed storage and cloud storage are two alternative ways for businesses to store their data without investing in expensive dedicated systems and data warehouses to put them in:

- ✔ **Distributed storage** is a method of using cheap, off-the-shelf components to rig up your own high-capacity storage solutions, which are then controlled by software that keeps track of where everything is and finds it for you when you need it.

- ✔ **Cloud storage** really just means that your data is stored remotely but is connected to the Internet and is accessible from anywhere you can get online. In current business usage it tends to mean that you're paying a third party such as Google or Amazon, or one of thousands of smaller, dedicated cloud storage operations, to store it for you online somewhere. So, you don't have to worry about physically holding onto the data yourself at all.

Ensuring data security

Security is a huge issue in big data (see Chapter 9 for more information on the data security layer). It's also pretty specialist, so it's a good idea to get some help from a data security advisor. Data needs to be secured just like any of your other business assets, like your property, your stock/ merchandise, your hardware and so on.

Most people think cloud storage is less secure, but that's not always the case. In-house storage systems are vulnerable too, sometimes more so. You need to weigh up the risks and the pros and cons of various storage methods. This is where expert help is invaluable.

Avoiding data breaches

Data breaches can lead to huge losses for businesses and there have been some very high profile breaches in recent years.

Hackers attacked American retailer Target's systems during the 2013 holiday season. Initially Target said that credit card and debit card information connected to 40 million customers had been stolen. Later it emerged that other personal data connected to between 70 million and 110 million people had also been taken. Approval has now been given for over 100 million victims of the data theft to claim compensation, which potentially leaves the retail giant facing claims of over $10 million.

A hundred million victims seems like a lot, but it's not even the biggest data breach in history. That dubious honour is currently held by Experian-owned data aggregation company, Court Ventures, who had 200 million records stolen! A slightly smaller but higher profile breach happened to eBay in 2014. Hackers accessed and stole millions of customer records by using employee details to log into eBay's computer systems. All users were forced to change their passwords in what turned out to be a public relations nightmare for the company.

Incidents like this – and the many other large-scale data thefts that frequently take place – show that even the biggest companies often fail to keep the promises they make about protecting data. It's something that businesses big and small absolutely must get right.

Big data analysis can do a lot of good – but it's reliant on people (and your customers) trusting that safeguards are in place to keep their personal information secure. It's therefore essential to protect your data against breaches.

Ways of securing your data and avoiding breaches include:

 ✔ Training your staff so they never give away secure information. This can be more of an issue in bigger companies where con artists can gain access to a system by pretending to be 'Joe Bloggs from IT' and asking unsuspecting employees for their login information. Regardless of the size of your company, your employees should never give their login information to anyone.

 ✔ Encrypting your data so that, even if it is breached, the hackers cannot decrypt the data.

 ✔ Have systems in place that detect and stop breaches while they're happening.

Establishing Infrastructure and Technology

Building a big data infrastructure is essential to data-based operations. This sounds terribly disruptive and expensive, but it really just means making sure you have the technology and systems in place to take advantage of data.

Assessing infrastructure needs

Your first step is to establish what infrastructure you already have and what you need to beef up or create from scratch. There's more detail on big data infrastructure needs in Chapter 9 and big data competencies in Chapter 8. Some companies build from the bottom up, their very existence made possible by big data.

When you're looking at using data to improve operations, there are three key areas of infrastructure to consider:

 ✔ Creating processes and tools to generate internal data and/or access external data. (I talk about sourcing and generating data in 'Sourcing the Required Data' earlier in the chapter.)

 ✔ Ensuring that you have the facilities and systems to store and secure that data. As data becomes increasingly important to your business, it's vital you protect that data – see 'Ensuring data security' and 'Avoiding data breaches' earlier in the chapter.

 ✔ Setting up the algorithms to automatically analyse that data and create the necessary outputs, whether that's dynamic maintenance schedules, better targeting of customers, dynamic pricing systems or anti-fraud measures.

If you've already been using data in your decision making (as discussed in Chapter 11), chances are you already have some of the technology and skills needed. If this is your first dip into big data, then you may need to start from the ground up, but thankfully there are lots of products and services available that make this process easier.

Creating the infrastructure

For most businesses, creating a big data infrastructure doesn't mean building a data warehouse and employing armies of analysts (unless you're a Facebook or Google that is). There are plenty of services out there that are aimed at small and medium businesses.

For example, HP made its big data analytics platform, Haven, available entirely through the cloud. This means that everything – from storage to analytics and reporting – is handled on HP systems that are leased to the customer via a monthly subscription – entirely eliminating infrastructure baggage and costs. This removes many of the hurdles associated with implementing big data. Competition with other similar services such as Amazon's Redshift and IBM's DashDB should keep subscription prices low and lead to a big increase in the number of businesses employing analytics to improve efficiency.

Testing and Piloting Operations

Once everything is in place, you need to test your systems to check everything is working as it should *before* you go live. It's no good finding out there are serious problems three months down the line and wasting valuable time, energy and money.

In general, there are two parts to testing your operations: infrastructure and algorithms.

Here are some things to consider when testing your infrastructure. If you're working with a data expert, they'll be able to identify additional items that are specific to your business. It's not an exhaustive list, but the idea is to get you thinking about what you should be checking:

- ✔ Is the data you need being collected/measured as you expected? Check that no data points are missing.
- ✔ Is the data being collected frequently enough?
- ✔ Is the data storage secure or are there any potential weak points?

You also need to check your algorithms and analysis:

✔ Are you seeing the results you expected? If not, you may need to tweak the algorithms.

✔ Is the analysis providing enough information for your needs? Do you need to add other variables or combine additional data to get a fuller picture?

Frustrating as it is to find that things aren't working as you expected, it's better to find out now so that you can make the necessary changes. If you do tweak things, even a little, repeat the testing process to check that your changes

✔ Worked

✔ Didn't introduce unintended consequences

Remember that you're in this for the long haul to systematically improve the way you do business, so take time to get this stage right.

Transforming Your Operations

You've tested and tested and you're ready to go. Now it's time to sit back and relax, right? Well, not exactly!

Running it

This isn't just a one-off project with a neat beginning, middle and end. Using data to improve your operations is an ongoing gig. As such, that means viewing data as just a part of your business from now on – as important as your product, your employees, your distribution channels, your customer service and so on. Like each of those areas, they need careful monitoring to check they're working the way you want.

You may start this journey in one area of your business, for example, using data to automatically optimise your delivery routes. Chances are, you'll soon identify other areas of your operations that could benefit from data. So, if you're using data in your deliveries, a logical next step might be to use sensors to monitor vehicle wear and tear, thereby automating vehicle maintenance schedules (servicing vehicles as they need it, instead of according to an arbitrary time frame). Once you have the infrastructure in place, it's relatively easy to extend the applications to other areas of the business.

Looking into the future

It's a good idea to review progress regularly to see how things are progressing. If you're not seeing the improvements you expected, you may need to tweak your algorithms or look at collecting additional data.

I'd say you should review progress at least every six months, although if your data is changing all the time, you'll need to revisit things on a much more frequent basis. Unfortunately, when it comes to reviewing progress, there's no exact timetable to follow – you'll need to work out what's right for your business, depending on the data you're using and what you're trying to achieve, through a process of trial and error.

The beauty (and I suppose the difficulty!) with big data is that things are changing all the time: new collection methods are being developed, new analytical platforms are hitting the market and storage options are increasing and getting cheaper all the time. Businesses are finding more and more ways to use data to improve how they do things and gain competitive advantage. As such, how you use data in five years' time, or even one years' time, may be different to how you start out using data now.

Knowing where to start is often the hardest part, which is why I place so much emphasis on building a big data strategy, which I talk about in Chapter 10. Once you have the foundations in place and you're starting to integrate data into your operations and decision making, it's important to keep that momentum going. In Chapter 13 I look at how to create a big data culture in your business. This means viewing data as an ongoing commitment to improving the way you do business, across all areas of the company and at all levels.

Chapter 13

Creating a Big Data Culture in Your Business

*B*y collecting and analysing data, you can transform your business in two ways: Firstly, you can use data to examine your existing business model and improve how you do business. This may involve understanding and targeting your customers better, increasing employee well-being, fighting fraud, or improving efficiency. Secondly, there is the possibility that data may eventually change your business model or lead to diversification. For example, if you manufacture products that have the ability to collect a lot of data, you may find that the data itself is more valuable than what it tells you about improving your business – enabling you to sell that data to interested parties or provide additional services to customers based on the data.

Most companies start with the aim of improving their current business model – and that is definitely what I recommend. Looking for new business models should be the cherry on top of the big data cake!

Using data to improve your business strategy and look for new commercial opportunities requires a bit of a mindset shift for most companies. This chapter is about building a culture of data-based decision making in your business and viewing data as an ongoing commitment to improvement, at all levels in the company.

Moving to Fact-Based Decision Making

Many business owners and managers make decisions based on gut feeling rather than hard facts. Sometimes this works out; sometimes it doesn't. The truth is, solid facts are far more likely to lead to consistently good business decisions – and that's where data can help.

In an age when everything can be measured, quantified and analysed to gain new insights, it makes sense to use that process to improve your decision making. Basing decisions on what data tells you helps you to implement your business strategy faster and more efficiently – whether you want to increase staff retention, cut wastage by ten per cent, increase efficiency in your manufacturing process or achieve some other meaningful objective.

Moving to fact-based decision making should be a company-wide effort; where possible, everyone in the business should be using data as the basis for what he does. This is no easy feat – it requires a change in organisational culture away from basing strategic decisions on gut feelings or assumptions to solid facts.

There are two key aspects of building a culture of data-based decision making:

- Get buy-in across the whole company.
- Emphasise the positive outcomes of using data to underpin company strategy.

Facilitating company-wide buy-in

Your ultimate aim should be to create a culture in which people naturally want to make better decisions and look to data to help them do so.

A good way to sow the seeds for improved decision making is to engage key personnel in developing your data strategy, which I talk about in Chapter 10. For example, if you want to use data to better understand and target your customers, then involve your marketing head from the outset. Or, if you want to improve manufacturing output and reduce unexpected downtime, then you'll need to get your manufacturing people on board. Encourage those key personnel to become data advocates, creating a trickle-down effect.

Another key step is to *use* the insights you gather; don't just sit on them. It sounds obvious, but, after identifying your strategic questions and analysing the data to get answers, you really need to act upon the insights found. What you do will encourage your people to shift their thinking towards evidence-based decision making. If you do nothing, you really can't expect the overall company culture to change. Use that valuable knowledge, demonstrate positive outcomes, and it will be much easier to get buy-in from others.

Here are my top tips for facilitating company-wide buy-in:

- There are naysayers in every company and negativity can be contagious! Identify sceptics or blockers and spend time engaging them. Use their pain points to show how fact-based decision making can make their jobs easier.

- Make it easy for people to understand data and pull out the key facts they need to make better decisions. Present insights in an attractive and engaging way. (There's more on this in Chapter 11.) It's of no use to anyone if key facts are buried in long, dull reports.

- With this in mind, build and maintain strong links between the people analysing the data, the people reporting the insights and the people making business decisions – knowing what the decision makers need to know makes it easier to present information to them.

- Be open about what you're measuring and why. For example, if you're focused on improving people management, then you're probably going to be measuring what your people do, when, for how long and so on. Understandably, this can make people nervous, with certain Big Brother overtones! Don't be sly about this. People are far more likely to be comfortable if you're honest from the outset and emphasise the positive goals (in this example, building a better workplace for everyone).

- Lead by example and use hard facts as the basis of everything you do. This is harder than it sounds; if you're a successful business owner or manager, good gut instincts have probably played a large part in where you are today! Make a commitment to changing the way you make decisions and your people will follow.

Following these pointers can help everyone in the business leverage data and move towards more fact-based decision making.

Emphasising the positive impact data can have

There's no denying it: change is difficult for many people and businesses. And implementing a cultural shift in an organisation, whether big or small, is not a quick and easy job. But it is crucial if your company is to make smarter decisions going forward. Focusing on the positive outcomes certainly helps smooth the way.

Broadcast positive goals and outcomes load and clear. If data has helped reduce wastage by ten per cent, then you should be shouting about that success. If you're only at the beginning of your data journey, share examples from similar companies. Seeing how other people have changed their decision-making processes can provide a helpful nudge in the right direction.

Focusing on the good that big data can bring, either with insights from your own business or examples from elsewhere, lays the foundations for fact-based decision making.

Allowing Data to Influence Strategy

Even after you answer your strategic questions (see Chapter 11), the fun doesn't stop there (or it doesn't have to). Data can help support ongoing business practices, challenge how you do things in your company, and influence all areas of your business strategy.

You can use data in your business in literally millions of ways, but here I focus on four key examples: managing talent, boosting employee satisfaction, increasing operational efficiency and optimising business processes. These examples give you an idea of how data can help improve decision making and change your organisational culture for the better.

Managing talent

Big data is now filtering through into human resource processes. Largely, this falls into two camps: finding the best talent and hanging on to that talent!

Recruitment has traditionally been a somewhat hit-and-miss affair; statistics show that almost half of appointments end up as failures within 18 months. That shouldn't be surprising; personalities are often the hardest things to accurately convey and interpret in an interview and around 90 per cent of appointment failures are down to attitudinal reasons.

Perhaps more surprising is that companies continue to make hiring decisions (with all the financial liabilities that they entail) based on an often brief interview and a cursory look at a CV. Much of the time the decision is based on an interviewer's gut feeling. Considering that a large proportion (40 per cent to 60 per cent by most estimates) of a company's revenue goes on staff salaries, it makes sense to be a bit more strategic about the recruitment process and base decisions on data rather than instinct.

Taking a more scientific approach to appointing staff enables you to find more suitable people who stay happy and on the job for longer.

Mining social networks for insights

Many companies are already using Google, Facebook and Twitter to search a potential new hire's name to make sure there's nothing lurking in the woodwork.

An American pizza company recently fired a woman for her Twitter comments the day before she was due to start after she indicated in some very strong language that she thought it was a pretty lame job, and she wasn't exactly looking forward to starting. In normal circumstances though, anything that a person wants hidden is unlikely to appear on his Facebook or Twitter feeds, so you need to look a little deeper.

Services are emerging that allow employers to assess a candidate's suitability using more subtle indicators. As well as semantic analysis of the language they use, patterns of behaviour (such as enthusiasm for subjects related to the job) can be monitored and compared against patterns shown by previously successful employees.

Using data to improve recruitment decisions

Tools such as Cornerstone (www.cornerstoneondemand.com) and TalentBin (www.talentbin.com) allow employers to crunch data in more ways than ever to find the right candidate for the right position. Some companies have taken it even further. For example, hotel chain Marriott created its own Farmville-style game that simulated the running of a hotel to test the abilities of potential candidates. The experiment was reportedly not a huge success (the game was apparently rather boring), but it demonstrates new ways of thinking that companies are applying to decision making.

Using data analysis to find patterns and correlations between personality traits, behaviour and capabilities that fit with particular roles means you can get more of the right people in the right jobs. In turn, this increases productivity, employee engagement and happiness – and that's got to be a good thing for everyone.

A bank was able to cut staff costs in one area by half simply by analysing the performance of staff recruited from different universities. The bank assumed its best-performing people would be those with excellent degrees from the top-rated universities in the country. Data analytics proved this assumption wrong. It turned out that candidates from non-prestige universities outperformed the top university candidates. This insight helped the bank recruit the best talent for it – and for less money.

Another often-cited example is that of office equipment manufacturer Xerox. An analytics firm was asked to monitor staff performance and then come up with a profile of an ideal candidate for its call centres. Among the surprising findings was that previous call centre experience was no indicator of success, and that candidates with criminal records often performed better than those without. The experiment led to a 20 per cent reduction in staff turnover.

If you're struggling to wean your people off gut-based recruitment decisions, let data help you make the case. Emphasise the proportion of revenue your company spends on staff wages each year and analyse staff turnover rates (the UK average is around 15 per cent a year, although it varies wildly across industries). The results may indicate a strong need to apply data to your recruitment strategies.

Most employers still rely on gut instinct to some degree – and that's not necessarily a bad thing. The best decisions are those that are informed by data but interpreted through experience and common sense. There will always be a need for the human touch when it comes to recruiting. But, as in many other areas of business, data is certainly helping to take the guess work out of recruitment.

Boosting employee satisfaction

Companies now have more data than ever on their employees and more tools and technology with which to analyse this data. As well as optimising talent acquisition, big data tools can help companies measure and improve company culture, staff engagement and overall employee satisfaction.

Google has regularly been voted the best company in America to work for – its staff get free meals, generous paid holidays, access to nap pods for power napping during the day and are even encouraged to grow fruit and vegetables at work. And, despite their 'don't be evil' motto, Google top brass hasn't done all this simply because they are lovely people. Like everything they do, their decisions were based squarely on data – and in this case, the data showed that treating staff well would increase employee satisfaction.

Employers have been using analytics for some time now to understand what makes their staff tick, using metrics such as staff engagement to understand what drives productivity and innovation in the workplace. The humble employee survey is a precursor of this.

Implications are also beginning to be realised for health, safety and well-being at work. Obviously, when people become ill at work or are absent for long periods of time, it's stressful for the individual involved, but it's also detrimental to the business and the people left picking up the extra workload. Personal analytics and health monitoring can change all that and give you a real-time insight into health and well-being. Hitachi's Business Microscope service enables companies to fit its staff with Radio Frequency Identification (RFID) tags that track their movements around the workplace and even monitor sound waves to identify how stressed or relaxed they are when they speak.

People who work in potentially dangerous or stressful environments are being measured to monitor their fatigue and stress levels so that employers can pull them off jobs before they get too tired and potentially cause an accident.

Data can provide a wealth of insights in terms of productivity, and even sales. In one trial, a retailer was able to increase sales by 15 per cent after it noticed that the presence of a member of staff in certain areas of the store had a high impact on products sold, while in other areas, staff presence had very little effect. In a seated office environment, technology can record how long employees spend at their desks, how much time they spend interacting with other staff, whom they talk to, the distance they stand from each other during conversations and the enthusiasm with which they contribute to meetings.

One of my clients uses analytics tools to scan and analyse the content of emails sent by staff as well as the social media posts they make on Facebook or Twitter. This allows the client to accurately understand the levels of staff engagement, and it no longer needs the traditional staff surveys, which were expensive, time-consuming and less accurate.

Big Brother approaches may sound suitably Orwellian and difficult to get staff to engage with. But how well they're received by staff depends very much on the way they're used. If used as a disciplinary tool focused on the behaviour of individuals, they will undoubtedly lead to resentment. But, when used as a way to gain an overview of the company as a whole and how people interact to get the job done, you'll get more buy-in – and far more useful insights. At the end of the day, people are far less likely to complain if the insights generated benefit them, whether it be nap pods or more annual leave!

Increasing operational efficiency

Operational efficiency can be defined as delivering products or services in the most efficient and cost-effective way possible. Often operational decisions are based on experience or 'the way things have always been done'. But data and technology have a lot to offer in terms of making your business as efficient as possible.

For a business, the ability to have its production, stock control, distribution and security systems all connected and talking to each other means greater efficiency and less waste.

The efficiency of every machine – and human for that matter – can be recorded so companies know what's working and can make improvements where they're needed. The possibilities are endless; it's about choosing what's best (and what's possible) for your business.

Big data analytics also help machines and devices become smarter and more autonomous (for more on sensor data, machine data and the Internet of Things, see Chapter 5). Manufacturers are monitoring minute vibration data from their equipment, which changes slightly as it wears down, to predict the optimal time to replace or maintain parts. Doing this too soon wastes money; doing it too late can trigger a failure and expensive work stoppage.

Operational efficiency is arguably one of the areas where it's easiest to convince people of the benefits of fact-based decision making. Hard facts related to performance, maintenance and the financial savings that come from greater efficiency take the guess work out of decision making. As such, this might be a good starting point for your business, particularly if you're in manufacturing or distribution of any kind.

Optimising business processes

Ideally, your people will look to data to improve all aspects of business decision making in all areas of the company. This includes everything from stock management to customer relationships to security.

Many retail companies are already using algorithms to understand what's trending in social media and what competitors are charging in real time. Algorithms are also great for recommending other products a customer might like – a strategy basically pioneered by Amazon and used to great effect.

I have worked with a number of hotel chains that want to move away from the traditional in-house surveys, which are costly and questionably accurate, to using social media to analyse what people are saying and posting about the hotel. This way, hotel managers can better understand their customers and improve their service. By running and using sentiment analysis (see Chapter 5) on Facebook posts, tweets and other social media sites and reviews on Trip Advisor, in addition to existing data, hotels are getting far more reliable information than they would from a survey.

Stock management is another area with enormous potential, using data from social media, web search trends and weather data, for example, to build predictive models for what your customers will want and when. One often-cited example is the supermarket chain Walmart that discovered a surprising correlation between hurricane warnings and sales of Pop-Tarts. Apparently, in a hurricane, people just want to hunker down and eat Pop-Tarts. Perhaps the UK equivalent is huge sales of charcoal, sausages and hot buns on the first vaguely warm day of the year – usually in April and usually when the temperature is only around 15 degrees Celsius (around 60 degrees Fahrenheit)!

It's easy to get caught up in fun insights like the Pop-Tart analogy, because data has the ability to tell you some mind-boggling things. The trick is to focus on what benefits your business's decision making and what you can actually act upon. For example, if you're a retailer that's already sold your shelf space to specific companies and guaranteeing space for particular products, then knowing that sales of a certain bottle of wine increase on Tuesday evenings isn't going to help you much beyond knowing to stock up on Tuesday and re-stock on Wednesday morning. You can't devote more space to that product on Tuesdays because the shelf space is allocated elsewhere. So, while it's an interesting insight, it's not necessarily useful in terms of your business strategy.

One particular business process seeing a lot of big data analytics is *supply chain* or *delivery route optimisation*. Here, GPS and radio frequency identification sensors are used to track goods or delivery vehicles and optimise routes by integrating live traffic data. For instance, if a delivery driver has an optimised delivery schedule, that schedule interacts in real time with weather data and traffic data so that if there is a traffic jam, accident or reports of delivery-impacting weather such as snow or storms, the schedule automatically calibrates an alternate route. Optimising this business process can also include delivery companies putting sensors on pallets and handheld devices that record delivery and monitor where drivers are, while also monitoring the engines of the delivery vehicles to create dynamic servicing schedules.

Technology can also improve business security and reduce fraud, with the potential for huge financial savings. In fact, big data is already applied heavily in improving business security through CCTV (closed-circuit television) video footage analytics. Credit card and insurance companies are already using data to prevent fraud. Insurance companies, for example, are using big data algorithms to check for fraudulent claims as well as anomalies in policy applications. Algorithms can now take into account the speed at which you complete a claim or application form – to spot those completed by machines versus people – as well as whether applicants have gone back and changed their initial application to reduce premiums by maybe not admitting a recent claim or decreasing their annual mileage.

How far you go in these processes is up to you. Some of much of it may not be relevant or feasible for your business at this time, which is fine. This process is not about becoming an all-singing-all-dancing data company overnight; it's simply about improving overall decision making and becoming more analytical in how your business operates.

How Uber uses big data – A practical case study

Uber is an example of a company that based its entire business model on big data, with data informing every part of the service it offers to customers.

Uber is a smartphone-app-based taxi booking service that connects users who need to get somewhere with drivers willing to give them a ride. The service has been hugely controversial, due to regular taxi drivers claiming that it's destroying their livelihoods and concerns over the lack of regulation of the company's drivers. This hasn't stopped it from also being hugely successful – since being launched in San Francisco in 2009, the service has been expanded to many major cities on every continent except for Antarctica.

The business is rooted firmly in big data, and leveraging this data in a more effective way than traditional taxi firms have has played a huge part in its success. Uber's entire business model is based on the very big data principle of crowdsourcing. Anyone with a qualified car who's willing to help someone get to where he wants to go can offer to get him there. Uber holds a vast database of drivers in all of the cities it covers, so when you ask for a ride, it can instantly match you with the most suitable drivers.

Fares are calculated automatically using GPS, street data and the company's own algorithms that make adjustments based on the time that the journey is likely to take. This is a crucial difference from regular taxi services because customers are charged for the time the journey takes, not the distance covered.

These algorithms monitor traffic conditions and journey times in real time, meaning prices can be adjusted as demand for rides changes, and traffic conditions mean journeys are likely to take longer. This encourages more drivers to get behind the wheel when they're needed – and stay at home when demand is low. The

company has applied for a patent on this method of big data-informed pricing, which it calls *surge pricing*.

This is an implementation of *dynamic pricing* – similar to that used by hotel chains and airlines to adjust price to meet demand – although rather than simply increasing prices at weekends or during public holidays, it uses predictive modelling to estimate demand in real time.

The service also relies on a detailed rating system – users can rate drivers, and vice versa – to build up trust and allow both parties to make informed decisions about whom they want to share a car with. Drivers in particular have to be very careful to keep their standards high. They have another metric to worry about, too – their *acceptance rate* (the number of jobs they accept versus those they decline). Drivers were told they should aim to keep this above 80 per cent in order to provide a consistently available service to passengers.

Uber will have to overcome legal hurdles – the service is currently banned in a handful of jurisdictions including Brussels and parts of India – and is receiving intense scrutiny in many other parts of the world. Several court cases are underway in the US regarding the company's compliance with regulatory procedures. If regulatory pressures do not kill it, then it could revolutionise the way you travel around crowded cities – there are certainly environmental as well as economic reasons why this would be a good thing.

Uber is not alone – it has competitors offering similar services on a (so far) smaller scale, and competition among these upstarts is going to be fierce. You can expect the winners to be those who make the best use of the data available to improve the service they provide to customers.

Identifying New or Additional Business Models

One way that big data can transform your business is by helping to identify new or additional business models. Thanks to the massive explosion in data available and our increasing ability to analyse that data, some companies have radically changed their commercial models and moved into new territory. For some, data is changing the very nature of their business. For an example of a company that's based its entire business model on big data, check out the sidebar 'How Uber uses big data - A practical case study'.

Applying data to improving existing operations should be your primary focus, and this is where your strategic questions come into play (I discuss them in Chapter 11). However, once you have identified and answered your strategic questions, you may find that the data also points to interesting new opportunities – something that may take your business in a new direction.

The key is to stay open to new opportunities that the data may shine a light on, whatever they may be. This could mean that the data exposes new strategic questions that you hadn't thought of before and will want to explore in future. It could mean discovering opportunities for additional revenue streams in your existing business model. Or, in some cases, it may expose a completely new business model.

This may sound so exciting that you get tempted to skip ahead to discovering what the data may tell you, without bothering with strategic questions. Don't fall into this trap. It's never a good idea to start with the data and see what it tells you; always start with strategic questions. Look at what *else* the data might tell you only after you have answered these questions.

What opportunities exist depend very much on your company and industry, but here are a few quick tips to help you identify opportunities for new business models in your data:

- Look for patterns in the data that point to new product ideas, perhaps in web trends or social media data.

- In many cases, the use of big data can change a business model from a classic manufacturing model to a service model. Rolls-Royce no longer sells its engines to airlines – it now sells flying hours. As a company, it remains responsible for the engine (its product) and monitors it remotely. In the same way, a fridge manufacturer could sell cooling hours and a bicycle manufacturer could sell miles cycled.

✔ If you have a large amount of data, this may prove a valuable revenue stream in itself. For example, if you manufacture a product with sensors, the user data generated from those products may help your customers make efficiency savings – valuable information that many customers would be happy to pay for.

Ultimately, access to data and the ability to analyse it allows you to review evidence and make better decisions based on fact, not assumption or gut feeling. With data at the heart of everything your company does and every key decision you make, you're in a position to apply insights for the better across the board.

It's clear that creating a big data culture in your company isn't an overnight job. It takes time and dedication to get company-wide buy-in, and it requires a shift in mindset away from gut-based decisions to data-based decisions. But the result is a smart, efficient company that continuously looks to improve the way it does business, and is able to spot and act upon new opportunities when they crop up.

How General Electric is transforming its business with big data

GE is transforming its business thanks to big data, evolving from its traditional manufacturing roots to data services.

GE makes products for a range of industries, including aviation, rail, healthcare, electrical distribution, lighting, energy, oil and gas. Its products now contain hundreds of sensors that collect data, and all that data is analysed to identify patterns that could be relevant to its clients.

So, using that data and insights gathered, GE now provides additional services for the clients that own GE machinery. These services deliver insights that help the clients improve real-time efficiency and minimize downtown caused by failures. This is must-have information for the clients concerned as unexpected downtime is enormously costly. And improvements in efficiency have the potential to save companies a fortune. For example, GE estimates that just a one per cent improvement in efficiency across the key sectors it sells to could lead to combined savings of $300 billion.

GE is investing heavily in its data business; it invested $1 billion since 2012 in a state-of-the-art analytics and software centre. It is paying off too; the additional, data-related servicing now accounts for one-third of GE's business.

Part V
The Part of Tens

You can find a bonus Part of Tens chapter, Ten Big Data Predictions for the Future, at www.dummies.com/extras/bigdataforsmallbusiness.

In this part . . .

- ✔ Avoid costly and time-consuming big data pitfalls in your business.
- ✔ Access key big data sources without spending a penny.
- ✔ Find out about the best big data collection tools for small businesses.

Chapter 14

Ten Biggest Big Data Mistakes to Avoid

In This Chapter

▶ Understanding the main big data blunders

▶ Knowing how to dodge them

▶ Making your big data journey as smooth as possible

As with any exciting new technology or business process, there is a danger of getting carried away, making costly errors or just getting so overwhelmed by the possibilities that you simply don't know where to start. This chapter is about understanding the main big data mistakes that businesses often make – and just as importantly, how to avoid them.

Collecting Data on Everything

Some companies aim to collect as much data as possible, thinking that the more data they have, the more their business will benefit. That may be fine for big corporations like Google and Facebook that have the manpower and resources to collect, manage and analyse vast amounts of data. For the majority of businesses though, there is simply no point trying to collect everything – it's stressful, expensive and ultimately unhelpful.

I'd argue that your focus should be as narrow as possible, not as wide as possible! The aim is to be really clear and specific about what data you need. Focus on finding the exact data that will benefit your business. This is where your strategy comes in (for more information on creating a big data strategy, see Chapter 10). You need to know what your goals are and what questions you want answered. Only then can you focus on collecting the data that will help you answer those questions.

Instead of collecting everything, collect X and Y to answer question Z.

Collecting Only the Fashionable Data

There are trends and fashions in data just as there are in all walks of life. Much like kipper ties and crimped hair, structured data may be seen as deeply unfashionable (see Chapters 4 and 5 for different data types). These days all the cool kids want unstructured data – and male clutch bags, apparently. But, when it comes to data, don't get caught up in what's hot or what's not – because the most fashionable data may not be the most helpful data for your business.

No type of data is inherently better or more useful than any other type of data. Focus on finding the best data for your business: the data that will answer your strategic questions and ultimately help you improve your business.

Going Straight to External Unstructured Big Data

Unstructured data is the rock star of the data world while structured data is often seen as old-fashioned. You also have a choice between internal data that you've already collected (or can collect easily) and external data. Heading straight for external unstructured data can be a costly mistake.

Unstructured data is incredibly powerful stuff, but don't focus entirely on external unstructured data at the expense of internal structured data. Starting with existing internal data is often easier, if less exciting. However, most businesses need a combination of datasets to answer their strategic questions.

Combining unstructured data with more traditional structured data often has real value – some of the best insights can be gained this way.

Getting Overwhelmed by the Volume of Existing Data

The sheer volume of data being generated each day is staggering. Half a billion tweets will be sent today, and in the time it took you to read this sentence, 20 million emails were sent!

It's easy to get lost in a sea of data. And, taking the first steps into big data can be daunting when you consider what the big guys like Amazon are doing on a daily basis. The truth is, the sheer array of data out there and what the big companies are up to doesn't really matter to your business. What matters is focusing on the data that will help answer your strategic questions, inform your decision making and transform your business.

Focusing on your SMART questions (see Chapter 11) and your big data strategy (see Chapter 10) will help you forget the hype and focus on where you want to be and how big data can help you get there.

Ignoring Small Data

I always advise my clients to think of SMART data, not big data (more on this in Chapter 11) because big may not necessarily help you achieve your business goals. Existing internal data, like transaction records, can provide a wealth of information such as the busiest time of day for sales. You may wish to combine your existing small data with other big data sources, like social media, and that's fine – I'd encourage that. The key is to not overlook the valuable small data you already have.

Small data can be just as helpful as big data and sometimes more so. The right solution for your business may in fact be a combination of big and small data.

Throwing Money at the Problem

Worldwide, in 2015, companies were expected to spend £80 billion on products and services related to big data analysis. There's big money in big data.

Although you undoubtedly need to invest some funds (or, at the very least, some time) into your big data efforts, throwing a ton of money at it and expecting results isn't the best way forward.

Spending big money is unlikely to yield results if you don't have a clear strategy at the outset. It's far better to have clear goals and questions and target your big data activities accordingly.

In fact, a lot of the software and analytics tools for big data analysis are available in the public domain and are free to use. And you don't need huge computing power or specialist in-house equipment. For example, Hadoop (see Chapter 9) is designed to run on cheap, commonly available hardware – making it accessible for organisations of any size.

Not Matching Big Data to Your Strategic Questions

I keep coming back to strategy, and for good reason. Too often I see big data being done in an ad-hoc, sporadic way. Without an underlying strategy, you may occasionally get lucky and stumble across a gem of insight. But with strategic questions in place, and by always bringing your activity back to those questions, insights will pop up with far more predictable regularity.

For example, do you want to increase sales? Or increase customer satisfaction? Or improve product quality? Your strategic questions affect the kind of data you need and how that data needs to be analysed. So, be very clear about what you're trying to find out from the start. In my experience, these questions are just as important as the answers themselves!

At each stage of the process, check to ensure that you're still on the path to answering those questions and not being led off on a tangent.

Not Involving the Right People in Your Big Data Strategy

Who's involved in creating your big data strategy depends on what you're looking to achieve. If you're looking to increase sales, then bringing your marketing and sales colleagues on board is an excellent idea. If you're looking to improve employee satisfaction and retention, then involving your human resources (HR) person or HR team is a smart move. Big data can throw up some incredible insights for improving your business; getting the right team members on board from the start is key to engaging them in the transformation process.

You also need to engage any key decision makers in your business. Ultimately, it will be their job (along with you) to take those insights and make the right decisions for the business – getting their buy-in and enthusiasm from the start makes the whole process run more smoothly.

It's likely you will also want to bring in some external help, such as a big data consultant, to help you formulate your strategy. This is a great idea, but remember that when it comes to your business objectives, you're the expert.

Collecting the Data and Not Analysing It

There are four Vs of big data: volume, velocity, variety and veracity (see Chapter 2). Analytics provides the fifth V: value. Analysing the data provides all the valuable insights that help you achieve your business goals.

The data itself is meaningless, no matter how much you have – it needs to be converted into insights that answer your key strategic questions.

The type of analysis you do really depends on the type of data you have and what you're looking for. See Chapter 9 for more information on analysing data.

Analysing the Data but Not Reporting the Results in a User-friendly Way

Reporting may not be as sexy as data analytics, but it's very important. You need to report insights in a way that people in the business can easily understand. If they can't identify or understand the key insights, they won't be able to make the right decisions (or get on board with your decisions) to improve the business.

Before NASA launched the Challenger Space Shuttle, some of the engineers at base had serious concerns about one of the components. The engineers gave detailed reports showing their findings and assumed that the launch would be abandoned. Unfortunately, the important findings were buried deep within detailed, lengthy reports and the key messages weren't clear to those making the decisions. As a result, the launch went ahead – with devastating consequences when the shuttle exploded.

Follow this advice for reporting your results in a user-friendly way:

- ✔ Do think about who the information is for and target it accordingly.
- ✔ Do link your results to your strategy. Show how the findings relate to your strategic questions.
- ✔ Do make your findings as easy to understand as possible. Visualise your data by using colour, photographs, charts and graphics to draw out the key insights.
- ✔ Do not bury key information in long reports.

Chapter 15

Ten Free Big Data Sources

In This Chapter

▶ Knowing where to look for free data

▶ Understanding what sort of data you can get your hands on

▶ Making the most of free data in your business

Data is everywhere – and a lot of it is freely available. These days companies don't necessarily have to build their own massive data repositories before starting with big data analytics. Many big companies and governments have made large amounts of information available in the public domain, meaning there's a wealth of data out there accessible to anyone and everyone.

Any company, from big blue chip corporations to the tiniest start-up, can now leverage more data than ever before. Many of my clients ask me for the top free sources they could use in their big data endeavour. Here's my rundown of some of the best free big data sources available today.

Data.gov (US Government Data)

In 2013, the US government pledged to make all government data available freely online. This site is the result of that pledge, and it's an absolute treasure trove of information. It acts as a portal to all sorts of government data on everything from climate to crime rates. You can use it for research purposes, or it can serve as a useful tool for developing web and mobile applications.

A security firm could use the portal to look up crime statistics, helping to narrow its focus on a particular area or type of service (linked to a rise in home invasions or burglaries, for instance). Or, if a company were looking to expand and set up a new factory or distribution centre, it could check out unemployment statistics to find a location where there's likely to be a large number of available (and keen) candidates.

Head to www.data.gov to find out more.

US Census Bureau

This site provides a mountain of information on the lives of US citizens covering population data, geographic data and education. You can get statistics from multiple surveys and there are some cool gizmos like data visualisations and interactive maps to make the information more digestible.

Demographic data like this can be a useful indicator of trends, which is especially helpful if you're developing a new product or service. It can also help you target products or services to particular local demographics. For example, a concentration of young families in a particular area would be of interest to someone looking for a place to set up a nursery or kindergarten.

To access the data, visit `www.census.gov/data.html`.

European Union Open Data Portal

The European version of the US census data, this site offers census data from European Union institutions. You can browse datasets by subject (such as industry, finance, and employment) or you can search for specific datasets using keywords.

Find out more at `www.open-data.europa.eu/en/data`.

Data.gov.uk

This is rather like the US government portal but specifically for the UK. Here you can find open data from the UK government, covering everything from census data to traffic information to energy consumption data. It also houses the British National Bibliography, which has metadata on all UK books and publications since 1950.

As well as published books, the British National Bibliography provides information on forthcoming books. This could be helpful to an independent bookstore looking to schedule events and promotions for the months ahead. If it were to combine that information with insights from local census data, it could predict which titles might be most valuable or appealing to the local clientele.

Visit `www.data.gov.uk` to access the data. You can submit data requests if you can't find what you're looking for.

HealthData.gov

Official site of the Health Data Initiative, here you can find US healthcare data stretching back 125 years. Information available includes claim-level Medicare data, population statistics, clinical care provider quality information, Food and Drug Administration recall data, databases of the latest medical and scientific knowledge, and much more.

This data could help identify trends in healthcare and would be extremely valuable for any company looking to develop health-related products or services in the US market. For example, if your company specialises in products related to quitting smoking, then the statistics and medical data will be a big help in product development.

You can find the data at `www.healthdata.gov`.

Google Trends

This is a very powerful and versatile tool, providing statistics on search volume (as a proportion of total searches) for any given term since 2004. You can see search popularity for certain phrases or words and how it has changed over time, either on a yearly basis or by drilling down to specific weeks (say, if you wanted to see how an event affected the popularity of a given search term). Given that there are 3.5 billion Google searches every day, the amount of data available is vast! You can narrow the results by geographic location, making sure you get the information most relevant to your business.

Google Trends can be used to understand trends in your industry, what is popular right now and what is becoming more popular (or less popular). It's a great way of gauging consumer interest.

To get started with Google Trends, visit `www.google.com/trends/explore`.

Facebook Graph

Although some of the information on users' Facebook profiles is private (depending on how savvy they are with their settings), a lot of information isn't private. Facebook has developed the Graph API (Application Program Interface) as a way of querying the huge amount of information its users share with the world. Even if you have your privacy settings cranked up to the highest level (which many people don't bother to do), Facebook can still provide information to companies about what you're saying – just not that you're the one saying it.

Facebook Graph provides lots of useful information for free, but you need to pay for access to the most detailed information. It's worth checking out the free access in the first instance, particularly if you're interested in monitoring consumer trends.

Find out more at `https://developers.facebook.com/docs/graph-api`.

Weather Data Sources

You can find a huge collection of environmental, meteorological and climate datasets from the US National Climatic Data Center, the world's largest archive of weather data. UK weather data from the Met Office is available through the `www.data.gov.uk` portal.

Weather data can be used in a number of ways, from estimating customer numbers to deciding how many sausages and hot dog buns to stock on a given weekend.

A farm and petting zoo was having trouble estimating visitor numbers and managing staffing levels. It used standard weather forecasts but with limited success and was frequently caught out by having too many or too few staff on hand. By using historical attendance data it already had in-house combined with detailed local climatic data, it was able to predict visitor numbers and plan staffing levels much more accurately. It was also able to better manage stock and increase sales in the on-site farm shop by targeting the products that best matched the weather.

Climatic data for the US is available at `www.ncdc.noaa.gov/data-access/quick-links#loc-clim`; go to `https://data.gov.uk` for UK data.

Federal Reserve Economic Data

Federal Reserve Economic Data (FRED to its friends) is a huge repository of data from the Federal Reserve and a number of government agencies, such as the Bureau of Labor Statistics. Datasets include financial data, business data, consumer price indices and employment and population data. Information from FRED is widely used, widely reported and plays a big role in the financial markets around the world. You can view the datasets in text or graph format and even download it to import into spreadsheets.

FRED's data can show where the overall business climate is going, which industries are booming, and which aren't, helping you make better long-term business decisions. For example, if you're considering expanding or investing in new infrastructure, then a strong economy may indicate it's a good time to go ahead. However, if the economy is on the slide, then it might be a good time to reduce business costs.

Head to `https://research.stlouisfed.org` to access the data.

Google Maps

Encompassing its interactive maps, satellite images and Street View, Google Maps is a huge time-saver for many businesses. The range of organisations using this data is huge – from small businesses right up to government agencies.

For instance, a local government planning office could review planning applications using Google Maps rather than having to make a physical visit to the site. Even a local window cleaner could use Street View when quoting for services, creating more accurate quotes quickly and efficiently.

Visit `www.maps.google.com` to get started.

Chapter 16

Ten Key Big Data Collection Tools

*T*he sheer volume of data available can be daunting – and so can the number of big data products, tools and platforms out there to help you collect and analyse data. What's the best way to collect data and how are other businesses going about things? In this chapter I identify my top tools for gathering big data and give helpful examples of how other businesses and organisations use these tools.

Keep in mind that you may well need a combination of tools to answer your strategic questions (I talk about those in Chapter 11). For example, when working with clients, I often find the most useful insights come from combining internal data (like transaction data) with external data (such as Twitter posts). A similar approach may work for you.

Smartphone GPS Sensor

GPS sensors track where you are by using satellite information. Many people use their phones to find things of interest near them or to get directions to a particular location, but GPS can do so much more. Your smartphone is constantly collecting data on where you are, and this information can be incredibly valuable for businesses.

If local is a key part of your business, you could develop a customer app that uses GPS data. For example, if you run a food delivery service, you could develop a customer app and use the GPS data on where customers are located. This could be useful if you specifically wanted to target customers within a ten-mile radius or want to send out a promotional offer and skip customers out of the area or on holiday.

Smartphone Accelerometer Sensor

This is the sensor that measures how fast the phone is travelling, which is particularly helpful for companies in which vehicles or transport play a big role. Today, some insurance companies are using these sensors to tell how fast customers drive so they can offer dynamic premiums (essentially, cheaper premiums for better drivers). A taxi firm or delivery company could use these sensors to see how well drivers are doing, helping them to improve driver performance, make financial savings and improve customer experience.

You can either develop your own app or make use of the many existing apps available.

Accelerometer data has been cleverly used by the City of Boston, which created an app to detect potholes. Bostonians were asked to download the app to their smartphone which would then run in the background as residents went about their daily lives. As residents drove around the city, the accelerometer in their phone would measure how fast they were travelling and when they slowed down or braked. A little algorithm was then applied to this data to identify potential potholes – because when you drive along a road and see a pothole, you usually slow down or swerve to avoid it and then speed up again. (Even if you didn't see it and slow down in time and end up driving right over the pothole, the sensor in your smartphone would detect the bump.) The algorithm identified potential potholes from the smartphone data, giving city officials a real-time picture of the condition of the city's streets. Needless to say, this was a much more efficient and cost-effective system than the old one, which involved someone physically driving down all the roads in the city twice a year!

Telematics System

Telematics is a combination of telecommunications and informatics, and it involves the collection and transmission of data from vehicles. It's a bit like a smartphone accelerometer sensor (see the preceding section) but is built into vehicles instead of smartphones. Telematics systems also tend to provide more detailed information than accelerometer systems.

Police forces are using telematics systems to monitor how officers drive their vehicles. Not only does the information collected help to improve driver education and performance, it can also help reduce emissions and tyre degradation and improve vehicle maintenance.

Businesses that might benefit from a system like this include bus companies, taxi firms, and haulage companies. Think of it as a more modern and accurate version of a 'How's my driving?' banner on the back of a truck! The information you find out can improve staff training and reduce costs overall.

Wi-Fi Signals

Wi-Fi signals are an excellent source of data, particularly for retail businesses. Nowadays, almost everyone has a smartphone and smartphones give out signals when the Wi-Fi option is switched on (because the phone is constantly scanning for local Wi-Fi networks).

Wi-Fi signals can monitor how many people pass your store, how many people stop and look in your window and how many people then choose to come inside. This technology is now incredibly cheap and easy to implement and it's an accessible option for retailers of all sizes.

Retailers are using these signals to varying levels of sophistication. Some track how customers physically move around a store and what they stop to look at. Some use personal information (for instance, if you've downloaded a store app or given your details to access the in-store Wi-Fi) to target promotions and make recommendations while you're in the store. As an example, iBeacons provide a way of communicating with smartphones in the store, alerting customers to products nearby.

Increasingly, Wi-Fi data will be combined with video data and facial recognition software to identify a shopper's age and gender, even her exact identity.

LinkedIn

With 300 million registered users, LinkedIn is one of the most popular social media sites in the world (currently ranked third). It's a great resource for professionals and businesses alike, from childminders to Fortune 500 companies.

Your business can use LinkedIn to find talent and make connections. If you operate in a niche field, it's a great way to find people with very specific skills. Or, if you're considering applications from candidates, you can check out their profiles, connections and recommendations before narrowing down the pile and selecting who gets invited for an interview.

Facebook

Currently the biggest social media site in the world, Facebook is likely to be your first stop for social media big data. Behind the cat pictures and humblebrag status updates is a vast amount of data on customer behaviour. Facebook offers incredibly useful breakdowns of customer information and analyses of all the data it has. Some of this you need to purchase, but plenty is available for free.

Facebook is scarily accurate when it comes to insights into peoples' behaviour. In fact, it can now predict very accurately when someone is about to change her status from 'single' to 'in a relationship' (presumably, the other way around too!).

Facebook data encompasses text data, photo data, video data, and user Likes. All this data can be analysed and used to your business's advantage – whether you want to target a promotion or understand how many pregnant women live in a certain area.

Twitter

Twitter is the second most popular social media site and, unlike Facebook, there are no privacy settings, which makes it very interesting to businesses.

Every time a Twitter user mentions a company or product, that information is visible to everyone, including the company. Even if a product isn't mentioned explicitly in the text of the tweet, companies can detect when their product features in a photo. Examples of this might include a drinks company finding pictures of people drinking its product, restaurants finding pictures taken in their restaurant and fashion houses finding out who is wearing their clothes.

Carrying out sentiment text analysis (which I talk about in Chapter 5) is a good way to tell how your business or product is doing in the Twitterverse. You can gain insights into the popularity of a product or service, understand customer satisfaction and deal with any problems swiftly.

In another example of Twitter analysis, researchers were able to predict which women were most at risk of developing postnatal depression. They analysed Twitter posts, searching for verbal clues in the weeks leading up to the birth. They found that negative language and words hinting at unhappiness, as well as an increased use of the word *I*, indicated an increased chance of developing postnatal depression. Sentiment analysis can tell a lot about users' feelings, opinions and experiences without having to trawl through individual tweets one at a time.

Machine Sensors

This includes any sensor on anything – whether it is a shop door or a tennis racquet. By incorporating sensors into your business or product, you can glean a ton of information about your customers. Thanks to the Internet of Things (discussed in Chapter 5), everything is becoming more intelligent, more data is being collected than ever before and it's easier than ever to analyse this data.

Even very traditional industries, like farming, are getting in on the sensor act: tractors have sensors that dynamically adjust maintenance schedules and fields have sensors that monitor soil condition and temperature. Even yoga mats can include sensors that monitor your position and send information on how to improve your yoga practice.

Sensors are tiny, affordable and very easy to add to products. They are revolutionising the way businesses interact with their customers, enabling them to understand how customers actually use their product and to make personal recommendations.

Transaction Data

Transaction data is a great place for any business to start its big data journey, since it is internal and therefore relatively easy to access and analyse. In a nutshell, it shows you what your customers bought and when. Depending on what you measure, it can also show where the item was purchased, how the customer came across the product and whether she took advantage of a promotion.

Even basic transaction records can be very useful for measuring sales, monitoring stock levels and predicting what you need to order (or manufacture). You may already have all the transaction data you need to answer your strategic questions (I talk about them in Chapter 11), or you may find you need to implement new transaction systems to fully answer those questions.

Finance Data

This includes all your company's financial data, not just the transactions. Finance data has many uses such as predicting cash flow and influencing investment and other long-term business decisions.

Often companies find that combining finance data with other kinds of data is particularly powerful. For example, you might look at your own internal financial data along with big data from open government sources about industry trends and the wider economy. Combined, this data could tell you whether now really is a good time to expand operations or invest in a new fleet of vehicles.

Index

E •

• **F** •

Notes

Notes

Notes

Notes

About the Author

Bernard Marr is the founder and CEO of the Advanced Performance Institute, an organization that specializes in improving business performance and decision making through the use of data.

Bernard is a best-selling business author, keynote speaker and consultant in big data, analytics and enterprise performance. He is one of the world's most highly respected voices anywhere when it comes to data in business. His leading-edge work with major companies, organisations and governments across the globe makes him a globally acclaimed and award-winning researcher, consultant and teacher.

Bernard is a regular contributor to the World Economic Forum, is acknowledged by the CEO Journal as one of today's leading business brains and by LinkedIn as one of the world's top 50 business influencers.

His articles and expert comments regularly feature in high-profile publications including *The Times, The Financial Times, Financial Management, Forbes, the CFO Magazine, The Huffington Post* and *The Wall Street Journal*. Bernard is an avid Tweeter and the writer of the popular The Big Data Guru column.

He has written a number of seminal books and hundreds of high profile reports and articles. This includes the best-sellers *Big Data: Using SMART Big Data, Analytics and Metrics To Make Better Decisions and Improve Performance, Big Data in Practice, The Intelligent Company, Key Business Analytics: The 60+ Business Analysis Tools Every Manager Needs to Know,* and *Key Performance Indicators For Dummies*.

Bernard has worked with and advised many of the world's best-known organizations including Accenture, Astra Zeneca, Bank of England, Barclays, BP, DHL, Fujitsu, Gartner, HSBC, Mars, Ministry of Defence, Microsoft, Oracle, The Home Office, NHS, Orange, Tetley, T-Mobile, Toyota, Royal Air Force, SAP, Shell and the United Nations, among many others.

If you would like to talk to Bernard about any data project you require help with or if you are thinking about running a big data event or training course in your organization, contact him at www.ap-institute.com or via email at: bernard.marr@ap-institute.com.

You can also follow @bernardmarr on Twitter, where he regularly shares his ideas, or connect with him on LinkedIn or Forbes, where he writes a regular blog.

Dedication

This book is dedicated to the people who mean most to me: My wife Claire and our three children Sophia, James and Oliver.

Author's Acknowledgments

I am so grateful to everyone who has helped me get to where I am today. All the great people in the companies I have worked with who put their trust in me to help them and in return give me so much new knowledge and experience. I must also thank everyone who has shared their thinking with me, either in person, in blog posts, books or any other format. Thank you for generously sharing all the material I absorb every day! I am also lucky enough to personally know many of the key thinkers and thought leaders in the field, and I hope you all know how much I value your inputs and our exchanges. At this point, I usually start a long list of key people but I always miss some, so this time I want to resist that and hope your egos will forgive me. You are all amazing!

Finally, I want to thank the team at Wiley for all your support. Taking any book through production is always a challenging process and I really appreciate your input and help.

Publisher's Acknowledgments

Executive Commissioning Editor: Annie Knight

Project Manager: Michelle Hacker

Development Editor: Word Mountain Creative Content

Special Help: Kathleen Dobie

Production Editor: Kinson Raja

Cover Photos: ©pictafolio/Getty Images, Inc.

Take Dummies with you everywhere you go!

Whether you're excited about e-books, want more from the web, must have your mobile apps, or swept up in social media, Dummies makes everything easier.

Visit Us

Like Us

Follow Us

Watch Us

Join Us

Pin Us

Circle Us

Shop Us

FOR DUMMIES

A Wiley Brand

BUSINESS

978-1-118-73077-5

978-1-118-44349-1

978-1-119-97527-4

MUSIC

978-1-119-94276-4

978-0-470-97799-6

978-0-470-49644-2

DIGITAL PHOTOGRAPHY

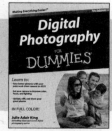

978-1-118-09203-3

978-0-470-76878-5

978-1-118-00472-2

Algebra I For Dummies
978-0-470-55964-2

**Anatomy & Physiology For Dummies,
2nd Edition**
978-0-470-92326-9

Asperger's Syndrome For Dummies
978-0-470-66087-4

Basic Maths For Dummies
978-1-119-97452-9

Body Language For Dummies, 2nd Edition
978-1-119-95351-7

Bookkeeping For Dummies, 3rd Edition
978-1-118-34689-1

British Sign Language For Dummies
978-0-470-69477-0

Cricket for Dummies, 2nd Edition
978-1-118-48032-8

**Currency Trading For Dummies,
2nd Edition**
978-1-118-01851-4

Cycling For Dummies
978-1-118-36435-2

Diabetes For Dummies, 3rd Edition
978-0-470-97711-8

eBay For Dummies, 3rd Edition
978-1-119-94122-4

**Electronics For Dummies All-in-One
For Dummies**
978-1-118-58973-1

English Grammar For Dummies
978-0-470-05752-0

French For Dummies, 2nd Edition
978-1-118-00464-7

Guitar For Dummies, 3rd Edition
978-1-118-11554-1

IBS For Dummies
978-0-470-51737-6

Keeping Chickens For Dummies
978-1-119-99417-6

Knitting For Dummies, 3rd Edition
978-1-118-66151-2

FOR DUMMIES®

A Wiley Brand

SELF-HELP

978-0-470-66541-1

978-1-119-99264-6

978-0-470-66086-7

LANGUAGES

978-0-470-68815-1

978-1-119-97959-3

978-0-470-69477-0

HISTORY

978-0-470-68792-5

978-0-470-74783-4

978-0-470-97819-1

Laptops For Dummies 5th Edition
978-1-118-11533-6

Management For Dummies, 2nd Edition
978-0-470-97769-9

Nutrition For Dummies, 2nd Edition
978-0-470-97276-2

Office 2013 For Dummies
978-1-118-49715-9

Organic Gardening For Dummies
978-1-119-97706-3

Origami Kit For Dummies
978-0-470-75857-1

Overcoming Depression For Dummies
978-0-470-69430-5

Physics I For Dummies
978-0-470-90324-7

Project Management For Dummies
978-0-470-71119-4

Psychology Statistics For Dummies
978-1-119-95287-9

Renting Out Your Property For Dummies, 3rd Edition
978-1-119-97640-0

Rugby Union For Dummies, 3rd Edition
978-1-119-99092-5

Stargazing For Dummies
978-1-118-41156-8

Teaching English as a Foreign Language For Dummies
978-0-470-74576-2

Time Management For Dummies
978-0-470-77765-7

Training Your Brain For Dummies
978-0-470-97449-0

Voice and Speaking Skills For Dummies
978-1-119-94512-3

Wedding Planning For Dummies
978-1-118-69951-5

WordPress For Dummies, 5th Edition
978-1-118-38318-6

Think you can't learn it in a day? Think again!

The *In a Day* e-book series from *For Dummies* gives you quick and easy access to learn a new skill, brush up on a hobby, or enhance your personal or professional life — all in a day. Easy!

Available as PDF, eMobi and Kindle